Two week loan

WITHDRAWN

Please return on or before the last date stamped below.
Charges are made for late return.

ERRATUM

Contents page v

MOVING IN MEASURE
Essays in honour of Brian Moloney

Hull University Press

MOVING IN MEASURE

Essays in honour of Brian Moloney

Edited by

JUDITH BRYCE AND DOUG THOMPSON

Department of Italian
University of Hull

HULL UNIVERSITY PRESS
1989

© Hull University Press

British Library Cataloguing in Publication Data

Moving in measure: essays in honour of Brian Moloney
    Brian Moloney
    1. Italy, 1300–1987
    I. Bryce, J.H. II. Thompson, A.D.
    III. Moloney, Brian
    945

ISBN 0-85958-475-5 hardback
ISBN 0-85958-474-7 paperback

Phototypeset in 10 on 12pt Times by Computape (Pickering) Ltd, North Yorkshire, printed by The University of Hull

Contents

Foreword

When Brian Moloney decided to take early retirement, early in 1986, he was characteristically deeply involved in the fight to maintain and if possible to strengthen the position of Italian in Higher Education, having been nominated chairman of the Society for Italian Studies' working party which had been set up to tender advice to the University Grants Committee and collaborate in the formulation of a national plan for the subject in British universities. It was in large measure due to Brian's careful orchestration and skilful diplomacy that Italian emerged from the UGC's inquiry on such a sound footing for the future. It was this particular achievement, which seemed to 'set a crown upon a lifetime's effort' in the interests of our subject, which provided the immediate stimulus to mark Brian's departure from professional life in some memorable way. If the idea of the special conference and subsequent *Festschrift* came from the department at Hull, it was at once espoused by the Society for Italian Studies, the Association of Teachers of Italian and the Italian Cultural Institute in London, all of which have contributed generously to the production costs of this present volume.

The conference in honour of Brian Moloney, which took place in Hull from Friday 27 to Sunday 29 March 1987 was very successful, the more so perhaps because until a couple of weeks before it was staged Brian himself knew absolutely nothing about it. With the invaluable assistance of Ruth, his wife, and Kathleen, our departmental secretary, and the occasional discreet telephone call to individuals whom Brian thought he had arranged to see within the period in which the conference was scheduled, we were able to steer him fairly easily towards the conference and the pleasure it so obviously gave him.

The criteria used in the selection of papers for the conference were very simple: the topics had to be sure to interest Brian and their presenters had to have worked with him in one of the universities in which he has taught. These, with a little more licence, were also the criteria used in the selection of articles for this present collection, with the result that of the sixteen essays nine are written by present and former teaching colleagues of Brian's, two by former students and another two by former teachers of his at Cambridge.

We should like to offer our thanks to all those friends and colleagues who helped to make the conference a success, whatever their role, and to those who have subsequently contributed the essays contained in this volume. In this latter context, further thanks are due to Mrs Kathleen Chatfield for her patient preparation of the various stages of the typescript, to Alan Best, Joyce Bellamy and Jean Smith of the Hull University Press for their valuable help and advice on technical matters, to SIS, ATI and the Italian Institute for their above-mentioned financial support, and to Osvaldo Böhm, Venice, for permission to reproduce the photographs.

At this point, it would seem fitting to wish Brian and Ruth a long and happy retirement, but not a bit of it! for while this volume has been in preparation, Brian has decided that retirement is not yet the career for him and thus from January 1989 he will be taking up a new appointment as the first incumbent of a newly-established Chair of Italian at the University of Wollongong, New South Wales. So we must postpone our intended good wishes for his retirement indefinitely and instead substitute our sincere hopes that he will enjoy a long, happy and rewarding career Down Under. We further hope that this volume of essays, a tangible mark of our esteem, gratitude and affection, will give him a great deal of pleasure and satisfaction in the years ahead.

Department of Italian   Judith Bryce
University of Hull   Doug Thompson
December 1988

Brian Moloney

Curriculum Vitae

1933	Born 6 June, Leicester.
1944–52	Pupil at Alderman Newton's Boys' School, Leicester.
1952	Awarded an Open Exhibition in French and German at King's College, Cambridge.
1954	Elected to an Open Scholarship at King's College.
1955	Awarded Bachelor of Arts degree and College prize.
1955–7	Military service in Cyprus
1957	Married Ruth Hirst. Awarded State Studentship and elected to R. J. Smith Research Studentship at King's College, Cambridge.
1960–1	Assistant lecturer in Italian and French, University College of Wales, Aberystwyth.
1961–5	Lecturer in Italian, University of Hull.
1962	Awarded the degree of Doctor of Philosophy of the University of Cambridge.
1965–70	Lecturer in Italian, University of Leeds.
1970–5	Senior Lecturer in Italian, University of Leeds.
1972–6	Hon. Treasurer of the Society for Italian Studies.
1975–87	Professor of Italian, University of Hull
1982–6	Chairman of the Society for Italian Studies.
1982–8	Senior Editor of *Italian Studies*.
1986–8	Hon. President of the Association of Teachers of Italian.
1989	Professor of Italian, University of Wollongong, NSW.

List of Publications by Brian Moloney

Books

Novelle del Novecento, edited and introduced by BM (Manchester, 1966); reissued 1968, 1971, 1975, 1978, 1982, 1984.

Florence and England. Essays on Cultural Relations in the Second Half of the Eighteenth Century (Florence, 1969).

Italo Svevo. A Critical Introduction (Edinburgh, 1974).

Articles

'The Third Earl Cowper: an English Patron of Science in Eighteenth-Century Florence and his Correspondence with Alessandro Volta', *Italian Studies*, 16 (1961) 1–34.

'Horace Mann in Florence: 1738–1786', in *Italian Studies presented to E.R. Vincent* (Cambridge, 1962) 154–65.

'Novecento', in *The Year's Work in Modern Language Studies*, 23 (1962) 271–84.

'Novecento', ibid., 24 (1963) 308–19.

'Novecento', ibid., 25 (1964) 268–78.

'The Modern Italian Novel', *Critical Survey*, 1 (1963) 128–32.

'The Della Cruscan Poets, the *Florentine Miscellany* and the Leopoldine Reforms', *The Modern Language Review*, 60 (1965) 48–57.

'Relazioni culturali fra l'Inghilterra e la Toscana nella seconda metà del Settecento', in *Atti del Quarto Congresso dell'Associazione per gli Studi di Lingua e Letteratura Italiana* (Wiesbaden, 1965) 156–64.

'Tematica e tecnica nei romanzi di Giorgio Bassani', *Convivium*, 34 (1966) 484–95.

'The *Discorsi* of Pietro Verri: Genesis and Revision', *Studies on Voltaire and the Eighteenth Century*, 56 (1967) 893–906.

'Anglo-Florentine Diplomatic Relations and the French Revolution', *English Miscellany*, 19 (1968) 273–93.

'The Novels of Francesco Jovine', *Italian Studies*, 22 (1968) 138–55.

'Zeno's Truth', in T. F. Staley (ed.), *Essays on Italo Svevo* (Tulsa, 1969) 48–56.

'Psychoanalysis and Irony in *La coscienza di Zeno*', *Modern Language Review*, 67:3 (1972) 309–18.

'Svevo as a Jewish Writer', *Italian Studies*, 27 (1973) 52–63.

'Italo Svevo e *L'Indipendente:* sei articoli sconosciuti', *Lettere italiane*, 25:4 (1973) 536–56.

'Italo Svevo and Thomas Mann's *Buddenbrooks*', in H.C. Davis, D. G. Rees et al. (eds), *Essays in Honour of J.H. Whitfield* (London, 1975) 251–67.

'Politics and the Novel in Mussolini's Italy', in D. Daiches and A. K. Thorsby (eds), *Literature and Western Civilization* (London, 1976) 295–314.

'Londra dopo la guerra: Five Unknown Articles by Italo Svevo', *Italian Studies*, 31 (1976) 59–81.

'Count Noris Changes Trams: an Unknown Article by Italo Svevo', *Modern Language Review*, 71:1 (1976) 51–3.

'Italo Svevo and the European Novel', Inaugural Lecture (Hull, 1977).

'Ignazio Silone', *ATI Journal*, 28 (1979) 3–6.

'La realtà del Mezzogiorno interpretata da Carlo Levi', *Civiltà italiana*, 4 (1980) 220–9.

'The Poetry of Praise', *The Franciscan*, 24:2 (1983) 84–94.

'Italo Svevo e James Joyce: affinità elettive', in E. Lauretta, *Il romanzo di Pirandello e Svevo* (Florence, 1984) 91–106.

'Italian Novels of Peasant Crisis', *ATI Journal*, 46 (1986) 41–6.

'Plot and Sub-plot in Italo Svevo's *Una vita*', *ATI Journal*, 48 (1986) 92–6.

'The Italian Peasant Movement since World War I: History and Literature', *Spunti e Ricerche*, 2 (1986) 1–8.

'Ortis's Cuckoo', in E.A. Millar (ed.), *Renaissance and Other Studies. Essays Presented to Peter M. Brown* (Glasgow, 1988) pp. 223–32.

Other

Italian. A Guide to First-Degree Courses in UK Universities and Colleges, Careers Research and Advisory Centre (Cambridge, 1966).

Italian. Degree-Course Guide 1969–70, CRAC (Cambridge, 1969).

Entries on Pavese, Pirandello and Svevo, in J. Wintle (ed.), *Makers of Modern Culture* (London, 1981).

Silone and Levi, Exeter Tapes I 914 (1983).

BBC Radio Talks on Svevo, Moravia, Silone and Carlo Gozzi.

List of Contributors

Roger Absalom	Reader in Italian, Sheffield City Polytechnic.
Z.G. Barański	Lecturer in Italian, University of Reading.
J.C. Barnes	Professor of Italian, University College, Dublin.
J.G. Bernasconi	Lecturer in the History of Art, University of Hull, and Fellow of the Royal Society.
P. Brand	Formerly Professor of Italian, University of Edinburgh.
Judith Bryce	Lecturer in Italian, University of Hull.
A.O. Bullock	Senior Lecturer in Italian, University of Leeds.
A. L. Lepschy	Professor of Italian, University College, London.
U. Limentani	Emeritus Professor of Italian and formerly Serena Professor of Italian at the University of Cambridge.
T. O'Neill	Professor of Italian, University of Melbourne.
L.A. Quartermaine	Lecturer in Italian, University of Exeter.
S. Rizzardi	Lettrice in Italian, University of Hull.
E. Schächter	Lecturer in Italian, University of Kent at Canterbury.
Doug Thompson	Senior Lecturer in Italian, University of Hull.
P.A. Williams	Lecturer in Italian, University of Hull.
J.R. Woodhouse	Lecturer in Italian, University of Oxford.

1

Dante's (Anti-) Rhetoric: Notes on the Poetics of the *Commedia**

Zygmunt G. Barański

These notes have their distant origins in Hull: in fact, their first glimmerings date from about the time when the recipient of this book returned to the University as the third incumbent of the Chair in Italian. I was then a research student working on the style of the *Commedia* in the wake of Patrick Boyde's book on Dante's lyric poetry.[1] However, as I proceeded with my investigation of Dante's use of rhetorical formulae and figures in his poem, I became increasingly dissatisfied with the directions of my research. The catalogue I was gradually building up of the poet's lexical choices and his use of tropes, *topoi*, and *colores rhetorici* seemed, paradoxically, to limit the originality of his great enterprise. The picture which was emerging from my data was well known to Dante scholarship: it showed that the overall stylistic texture of the *Comedy* was the result of formal syntheses and dislocations of current compositional practices. At the same time, however, I was becoming increasingly aware that the compartmentalising rhetorical tradition of the day could not account for Dante's experiments, but could only condemn them as *vitia*. What continued to remain obscure were the artistic reasons and literary precedents for his experimentation. The kind of stylistic analysis in which I was engaged highlighted effects without accounting for their causes; it offered a description of a poetic universe without explaining the general textual principles which lay behind its

* I should like to thank Maggie Barański, Giulio Lepschy, Lino Pertile and Shirley Vinall for their comments on an earlier version of this article. I have used the following editions of Dante's works: *Il Convivio*, ed. G. Busnelli and G. Vandelli, 2 vols, 2nd revised edition by A. E. Quaglio (Florence, 1964); *De vulgari eloquentia*, ed. P. V. Mengaldo, in Dante Alighieri, *Opere minori*, 2 vols (Milan–Naples, 1979–) II, 1–237; *La Commedia secondo l'antica vulgata*, ed. G. Petrocchi, 4 vols (Milan, 1966–7).

genesis. More worryingly, it did not cast light on how Dante might have legitimately justified his radical artistic practices, which so obviously challenged conventional literary wisdom, in a culture which was so concerned with the proper respect for precedents and *auctoritates*.

Seeking solutions to these problems in the *mare magnum* of Dante criticism, I came to realise that while much work had been done on the possible biographical causes and the ideological – political, theological, philosophical – origins of the *Comedy*, less attention had, in fact, been paid to the more strictly literary stimuli behind its composition. What seemed especially to be missing was a study of the poetics of the *Commedia* which could both substantiate in formal and ideological terms Dante's obsessive desire to experiment, and locate this in relation to contemporary ideas on literature.[2] At this juncture, I was especially fortunate to find myself in the sympathetically supportive environment of the Italian Department at Hull, where Brian Moloney and others encouraged me to turn my eyes to this new question. Now, as I at last approach the completion of my research,[3] I feel that it is especially appropriate that I should give a first outline of my conclusions in a collection brought together to honour the career of the person towards whom I and what follows owe a particular debt.

It is, of course, somewhat misleading to claim that Dante scholars have generally neglected what might loosely be described as his contacts and concerns with literary theory and criticism. In relative terms this is true, but what has been written, given the centuries-long fascination with the poet, still amounts to a substantial body of work, and one which has grown considerably during the last decade. In fact, the first part of my title intentionally (and, as I hope to show, polemically) calques the titles of a number of studies which focus on Dante's relationship to medieval rhetoric.[4] Although my research would have been much poorer without these and similar contributions, my main objection is that, while they undoubtedly help anchor the poet to his intellectual world, the vast majority end up by presenting a distorted and reductive picture of his views on literature and, in particular, of the poetics of the *Commedia*. Most notably, too, much emphasis – and not just in Dante studies – has been placed on rhetoric as the prime mover behind a medieval writer's creative practices and his reflections on his art. Thus, for instance, it is often forgotten that it was grammar's brief, and not rhetoric's, to encourage, *inter alia*, the explication and *imitatio* of literary works (*poetarum enarratio*). Furthermore, the critics' concentration on rhetoric has led to a considerable number of analyses of literary technique – the area with which rhetoric in the Middle Ages was most concerned – and to only a few studies of the theory of literary creation, about which it had little to say.[5]

My aim in this article is briefly to present the limits of rhetoric's possible influence on Dante, in particular when he came to write the *Comedy*, and to sketch summarily how other ways of thinking about literature also affected him (as important as rhetoric in the Middle Ages were grammar, allegory,[6] logic, theological writing, and the various forms of exegesis from the *scholia* to the *accessus ad auctores*, and from the interlinear and marginal glosses to the commentaries and to the *vitae*.[7] Yet, it nevertheless remains true that rhetoric – or rather, Dante's idiosyncratic reinterpretation of rhetoric – does hold a key place in the composition of the *Commedia*. And this influence continues to appear especially potent to scholars not just for reasons internal to the poem – which I shall presently examine – but also because of a number of external factors: firstly, the significant role played by rhetoric in Dante's education; secondly, the contacts which can be established between Brunetto Latini's recovery of an Aristotelian-Ciceronian 'civic' rhetoric and the poet's 'political' and ethical views on language; thirdly, Dante's fidelity to rhetorical norms in his 'minor' works; and, finally and most importantly, the fact that Dante himself started to write a rhetorical treatise, as the emphasis on eloquence in its title immediately shows (and which at least in one manuscript is called *Rectorica Dantis*) – all questions which critics have widely discussed. However, as with the study of other areas which are relevant to the general topic of the *Comedy*'s poetics (such as Dante's aesthetic views, his manipulation of his literary sources, his allegory, his attitudes to medieval semiotics, and his comments on other texts and authors), scholars have tended to consider the poet's different contacts with the rhetorical tradition in isolation from each other; and this, too, has enhanced the impression of rhetoric's all-pervasiveness, as against a more sober perspective stressing that there was considerable overlap between different rhetorical activities; that rhetoric was simply one intellectual system, among many, bearing upon literature; and that it is necessary to examine the interrelationship between these systems if a more complete idea of medieval, and specifically Dante's, poetics is to be achieved.[8] Unfortunately, with one or two shining exceptions (most notably, Battaglia Ricci, Mengaldo, Nencioni and Schiaffini),[9] the trend has been to fragment and to compartmentalise, resulting in a piecemeal approach to the poetics of the *Commedia* which, I believe, has downplayed the originality and wealth of Dante's technical considerations.

The critical enthusiasm for rhetoric has taken different guises, though the final effects of these has been the same; they have over-determined its importance to the detriment of other approaches to literature. Where this attitude is most pronounced, there is evidence that some scholars have come to consider rhetoric and poetry as just about synonymous.[10] This is unfortunate because not only does it deny the specificity which both clearly had in the Middle Ages, but it also masks the 'ancillary' status of rhetoric in poetic composition; points, which Dante's famous definition in the *De vulgari eloquentia* boldly underlines: *poesis* 'nichil aliud est quam fictio rethorica musicaque poita' (II, iv, 2).[11] For Dante, poetry was constituted through a complex synthesis of ideological ('fictio') and formal ('rethorica' *and* 'musica') properties.[12] Nor does he depart from this basic position anywhere in the *Commedia*. And, as he made even clearer in the *Convivio*, rhetoric inspired only part of the formal texture of a poem: 'la sua bellezza [of 'Voi che 'ntendendo'], ch' è grande sí per construzione, la quale si pertiene a li gramatici, sí per l'ordine del sermone, che si pertiene a li rettorici, sí per lo numero de le sue parti, che si pertiene a li musici' (II, xi, 9). Dante's rhetoric, like that of all his contemporaries, specifically concerned itself with those features of language ('toute expression non fortuite, c'est-à-dire . . . fonctionna-lisée en vertu de règles connues et indubitables')[13] which would make an argument more pleasing and persuasive: 'la chiarezza del suo [of rhe-toric] aspetto che è soavissima a vedere' (*Convivio* II, xiii, 13). Essen-tially, such 'clarity' was achieved through the judicious application of the rules of *convenientia* in the selection of vocabulary and figures to match one's chosen subject-matter. The whole thrust of the Second Book of the *De vulgari eloquentia*, as is well known, revolves around the doctrine of discrete rhetorical 'styles' each with its own range of *materia* and of formal procedures:[14]

Deinde in hiis que dicenda occurrunt debemus discretione potiri, utrum tragice, sive comice, sive elegiace sint canenda. Per tragediam superiorem stilum inducimus. . . . Stilo equidem tragico tunc uti videmur quando cum gravitate sententie tam superbia carminum quam constructionis elatio et excellentia vocabulorum concordat ... illa que summe canenda distinximus isto solo sunt stilo canenda: videlicet salus, amor et virtus et que propter ea concipimus, dum nullo accidente vilescant.   (II, iv, 5–8)

Given the close proximity, as Paul Zumthor has noted ('Rhétorique', p. 62), between this medieval conception of rhetoric and our modern notions of literary style, it is not surprising that so many scholars, even when they avoid conflating poetry with rhetoric, have limited their analyses of the form of the *Comedy* to its rhetorical surface and have tried to define its poetics simply in rhetorical terms; especially as they are able to call on the illustrious example of, say, a Curtius to guide them.[15] And Dante's poem is undoubtedly full of single elements which have their precedents in and are legitimated by the rhetorical tradition: from the 'exordial' functions of *Inferno* I to the parallel structuring between *Paradiso* XI and XII; from the linguistic artifices and contortions of *Inferno* XIII to the smooth sequence of images of the Triumph of Christ; and from the *comico-realistico* violence of the episode of the barrators to the erudite and elegant Latinate patina of so much of the second and third *cantiche*. Yet, both the discovery of rhetorical 'sources' for areas of the *Comedy* and the compilation of catalogues of individual rhetorical figures or procedures have their potential dangers. Detached as such studies normally are from the broader theoretical questions of the *Commedia*'s poetics, they give the misleading impression that the poem is ultimately like any other medieval work which is organised around similar rhetorically moulded elements, while the crucial point, it seems to me, is that the range of different 'styles' (from the 'lowest' to the 'highest', as the examples I have just given demonstrate) which it embraces is irrefutable evidence of its distinctive, unique, and anomalous character precisely when assessed in rhetorical terms.

To explain the *Comedy*'s hybrid, and thus rhetorically 'deficient' style, a number of critics, as I mentioned earlier, has continued to insist that the answer is nevertheless to be sought in the precepts of the *artes poetriae*. For them, Dante is original because he applied rhetorically established *convenientiae* in a flexible manner and incorporated the whole of the *rota Vergilii* in a single text.[16] This, in itself, is obviously true; though, as far as I have been able to ascertain, no medieval rhetorical work presents a

justification for the sort of experimentation which Dante pursued in his
Commedia.[17] In addition, the implications of the poet's formal choices
should not be seen so much as a further sign of the all-embracing power
of rhetoric, but as evidence of Dante's sense of its limitations. His
stylistic syncretism is both a challenge to contemporary rhetorical
convention and to the literature which this had produced, and proof that
alternative forms of literary composition are eminently possible. It is
clear that the poet could not comfortably find support for this break in
the rhetorical tradition nor in classical and medieval literature: most
significantly, even the paternal *Aeneid* was constrained by the 'bello stile'
befitting *tragedìe* (I shall return to this crucial question). Thus, one
cornerstone of Dante's poetics rests on the belief that the hierarchical
system of *genera dicendi* was not appropriate for the overall organisation
of his *Comedy*; yet, at the same time, he was also quite willing to carry on
exploiting individual aspects of the rhetorical tradition in his poem.

This seemingly ambivalent attitude is in some ways the most vital
aspect in understanding the *Commedia*'s poetics; and it does not just
affect Dante's assimilation and manipulation of rhetoric, but also that of
the other contemporary approaches to literature. He considered that his
poem, given its divinely instituted responsibilities ('. . . 'l poema sacro /
al quale ha posto mano e cielo e terra', *Par.* XXV, 1–2), necessarily
transcended the works of other writers, and was thus not subject to the
same compositional restrictions: 'Da questo passo vinto mi concedo / piú
che già mai da punto di suo tema / soprato fosse comico o tragedo' (*Par.*
XXX, 22–4) – and, in the *Comedy*, such disclaimers are always more than
simple modesty or ineffability *topoi*. Nevertheless, Dante was acutely
aware too that he needed to communicate within a culture which set
great store by convention and which, almost unconsciously, associated
particular formal procedures with certain connotations. Thus, in the
broadest comparative terms, Dante did rhetorically 'raise' his stylistic
register as he moved from one *cantica* to the next. Quite simply, if his
great work of reform was to succeed, he needed to speak to his audience
in a manner which it could still appreciate. Dante was not an 'avant-
garde' artist in the twentieth-century sense; his respect for the tradition
was, one might say, 'religious' (it is enough to recall his treatment of
Virgil and his work). On the other hand, he was aware of the unreasonable constraints which a dogmatically preceptive approach could impose.
His aim was to innovate – and even criticise – in a measured manner from

within the tradition, rather than to rebut this; in fact, if he had not created a tension, from in the *Comedy* itself, between, for example, the models of writing sanctioned by rhetoric and his own personal solutions, Dante would have found it difficult to draw attention to the originality of his poem. Although he challenged the rhetorical *forma mentis*, his basic understanding of what constituted rhetoric's concerns remained that which he had learned in school.

Dante was under no illusion about the interpretative difficulties which his experimentation might cause. However, not unreasonably, he expected his readers to 'work at' deciphering his poem, as they had been taught to do in their grammar classes and as the entire exegetical tradition continually reaffirmed. His addresses to the ubiquitous *lettor* are simply the most accessible examples of this design. Dante believed that he would be able to count upon the refined literary-technical memories and reading skills of, at least, the most sophisticated among his audience in order to make clear the *Comedy*'s original features. To help and guide his readers in this operation, the poet introduced a quite astonishing array of metaliterary elements with which he hoped to illuminate his poem's *novitas*.[18] As Gianfranco Contini said, in what remains the most fundamental contribution on Dante this century, 'una costante della personalità dantesca è questo perpetuo sopraggiungere della riflessione tecnica accanto alla poesia'.[19] In the *Comedy*, the poet did this in ways which would have been immediately recognisable to his contemporaries. Thus, his very use of metaliterary features as stimuli to exegesis is typical of medieval literature; however, both their number (there is scarcely a canto which does not include one or more such references) and the carefully planned way in which they are introduced distinguish Dante's approach from that of other writers. Similarly, if one considers the technical definition of *Purgatorio* – 'questa cantica seconda' (*Purg.* XXXIII, 140)[20] – the distance between Dante's and other current uses of the term *cantica* is quickly apparent; though he obviously did want some connection between these to be recognised.[21] Dante spoke about the *Comedy* in a language and in structures familiar to his time (it is especially noteworthy that, as far as I know, he did not invent a single new technical term with which to describe his radically innovatory poem, but instead drew on the established terminology of the different medieval discourses on literature). Yet, a semantic discrepancy is almost always noticeable between the subject-matter and style of the passages and

contexts in which he placed his metaliterary statements and the custom-
ary associations that this same technical vocabulary had at the time. For
instance, in the ideological 'gap', which he thought would develop
between a reader's conventional literary expectations at finding *Purgatorio* described as a *cantica*, and the *Comedy*'s original and unexpected
artistic solutions bearing this name, Dante believed that the explanation
for his experimentation would begin to emerge. To overcome her or his
confusion, the reader would be forced to interpret, and Dante, once
more, underlined the peculiar standing which his work had in relation to
the tradition.

To complement this more strictly technical (if not quite theoretical)
description of the *Comedy*, Dante also defined it in more concrete terms.
As a number of critics has shown, developing one of Contini's many
brilliant insights, Dante, by means of a complex series of poetic and
ideological manoeuvres, similarly highlighted the distance between his
poem and other literary experiences: from the writings of the Latin
classics (including Virgil) to those of the Provençal poets, and from the
French *chansons* and *romans* to the poetry of the *dolce stil novo*
(including his own youthful writings).[22] In particular, the *Comedy*
assimilates and goes beyond these traditions by stressing how inadequate
these are, on account of their rigid attachment to the categories of the
genera dicendi, in dealing with 'ciò che per l'universo si squaderna' (*Par.*
XXXIII, 87).

The other principal deficiency of these works, according to the poet, is
that none participates as directly as his *Comedy* in God's providential
scheme of things.[23] Dante, unlike his predecessors, had the divinely
willed responsibility to report all that he had learned on his eschatologi-
cal voyage (*Purg.* XXXIII, 52-7) – an experience which seems to have
evoked and touched upon every aspect of creation; and he had to do this
as completely as possible (*Par.* XVII, 127-9). Dante could, therefore,
only achieve his purpose if he was free to use those linguistic solutions
which his discrimination – sharpened by his journey and his artistic gifts
(*Par.* XXII, 112-14) – suggested as most suitable for his ends. Quite
simply, Dante claimed to be using language and literature to do God's
work. It thus no longer made sense for him to be limited by human
conventions. These, in fact, are remodified by their contact with the
divine, since the authority for his revolutionary poetics came from
Heaven itself. In writing the *Commedia*, Dante's most direct models

were God's two 'books': the universe which includes the whole of creation 'in un volume' (*Par.* XXXIII, 86), into whose pages the pilgrim had been granted the unique privilege of looking, and the Bible which is written according to the stylistically and thematically all-embracing conventions of the *sermo humilis.*[24] Dante, in his turn, dutifully strove to create a similar synthesis by constraining the different rhetorical 'styles', literary genres, and languages of his culture within a numerically harmonious structure of threes and tens which would serve as a textual *exemplum* of the principles and *ordo* of God's creation. It was also meant to display the divine hand behind the *Comedy*'s genesis. By imitating the supreme artist, source for every book, Dante drew legitimacy for his experimentation from the one place where no pedantic and conservative school-master could find fault. And the duty of humanity, inspired by the *Comedy*, was to follow the lead of its author and imitate the divine example, thus achieving a properly ordered balance in all its activities. By claiming God as his *auctoritas*, Dante was able to weave his artistic and didactic concerns into a single skein.

Dante's 'theological poetics',[25] does, in effect, institute and subscribe to a 'new rhetoric' – one which, in opposition to the 'old rhetoric', makes a virtue of plurality in oneness. This is the only literary ideal fit for one of Western culture's most committed syncretists; and it is, thus, inevitable that his attitude, whether to grammar, or to rhetoric, or to the literary tradition, or even to the world in which he found himself, is always a synthesising one. At every level of Dante's poetics, the macroscopic syncretist model of divine origin is reiterated. He imposed it too on the *Comedy*'s allegory which blends 'allegory of the theologians' with that 'of the poets', and both of these with conventional and personification allegory.[26] In this case, as elsewhere, Dante tried to match religious and secular culture; or, to put it more crudely – though perhaps more accurately – the Bible with Virgil. This, I feel, is the ultimate inspiration for the *Comedy*'s poetics.

One of the main reasons why Dante forged an especial allegorical and intertextual relationship between his poem and the Bible was to sanction the truth of his story. With Thomas Aquinas, the literal-historical level of the holy book had once again become crucial, while the 'letter' of secular writing was increasingly debased.[27] At the same time, although the Bible was indubitably regarded as a divinely inspired work, many exegetes had begun to praise the artistic skill of its human authors in fashioning its *littera*.[28] Thus, for Dante, the 'biblical' status of his 'letter' was the guarantee that his literary skill, too, would be appreciated and not ignored Thomistically as the dubious coating for 'belle menzogne' whose only value lay in their moral explication. Furthermore, one of the ways in which Dante demonstrates the insufficiency of the other literary traditions which he recalls in the *Comedy* is by measuring them against the Bible. Thus, only his poem can be said even to begin to have the formal, ideological, and ontological range of God's book. In Dante's literary universe ruled by the Bible, one other work, besides the *Commedia*, gains advantage from being compared to the Scriptures. The *Aeneid*, too, as Statius astonishingly reveals, has the power of salvation (*Purg.* XXII, 37–45).[29] In this way, Dante succeeds in honouring his principal sources and in drawing together this trinity of texts (and it is unlikely that the number is fortuitous). In addition, this process helps to underline the unique quality of each work: the Bible is the pinnacle of ideological and formal achievement which can only be properly enjoyed by God; the *Aeneid* represents the finest possible example of an ideologically and rhetorically constrained text; while the *Comedy* takes all that is best from the latter and endeavours, however falteringly, to follow the lead of the former.

Dante never thought of the *Comedy* as a new 'Bible', in the way that he considered it a new '*Aeneid*'. His poem's subordination to the Bible is immediately evident, since he nowhere claims that it can achieve that perfect synthesis of *verba*, *res*, and *signa* which is the Bible's hallmark.[30] Thus, given his human limitations, it would have been fruitless for Dante merely to try to 'imitate' God's 'writing'. Therefore, as I have argued, he drew on every human literary tradition in order to make his weak human voice fit to carry God's redemptive message.[31] This is crucial, since 'nello spazio tra il *verbum* divino e quello dantesco, non solo si trova la differenza tra la Bibbia e la *Commedia*, ma è anche il luogo in cui Dante rivendica il proprio genio poetico'.[32] In order to appreciate the singularity of the *Comedy* and its poetics, it is necessary always to keep in mind the full range of its allusiveness and the constant interplay between its wealth of sources. Of such stuff are the schemes of the syncretist.

Yet, at one level, Dante might be considered a failure. His immediate audience, as evidenced by the Trecento commentators, failed to unravel his new poetics.[33] However, so intimately does the *Comedy* fuse didacticism and poetry, ideology and art that it still succeeds in its powerful dramatic and intellectual effect even when its literary machinations are but vaguely glimpsed. This might seem an odd conclusion with which to finish a survey of almost a dozen years' work on Dante's poetics; nevertheless, this is precisely the yardstick with which to measure his consummate skill in marrying 'poesia' and 'riflessione tecnica'. To dismantle Dante's poetics can be a source of great intellectual pleasure, but so too can be the contemplation of the poem in its entirety. This is the lesson which the *Comedy* teaches and embodies, and which is its ideological bulwark: the harmonious coming together, in imitation of the divine model, of discrete elements in a single work. Dante gave his new artistic project a conventional rhetorical name – 'comedía' – ; and, in his choice of title, he enshrined the pride he felt for his poetics by intimately associating his technical reflection with his finished poem. His 'comic' style, unlike the usual entirely nominal *stilus medius*, was a truly 'middle' style where every idea, subject, and formal register could come together.[34] But *comedía* is more than this. As a technical term it did not belong just to the rhetorical tradition, but also spanned all those approaches to literature which underpinned Dante's poetics.[35] The clue to the poem's manifold syncretism and the key to its exegesis commence at its title, precisely one of the places which the *accessus ad auctores* recommended for especial attention when interpreting a work.[36]

Notes

1. P. Boyde, *Dante's Style in his Lyric Poetry* (Cambridge, 1971).
2. By 'poetics' I understand the literary and technical ideas which underlie and, in fact, generally precede a work of literature; see C. Segre, 'Poetica', in *Enciclopedia Einaudi* (Turin, 1980) X, 818–38.
3. I am about to complete a book with the provisional title *Dante 'Comico'. An Analysis of the Comedy's Poetics* to be published by Brill.
4. See E. Bigi, 'Caratteri e funzione della retorica nella *Divina Commedia*', *Letture Classensi* (Ravenna, 1973) IV, 183–203; A. Buck, 'Gli studi sulla poetica e sulla retorica di Dante e del suo tempo', in *Atti del Congresso Internazionale di Studi Danteschi*, 2 vols (Florence, 1965–6) I, 249–78; F. Di Capua, 'Insegnamenti retorici medievali e dottrine estetiche moderne nel *De vulgari eloquentia* di Dante', in his *Scritti minori*, 2 vols (Rome–Paris–Tournai–New York, 1959 [1945]); F. Tateo 'Rettorica', in *Enciclopedia Dantesca*, 5 vols (Rome, 1970–6) IV, cols 895b–8b.
5. See G. Dahan, 'Notes et textes sur la *Poétique* au Moyen Âge', *Archives d'histoire doctrinale et littéraire du Moyen Âge*, 55 (1980) 171–239 (pp. 171–2).

6. Although it is a critical commonplace to associate medieval literature with allegory, or, more precisely, with 'personification' and 'conventional' allegory, it is frequently forgotten that, in the Middle Ages, allegory principally had exegetical and structural functions; see Z. G. Barański, 'La lezione esegetica di *Inferno* I: allegoria, storia, e letteratura nella *Commedia*', in *Dante e le forme dell'allegoresi*, ed. M. Picone (Ravenna, 1987) pp. 79–97 with an extensive bibliography, and, in addition, see J. Whitman, *Allegory. The Dynamics of an Ancient and Medieval Technique* (Oxford, 1987).

7. See, for example, J. B. Allen, *The Ethical Poetic of the Later Middle Ages* (Toronto, 1982); R. W. Hunt, 'The Introductions to the *Artes* in the Twelfth Century', in *Studia medievalia in honorem R. M. Martin* (Bruges, 1948) pp. 85–112; A. J. Minnis, *Medieval Theory of Authorship* (London, 1984); *Medieval Semiotics* (special issue of *Style*, 20, ii (1986)); S. G. Nichols Jr, *Romanesque Signs* (New Haven and London, 1983); *Semiotica Mediaevalia*, ed. J. Evans (special issue of *Semiotica*, 63, i/ii (1987)); B. Stock, *The Implications of Literacy* (Princeton, 1983); E. Vance, *Mervelous Signals: poetics and sign theory in the Middle Ages* (Lincoln, 1986). And see also E. de Bruyne, *Études d'esthétique médiévale*, 3 vols (Bruges, 1946). It should not be forgotten that there was considerable overlap between the different medieval treatments of literature; this is especially true of grammar and rhetoric, see P. Bagni, 'Grammatica e retorica nella cultura medievale', *Rhetorica*, 2 (1984) 267–80.

8. See Bagni, 'Grammatica', pp. 270, 280.

9. See L. Battaglia Ricci, *Dante e la tradizione letteraria medievale* (Pisa, 1983); P. V. Mengaldo, *Linguistica e retorica di Dante* (Pisa, 1978); G. Nencioni, 'Dante e la retorica', in *Dante e Bologna nei tempi di Dante* (Bologna, 1967) pp. 91–112; A. Schiaffini, 'Dante, retorica, medioevo', in *Atti* (see n. 4 above) II, 155–86.

10. See, for example, R. Dragonetti, *Aux frontières du langage poétique* (Ghent, 1961) p. 53; Tateo, 'Rettorica', col. 895b. Similarly, for instance, both Tateo (and see also his *Questioni di poetica dantesca* (Bari, 1972)) and M. Shapiro, 'On the Role of Rhetoric in the *Convivio*', *Romance Philology*, 40 (1986) 38–64, assign to rhetoric concerns which belong to other medieval treatments of literature. Paolo Bagni (*La costituzione della poesia nelle 'Artes' del XII–XIII secolo* (Bologna, 1968) pp. 29–32) gives a brief explanation for the diffusion of rhetoric into other areas of medieval intellectual life; it is noteworthy, however, that in his most recent work, Bagni has attenuated the scale of rhetoric's influence in the Middle Ages.

11. For an excellent discussion of this definition, see Mengaldo ed., pp. 161–3.

12. See Mengaldo ed., pp. 161–3.

13. P. Zumthor, 'Rhétorique et poétiques latines et romanes', in *Grundriss der romanischen Literaturen des Mittelalters*, ed. H. R. Jauss and E. Kohler (Heidelberg, 1972) vol. I, pp. 57–91 (p. 62).

14. See F. Quadlbauer, *Die antike Theorie der 'genera dicendi' im lateinischen Mittelalter* (Vienna, 1962); P. V. Mengaldo, 'L'elegia "umile" (*De vulgari*

eloquentia, II, iv, 5–6)', *Giornale storico della letteratura italiana*, 143 (1966) 177–98.

15. E. R. Curtius, *European Literature and the Latin Middle Ages* (1948) (London and Henley, 1979).
16. See, for example, I. Baldelli, 'Lingue e stile delle opere in volgare di Dante', in *Enciclopedia Dantesca*. *Appendice* (Rome, 1978) pp. 55–112 (pp. 93, 109); Tateo, *Questioni*, passim, and 'Rettorica', cols 987b–8a. For a fuller critique of this position, see Z. G. Barański, ' "Significar *per verba*": notes on Dante and plurilingualism', *The Italianist*, 6 (1986) 5–18 (pp.13–14).
17. There is some evidence that classical rhetorical works were less rigid than their medieval counterparts (see, for example, *Ad Herennium*, IV, xi, 16; Horace, *Ars Poetica*, 73–98); however, the implications of this for Dante's experimentation in the *Comedy* are too complex for me to discuss in this short article.
18. See Barański, 'Lezione', pp. 79–85.
19. G. Contini, 'Introduzione alle Rime di Dante' (1938), in his *Un'idea di Dante* (Turin, 1976), p. 4.
20. It should be remembered that, in the *Comedy*, Dante described only *Purgatorio* directly by this term; thus, he defined *Inferno* as a *canzone* (*Inf.* XX, 3).
21. See *Thesaurus Linguae Latinae*, s. v. 'canticum'.
22. G. Contini, 'Dante come personaggio-poeta della *Commedia*' (1965), 'Un'interpretazione di Dante' (1965), and 'Filologia e esegesi dantesca' (1965), all in his *Idea*, pp. 33–62, 69–111, 113–42. See also, for example, G. Bàrberi Squarotti, 'L'artificio dell'eternità', in his *L'artificio dell'eternità* (Verona, 1972) pp. 383–534; M. Barchiesi, 'Catarsi classica e "medicina" dantesca', *Letture Classensi* (Ravenna, 1973) IV, 9–124; R. Hollander, *Il Virgilio dantesco* (Florence, 1983); A. A. Iannucci, 'Dante's Theory of Genres', *Dante Studies*, 91 (1973) 1–25; M. Picone, 'I trovatori di Dante: Bertran de Born', *Studi e problemi di critica testuale*, 19 (1979) 71–94, 'Giraut de Bornelh nella prospettiva di Dante', *Vox Romanica*, 39 (1980) 22–43, 'Paradiso IX: Dante, Folchetto e la diaspora trobadorica', *Medioevo Romanzo*, 8 (1981–3) 47–89, and 'Dante e la tradizione arturiana', *Romanische Forschungen*, 94 (1982) 1–18.
23. See Barański, 'Lezione', pp. 95–7.
24. See, in particular, E. Auerbach, *Literary Language and its Public in Late Latin Antiquity* (London, 1965) pp. 27–66, and 'Sacrae Scripturae sermo humilis', in his *Studi su Dante* (Milan, 1978) pp. 165–73. See also de Bruyne, *Études d'esthétique*, II, 314–18.
25. See Z. G. Barański, 'Re-viewing Dante', forthcoming in *Romance Philology*.
26. See Barański, 'Lezione', p. 96.
27. See Thomas Aquinas, *Summa Theologica*, I, i, 10. Resp.
28. See Minnis, *Medieval Theory of Authorship*.
29. More conventionally, Statius also acknowledges the 'Christian' message of Virgil's Fourth Eclogue (*Purg.* XXII, 67–73). However, this is the only

instance in the *Comedy* in which Dante grants a position of note to this work; instead, throughout his poem, he stresses, in a remarkably original move, the *Aeneid*'s privileged position in God's plan for humanity; see also G. Mazzotta, *Dante, Poet of the Desert* (Princeton, 1979).

30. See de Bruyne, *Études d'esthétique*, II, 302–13; Battaglia Ricci, *Dante e la tradizione*, pp. 90–100 (both include many references to primary sources).
31. See M. Corti, 'La teoria del segno nei logici modisti e in Dante', in *Per una storia della semiotica: teorie e metodi*, ed. P. Lendinara and M.C. Ruta (Palermo, 1981) pp. 69–86 (p. 78) (nos 15–16 of *Quaderni del circolo semiologico siciliano*).
32. Barański, 'Lezione', p. 96.
33. See G. Padoan, 'La "mirabile visione" di Dante e l'Epistola a Cangrande', in his *Il pio Enea, l'empio Ulisse* (Ravenna, 1977) pp. 30–63 (p. 41); Barański, 'Lezione', pp. 79–82, 97.
34. See Barański, ' "Significar" ', pp. 11–12, and 'Re-viewing Dante'.
35. A discussion of this point constitutes a significant part of my book.
36. See Minnis, *passim* (s.v. *titulus operis/libri*, in 'Index of Latin Terms', pp. 312–16 (p. 316)). It might be wondered why I have made no mention of the Letter to Cangrande in my article. My silence is not so much the result of my doubts regarding Dante's authorship of this work (in support of my reservations, I would cite, for example, the conservatism of the Letter's technical explanations – with the exception of its discussion of the *Comedy*'s allegory – when compared both to the poem's artistic practices and to its metaliterary statements). Rather, even if the Letter were by Dante, this would not change one basic fact. When Dante wrote and circulated the bulk of his poem, he could not count on the Letter's exegetical support. Thus, as I have tried to show, explanations for the *Comedy*'s poetics and clues on how it should be read need to be sought in the poem itself.

2

Lectura Dantis: *Paradiso* XXIII

C. P. Brand

Canto XXIII of *Paradiso* takes us into the eighth Heaven, the Heaven of the Fixed Stars which divides the Primo Mobile from the first seven planetary spheres. The function of the eighth Heaven in the divine cosmology has been explained in *Paradiso* II, 130–8:

> 'e 'l ciel cui tanti lumi fanno bello,
> della mente profonda che lui volve
> prende l'image e fassene suggello.
>   E come l'alma dentro a vostra polve
> per differenti membra e conformate
> a diverse potenze si risolve,
>   cosí l'intelligenza sua bontate
> multiplicata per le stelle spiega,
> girando sé sovra sua unitate.'

This Heaven then receives from the Primo Mobile the imprint of God's virtue which is multiplied in the different stars and thence distributed via the lower spheres to man on earth.[1]

There is thus a difference in kind between the eighth and the preceding seven spheres and it is not surprising that in Dante's account of his passage through Paradise his entry into the eighth Heaven is prepared in a distinctive way that marks it off from his arrival in the spheres below. In each of these the poet rises from sphere to sphere without any conscious awareness of his ascent – he arrives in each successive Heaven before he realises it and he can only report his experience in the past tense:

15

Io non m'accorsi del salire in ella . . .   (VIII, 13)

. . . ma del salire
non m'accors'io . . .   (X, 34–5)

'Noi sem levati al settimo splendore . . .'   (XXI, 13)

And no sooner has he arrived than he is plunged into a new sequence of experiences which allow no time for pondering on what has passed. Thus the speed of Dante's ascent through the seven planetary spheres is such that the distinctions between them are somewhat blurred – it is only when he stands on the threshold of the Heaven of the Fixed Stars that the passage from one Heaven to another is explicitly signalled by the poet. Here for the first time he stops to look down at the world he is leaving beneath his feet,

> L'aiuola che ci fa tanto feroci,
> volgendom'io con li etterni Gemelli
> tutta m'apparve da' colli alle foci.   (XXII, 151–3)

thus setting in perspective the pettiness of man's physical and emotional condition against the grandeur of God's creation and purpose. It is one of the high points of his journey, as visually arresting as a space-fiction scene, but also spiritually uplifting in its imaginative contrast between earth and Heaven. The concept is taken from Cicero's *Somnium Scipionis*, but Cicero's rather bare and explicit prose, 'iam ipsa terra ita mihi parva visa est ut me imperii nostri quo quasi punctum eius attingimus paeniteret', is here conjured into some of Dante's most memorable lines. Noteworthy is his replacement of the geometrical 'punctum' with the human 'aiuola' – perhaps deriving from Boethius: 'vix angustissima inhabitandi hominibus area reliquetur'.[2] (Contrast Chaucer's more literal rendering of Cicero in his picture of himself on the eagle's back in *The House of Fame*: '. . . flowen from the ground so high / That all the world as to my eye / No more seemed than a prikke', ll. 905–7.) Significant also is the typical Dantesque reticence in concealing in a quiet relative clause the sting which Cicero so rhetorically underlined at the climax of a consecutive clause, and which Boethius elaborates in a quite lengthy passage. The preceding canti have indeed been preoccupied with 'l'aiuola che ci fa tanto feroci' (the corrupt Benedictines, the wicked Christian kings etc.), and we turn away with relief and hope for the 'ultima salute' which Beatrice promises Dante is now close.

What is to follow in the next canto is the next stage in the ascent to God, a vision of all the blessed souls lit up by the light of Christ and the presence of the Virgin who come down to him not singly or in small groups but in their entirety, in anticipation of their final appearance in the Rose. What we are about to witness is the triumph of Christ in a scene parallel to the triumph of the Church Militant in the Earthly Paradise, as Beatrice has already explained to Dante

> 'sí che 'l tuo cor, quantunque può, giocondo
> s'appresenti alla turba *triunfante*
> che lieta vien per questo etera tondo'.   (XXII, 130–2)

and as she will repeat

> . . . 'Ecco le schiere
> del *triunfo* di Cristo e tutto il frutto
> ricolto del girar di queste spere!'   (XXIII, 19–21)

This canto therefore effectively concentrates our vision so that we can embrace the diverse experiences of the lower Heavens which are, in a sense, now superseded. What we shall see now is a great gathering of all the souls, the full harvest garnered under the influence of the starry sphere, a triumphant throne presided over by Christ and Mary thanks to whom their redemption was possible. While this vision has been anticipated frequently in the poem, it still is only a foretaste of the ultimate spectacle of the Rose. Its purpose is both to inform Dante about the working of God's purpose and also to encourage him to proceed. He has literally some stiff examinations ahead. The narrative structure of Canto XXIII is thus based on two events: the appearance, and disappearance, first of Christ and then of Mary with the attendant souls. These supernatural events are shown from the point of view of the two spectators, Beatrice and Dante, and much of the canto is devoted to the effects of these events, first on Beatrice, and then on Dante, and further, the effect on Dante of Beatrice's reactions to the two spectacles.

This is the basic material of Dante's canto and it determines closely the nature of his poetry. He is trying to describe a supernatural vision, an experience of great beauty and excitement, which, by its very extra-ordinary nature, is difficult if not impossible to communicate. He meets no ordinary souls here from the biblical, classical or medieval worlds to bring their individual experiences into this ethereal Heaven. Dante has moved on, apparently beyond his preoccupation with the temporary and contingent. Nor is he here questioning the divine intention (as he has done so often before) or being questioned on *his* beliefs, as will happen in the next canto. He is not concerned here with theological niceties but with the reality of a spiritual experience, and his poetry is at its least intellectual in any arid sense. He has, as he explains, a task of extreme difficulty and his style has to rise to meet it – which it does with a strongly Latinate, elevated vocabulary, and an unusually dense imagery of simile and metaphor.

Dante's gaze back at the petty earth is the termination of his passage through the seven planetary spheres and it forms a natural termination of Canto XXII. But a single line at the very end of that canto prepares us for what is to follow: 'Poscia rivolsi li occhi alli occhi belli' (l. 154). He looks from the earth to Beatrice, and the following canto opens directly and arrestingly with his comment on what he saw: 'Come l'augello, intra l'amate fronde . . .' (l. 1). The contrast between Dante gazing down on the strife-torn earth, and Beatrice gazing intently up to the peaceful Heavens is brought out in one of Dante's most beautiful similes: the mother bird waiting eagerly for the sun to rise so that it can collect food for its young, like Beatrice waiting tensely poised and expectant for the Sun of Christ Triumphant which will enable her to supply Dante with the spiritual nourishment ('quelle dape', l. 43) for his continued progress. (In the first canto of *Paradiso* Dante creates the same sense of tense expectancy in his description of Beatrice gazing more intently than another bird, the eagle, on the sun.) It is a beautiful picture, blended of outward calm and inner tension – the calm of the scene (stillness, dark-ness) underlined by the long vowels and formal structure of the opening tercet, each line with its own autonomy, uncomplicated by hiatus or enjambement – the tension of the bird stressed by the quickening rhythm, 'e con ardente affetto il sole aspetta' (l. 8), and the tension of Beatrice by her association with the bird and metrically by the enjambement of the fourth tercet which stresses her forward-looking, searching eyes:

Cosí la donna mia stava eretta
e attenta, rivolta inver la plaga
sotto la quale il sol mostra men fretta.   (ll. 10–12)

There is thus from the beginning a sense of longing, of tense expectancy, an urgency towards the ultimate goal, the Supreme Good which characterises this canto. We are not yet in the presence of God, but the mystic *élan* has already caught up Beatrice, poet and reader. Beatrice is already different: the bird simile shows this. She is still tender, and motherly like the bird, but she is also 'sospesa e vaga', bird-like in this too, 'eretta e attenta'. She takes on somehow the attributes of the bird, acting instinctively in response to some inner necessity which compels Dante to fall silent and wait patiently and deferentially himself. This simile has attracted a good deal of praise from the commentators; it does seem to bring this supernatural scene into the context of the real world, although no one, in Dante's time at least, could ever have witnessed such a scene – and this is probably a literary reminiscence from Lactantius's account of the phoenix, although the context of Lactantius's image is very different. His phoenix has no young to fret over, and the 'dolci nati' seem rather like a derivation from the 'dulces natos' of the *Georgics* (II, 523). This blending of the personal or intimate with the literary or derived elements is a marked feature of Dante's style here. In this very subjective impression of a spiritual, Christian experience the classical poets are frequently present – Statius, Virgil, Horace and Ovid notably – leading Trompeo to speak of the 'entusiasmo umanistico' of Dante here.

Dante sees Beatrice's preoccupation and is content to wait (ll. 14–15, 'qual è quei che disiando'); he is himself a man who desires something he does not have and waits hopefully – but the pseudo-simile is not empty. It stresses Dante's common humanity with us, who often have to wait hopefully for our wishes; he still has not seen the triumphant Christ and he reacts still much as we should do: the pseudo-simile brings the scene within our experience without introducing a new image to conflict with or dilute that of the bird.

But there now follows a section (ll. 16–39) in which Dante casts off some of his human deficiencies: the sky lightens. Beatrice explains that this is due to the descent of Christ and the blessed. Dante describes its effect on Beatrice and then tries to convey the appearance of this descent to him, turning again to Beatrice who explains further the reasons for Dante's bewilderment. Most significant here is the second remarkable simile

> Quale ne' plenilunii sereni
> Trivia ride tra le ninfe etterne
> che dipingon lo ciel per tutti i seni . . .   (ll. 25–7)

which serves to convey the extraordinary beauty of the resplendent Christ – not yet visible in his double nature of God and man, which Dante will not see until the Empyrean – but a 'viva luce', a sort of halo through which the shining substance of the body of Christ dazzles the poet. After the longing and the urgency of the opening simile we have a static picture of a peaceful skyscape, a full moon and a starry sky – Trivia smiling among the eternal nymphs (a celestial image for the moon and stars as compared with that of the terrestrial Diana and her mortal nymphs, cf. *Purgatorio* XXXI, 106, 'Noi siam qui ninfe/ e nel ciel siamo stelle').[3] Here they are eternal, incorruptible as stars according to the science which Dante followed, immortal souls whose flashing about Christ will continue for eternity. It is a justly famous passage which leads one to wonder at Dante's compelling correlation of sound and image: the long stressed vowels of the first line setting the scene of the clear sky, and contrasting with the stressed short 'i's ringing through the second line like a light flashing out through the darkness. Fubini has a fine analysis of this tercet in his *Metrica e poesia* where he comments *inter alia* on that 'u' in 'plenilunii' 'tenuto come in sordina', as though muted, and suggesting 'l'oscurità della notte'. And phonetic associations apart, 'plenilunii sereni' is itself a striking ellipsis for the full moon in a serene or clear sky. The association of the planets' light with smiling is familiar to us from the opening of *Purgatorio*, where Venus 'faceva tutto rider l'oriente'; here it links the smiling Trivia with the smiling Beatrice of line 48 and the awe-struck Dante who is now acquiring the power to withstand the brilliance of such smiles. In his rapture Dante lets out an exclamatory: 'Oh Beatrice dolce guida e cara!'. The long flowing sentence in which the vision is described with its literary and mythological allusion is contrasted with the staccato effect of the exclamation and the syntactically clumsy 'Oh Beatrice . . ./ Ella mi disse . . .' – the heavenly serenity with the bewildered poet.

Beatrice's two brief speeches of explanation (ll. 19–21 and 35–9) are of a theological nature, each employing a striking metaphor. In the first she explains the reasons for the lightening of the sky: here are the throngs of the triumph of Christ and all the fruit garnered in the wheeling of the spheres. To achieve salvation men need 'Christ's triumph' – that is the redemption through the Crucifixion and Resurrection – and the wheeling of the Heavens with their divine influence on human conduct. Man's natural endowments are the seeds which receive nourishment from the revolving spheres and are brought to maturity in a harvest which will ultimately fill the empty places in the Rose. The seed-sowing, harvest metaphor is repeated at the end of the canto in relation to the throng of souls surrounding Mary (ll. 130–2).[4]

But who precisely does Dante mean by this? The traditional view has been that he includes in the eighth Heaven all those redeemed by Christ's Passion, or all the blessed from the Empyrean. This would mean that the eighth Heaven does not have its own category of spirits – while distributing influence to the other spheres it would not have direct influence on any one man. Against this Porena has argued for a special category of those subject specifically to the influence of the fixed stars, and not including those who have already appeared in the first seven Heavens–so we have in the eighth Heaven Christ, Mary, the Apostles and Adam who possessed such virtue and grace as to be raised above the others and brought nearer to the angelic nature. But there are considerable objections to this – from Dante's normal concern with the number 7 (which makes us reluctant to accept an eighth category of souls) to the difficulty of accepting Christ, Mary, Adam and the Apostles together in a single category, and Dante's own explanation in *Paradiso* II, 112 dividing the three upper Heavens from 'li altri gironi'. The eighth Heaven therefore would seem to contain, for this period of their triumph, all the blessed souls who descend there temporarily to meet the poet, and then return to the Empyrean (just as some had temporarily appeared to the poet in the lower Heavens). The *beati* may therefore appear to the poet three times. The appearance of Christ here as well as in the Empyrean is explained by this first brief visit being a special dispensation to Dante in which the poet is the object of a revelation parallel to that of pre-Christian man (and it is no arrogance on Dante's part, as Porena suggests, to imagine Christ descending to meet him). So the way between Heaven and earth, blocked previously in the conflict between man and God, is cleared by the triumphant Christ, historically for mankind, allegorically for Dante's mystical journey. Indeed the four appearances of Christ to Dante between Earthly Paradise and Empyrean show a clear progression through the mystic light of the cross (*Paradiso* XIV) to the clearly defined light briefly visible in *Paradiso* XXIII, but inscrutable in its essence, to the clearly intelligible vision of *Paradiso* XXXIII

> ché la mia vista, venendo sincera,
> e piú e piú intrava per lo raggio
> dell'alta luce che da sé è vera.   (ll. 52–4)

The canto divides here, almost exactly in the middle (l. 69) with Beatrice drawing Dante's attention to a new vision, that of the Virgin, which occupies the remainder of this canto. Christ has withdrawn to the Empyrean and this first narrative action is complete. We can pause for a moment therefore to review the response of Dante's poetry to this single spiritual experience. Two features are particularly striking. The first is the adoption of a dignified, noble style in keeping with the solemnity of the occasion: the biblical 'la sapienza e la possanza'; the ritual 'triunfo di Cristo'; and the Latinate, elevated vocabulary ('labor', 'aggrati', 'superne', 'cape', 'dape', 'oblita', 'proferta', 'preterito'). All these contribute to what Sapegno has called 'la patina singolarmente nobile e sostenuta del discorso'.

The second feature is the density, pertinence and effectiveness of the figurative language. Of the six similes three relate to natural, three to human phenomena. At the narrative and emotional peak are those relating to the appearance of Christ: two grandiose scenes of inanimate nature (the moonlit landscape and the thunder-cloud). At a lower level a natural scene is used (the anxious bird) relating to a less exalted person (Beatrice). And for the lowly figure of the poet we have the two pseudo-similes of the waiting man and the wakening man, and the true simile of the man with his path blocked. The two grandiose and spectacular similes are placed centrally, like the mystical peak they represent, and they are prefaced and concluded by the lesser, more lowly pictures of animal and human experience, thus creating a sort of crescendo and diminuendo effect. The simile here, as Pagliaro suggests, is a 'vera e propria necessità di espressione', used where 'l'intuizione astratta trova in un'immagine concreta un tramite necessario di comunicabilità'.[5] It both clarifies and underlines the emotional reaction of the poet to an experience which is unique and for which there is no traditionally appropriate language. So the Trivia simile conveys the radiance of Christ's appearance but in a context of joy. The one that follows conveys a sense of stunned confusion.

The comparison of Dante's mind to the lightning in a cloud (l. 40) is a difficult one to engage with, perhaps intentionally so – the experience itself is confusing. Beatrice's explanation that Dante's brilliant vision is of 'la sapienza e la possanza/ch'aprí le strade tra 'l cielo e la terra' seems strikingly parallel to the image of the lightning which comes down from Heaven to earth 'fuor di sua natura'. Aristotle's words for fire moving downwards might equally well be applied to God made man. Yet this image is not explicitly referred back to Christ, but forward to Dante whose mind swells like the lightning in a cloud and comes bursting out – not presumably downwards but up to Heaven, thus reopening the 'path between Heaven and earth' in an experience which stuns the poet so that he cannot recall it. The simile thus links Christ's appearance with Dante's reaction in a subtle and compelling fashion.

These similes are thus reinforced by the metaphorical language of the passages not within the simile: the moon and the lightning striking the earth by Christ 'ch'aprí le strade tra 'l cielo e la terra' (l. 38); the birds awaiting food by 'quelle dape' (l. 43) with which Dante is fed; his struggle to recall his vision by the book that recalls the past (l. 54); the blocked passage by the poet's 'ponderosa tema' and 'picciola barca' (ll. 64, 67). It is a rich poetry in which the dense images reflect and sustain each other.

The second half of the canto (ll. 70 ff.) is devoted to a separate vision, that of the Virgin who appears with the Apostles among 'turbe di splendori' lit up from above. It opens suddenly with Beatrice's appeal to Dante to turn his gaze away from her to this new spectacle, the beautiful garden blooming under the rays of Christ. The language is scriptural, the tone mystical – the *rose* for the Virgin, the *lilies* for the Apostles, the *scent* that indicated 'the true path'. Beatrice's last words to Dante (ll. 46–8) were an injunction to look at her and her smile: now she rebukes him for gazing at her and tells him to turn his eyes elsewhere (not so sternly perhaps as in *Paradiso* XVIII – 'che non pur ne' miei occhi è paradiso'). We are not told explicitly what has happened in the meantime – only that he hears the first order in a daze so that he could not possibly describe the smile of Beatrice – small wonder, he says, that he trembles under the task that he has set himself. We infer therefore that he is wrapt in wonder at Beatrice's beauty when her words break into his rêverie. They come abruptly, unannounced, and take the reader by surprise, as they must have taken the poet.

This is in fact the fourth of Beatrice's addresses to Dante since the opening of the canto – four brief but insistent, almost nagging interruptions in the poet's fascinated absorption in the scenes before him: 'Ecco le schiere . . .' she points out (l. 19); 'Quivi è la sapienza . . .' (l. 37); 'Apri li occhi . . .' (l. 46); 'Perché la faccia mia . . .' (l. 70). The structure of the canto up to this point is characterised by this alternation of narrative and direct speech or monologue – the narrative embracing a sequence of supernatural events described in figurative language (Dante marvelling at the spectacle before him), and the monologues, Beatrice's interventions, illustrating, explaining, exhorting. What is the purpose and effect of this? Is it primarily artistic – to break up the succession of dazzling and startling images? Or is it narrative convenience – the first two of Beatrice's speeches are explanations for the reader's benefit, as well as for the poet, of the identity of these otherwise unidentifiable splendours? These are surely part of the explanation, but equally important is another factor. Dante is describing a mystical experience, a journey towards the Divinity; he has to progress from stage to stage, seeing and understanding successively the vision of Christ Triumphant and of the Virgin and Apostles. He is not permitted to rest or stagnate, but he is urged on in this mystical ascent by Beatrice, without whom he might never proceed. Her exhortations first to look on her and then to look away were seen by the ancient commentators as allegorical – he needs the light of faith or of Theology, to understand the visions he is witnessing, but he must then, with the aid of his faith, turn again to the mystical presence of the Virgin. But whether we read them allegorically or not, such minimal dramatic actions, consisting of mere movements of the eyes, are remarkably effective in underlining the tension of Dante's progress through Paradise. Beatrice urges him on and the emphasis of her words is all on the upwards surge of Dante's spirit. The poet tends to be static, resting in the beauty and splendour of those superb visions. Beatrice's words convey the mystic *élan*:

'*Quivi* è la sapienza e la possanza
ch'aprí le strade tra 'l cielo e la terra'.   (ll. 37–8)

'*Apri* li occhi . . .'   (l. 46)

'*Quivi* è la rosa in che il verbo divino
carne si fece; quivi son li gigli
al cui odor *si prese il buon cammino*'.   (ll. 73–5)

The emphasis is not on the conventional, static images ('rosa', 'gigli') but on the words conveying movement and progression.[6]

The structure of the canto is repetitive therefore: simile ('augello') – speech ('Ecco le schiere'); simile (Trivia) – speech ('Quel che ti sobranza'); simile ('come foco di nube') – speech ('Apri li occhi'); simile ('Io era come quei') – speech ('Perché la faccia mia'). It is reminiscent of the medieval concept of *commedia* as a succession of 'parti espositive' or expository elements, and 'parti didascaliche' or didactic elements, in dialogue; and some critics have seen in this canto something of the nature of the *sacra rappresentazione*. What is noteworthy here is how this structure is related to the essential material of the canto. Each successive state of bliss is conveyed in a simile; each speech of Beatrice's prods Dante further along 'il buon cammino', his mystical journey.

So Beatrice's last words to Dante, to look at the garden with the rose and the lilies, evokes another powerful simile ('come a raggio di sole . . .', l. 79) where the poet likens the sight of the Virgin and Apostles lit up from above to a striking natural scene – a ray of light penetrating the clouds, so that the light is visible, but not its source, the sun. The subjunctive 'mei' suggests a generic allusion so that the particularised 'vider' at the head of the line has a special urgency appropriate to the scene. The metaphorical garden comes to life as a real field, a landscape from Tuscany or Umbria with Dante himself looking out of the shadows on the sunny meadow dotted all over with flowers. Christ has disappeared aloft ('su t'esaltasti') in order to relieve Dante's eyes of the brilliance which would prevent him seeing Mary and the blessed. Dante is not yet ready to enter the next Heaven, any more than Christ's contemporaries were, during His stay on earth. Christ's withdrawal here parallels His resurrection which made possible the redemption of mankind. Here we have an idea of the Marian thesis that only by the intercession of the

Virgin, or via the Incarnation, can man reach God, an idea explicitly
declared in *Paradiso* XXXIII:

> 'Donna, se' tanto grande e tanto vali,
> che qual vuol grazia ed a te non ricorre,
> sua disianza vuol volar sanz'ali.'   (ll. 13–15)

Christ then has withdrawn, but Dante had not noticed, he was so intent
on Beatrice, and with his habitual graphic sense he does not therefore tell
the reader of Christ's disappearance until now. Nor had he noticed the
descent of Mary, whose presence, not her arrival, is announced by
Beatrice.

The sight of the new 'turbe di splendori' (ll. 85–93) provokes another
exclamation of gratitude (just as the vision of Christ Triumphant occa-
sioned his 'Oh Beatrice') – gratitude for the withdrawal of the dazzling
vision of Christ so that he can look on the 'bel fior', the Rose – that is
Mary. The language is studied, learned, high-flown, in accordance with
the tone of the material ('su t'esaltasti'; 'il quale e il quanto della viva
stella'; 'che là su vince come qua giú vinse' (which outstrips the stars in
Heaven in brightness just as it once outstripped in virtue all others on
earth). Yet within it is a lowly, humble image ('il nome . . . ch'io sempre
invoco / e mane e sera') of Dante reciting his prayers morning and
evening to the Virgin. As we have seen elsewhere there is a studied
contrast between the poet, who is human, and his surroundings, which
are supernatural, and this is underlined repeatedly in the imagery and
style, which are not uniform, but varied as the narrative requires. So the
high-flown, learned and solemn style gives way here and there to an
intimate, domestic note – note how later the image of Mary soaring up to
the ninth Heaven is broken by the simile of the baby stretching out its
arms to its *mamma* (l. 121).

But now the vision of Mary is withdrawn, in an interesting way. Her
descent and departure in the second half of the canto are parallel with the
descent and departure of Christ in the first – but Dante does not repeat
himself. Christ flew off unannounced and unnoticed. Mary is fetched,
and we see the descent of a blazing torch which circles round the Virgin
and gently reminds her that she is needed elsewhere (to make the
Empyrean more divine, 'dia piú'). The identity of the torch is disputed by
the commentators. Its own words 'Io sono amore angelico' (l. 103),

apparently addressed to Mary, are surely unnecessary as a self-introduc-
tion for the Virgin. Some see the torch as the Archangel Gabriel (here
renewing the mystic rite of the Annunciation) and interpreting *Paradiso*
XXXII, 94 ('quello amor che primo lí discese') as an allusion to this
occasion – while others see it as an unspecified angel, probably a Seraph,
or perhaps a number of angels which together form a crown, like the
various strings making up a lyre (the 'lira' of l. 100). Our imagination is
strained to the utmost to follow the metaphors of this passage – the *lyre
crowning* the *sapphire*, the *love circling* the *joy* which *breathes* from the
womb (the Virgin) that was once the *inn* of our *hopes* (Christ). Momi-
gliano points out how the ritual language (*'Benedictus fructus ventris tui'*)
is spiritualised. The reader is compelled to jettison any prejudices against
mixed metaphors, and the metaphors tumble thick and fast here, because
we are not in the normal world of the senses. We have here a blend of
movement and sound, a wheeling, circling melody ('circulata melodia').
No melody on earth can compare with this.[7]

   Now, in the last section of the canto (ll. 112–39) Dante sees Mary
return, up through the ninth Heaven to the Empyrean, following Christ,
but leaving behind the other blessed spirits with some of whom Dante
will speak in the following cantos, and he ends with an apostrophe to the
crowd of the blessed and especially to St Peter, the triumphant leader of
the army of saints. The fact of Mary's disappearance is only revealed in a
relative clause at the end of the first three tercets (ll. 112–20) which
emphasise the vastness of the spaces into which Dante is gazing: that is of
the Primo Mobile, conceived as a sphere the inner edge of which is
beyond the limits of Dante's sight. This is the sphere 'che piú ferve', that
is most ablaze with love, and is most quickened with life by the breath of
God (the Holy Spirit) and His working. This striking picture of the ninth
Heaven

>   Lo real manto di tutti i volumi
>   del mondo, che piú ferve e piú s'avviva
>   nell'alito di Dio . . .   (ll. 112–14)

shows how Dante's poetry is often built on the tight theological and
intellectual reasoning of his prose, here extending the metaphor and
repeating the superlatives of *Convivio* (II, iii, 9): 'E questo è cagione al
Primo Mobile per avere velocissimo movimento, che per lo ferventissimo

appetito . . . d'esser congiunta con ciascuna parte di quello divinissimo ciel . . .'. The language remains predominantly elevated and imprecise – so that commentators have not been sure if Dante is alluding to the ninth or tenth Heaven: the metaphorical 'royal cloak' for the Primo Mobile, as the top layer of a series of garments covering the earth, concrete though it is, does not really change the generally abstract character of the passage, because it is impossible to pursue visually this image through the subsequent verbs ('ferve' and 's'avviva'); the appearance ('parvenza') of the ninth Heaven is mentioned barely in time to be denied ('non apparve'), and the names of Mary and Christ are avoided and instead we have 'la coronata fiamma' and 'sua semenza'.

This language is contrasted with the realistic, even lowly style of the simile that follows (ll. 121–6) – the babe after it has been fed, stretching out its arms to its mother in an impulse of affection. The intimate form is chosen, *mamma*, not *madre*, and is set in a stressed and dominant position in rhyme; but even here the concrete gives way to the spiritual in the third line of the simile ('per l'animo che 'nfin di fuor s'infiamma') where the gesture ('di fuor') and the flushing of the cheeks ('s'infiamma') are merely the outward manifestation which is itself made here to 'blaze forth outwardly'. And the simile which, as we read, we expect to refer to Dante, in fact is used *not* in a concrete image of the poet stretching up his arms to the departing Mary (has not he just been fed with the sight of the Virgin), but of the spiritual impulse of the blessed (l. 124) who shoot up to Heaven in their reverence for Mary. They sing the first words of the antiphone of the Easter service, 'Regina coeli, laetare, alleluia'.

The language of the three concluding tercets is densely metaphorical and has been criticised as being not perhaps so controlled as is usual in the *Comedy*. The first of the three is troublesome, and however one interprets *bobolce* (whether more conventionally as those who sow, or less so as fields for sowing) either reading is related with difficulty to the chests which must refer to the blessed spirits. The figurative language of sowing, abundant crops and laden chests recalls effectively Beatrice's metaphor earlier in the canto ('tutto il frutto/ricolto del girar di queste spere' (ll. 20–1), and even the flowers blooming 'sotto i raggi di Cristo' (l. 72). But Dante does not persist with this image. He is looking, I assume, for a way to introduce St Peter, who is to appear in the next canto, and whose keys therefore are employed to guard a treasure analogous to that in the 'arche ricchissime'. So that although we pass through three different metaphors (the harvest, the treasure and the triumph) in what seems an incoherent and irrational fashion, the three tercets are in fact linked imaginatively and semantically – the 'ricchissime arche' look forward to the 'tesoro', and the 'tesoro' to the 'chiavi'. The rich harvest of the good sowers is the spiritual treasure acquired during the exile of the blessed on earth where they scorned material wealth, as did Peter in his triumph over worldly temptations.

Each of the last three tercets opens with an exclamatory and allitera-tive expression: 'Oh quanta . . .', 'Quivi . . .', 'Quivi . . .', building up an imposing *entrée* in the very last line for St Peter, who is to hold the centre of the stage in Canto XXIV where he will examine Dante on faith; and this rhetorical climax seems to contrast consciously with the quiet opening of the canto. We have commented on the marked sense of mystical progression in this canto, and on the careful use of stylistic effects to underline this. The growing mystical fervour is paralleled by the sense of growing light and richness as the canto proceeds: from the dark night to the sky brightening, the full moon, the flash of lightning, the beams of sunlight and finally the 'turbe di splendori'; from the hungry birds to the fruit of the heavens' calling, the flowering garden and finally the abundant harvest garnered in the chests; from the still nest and the silent Beatrice, through her successive speeches with their rising fervour, to the circling melody of the angels and the final hymn to the Virgin. The canto ends thus with the ascent of Mary and the blessed in a flood of light and a resounding hymn of praise, having begun in the darkness and quiet of a humble nest.

Notes

1. All references are to the edition by Natalino Sapegno (Florence, ninth reprint 1977). Apart from the standard commentaries see F. Pellegrini, *Lectura Dantis* (Orsanmichele, 1904); M. Porena, *La mia Lectura Dantis* (Naples, 1932); L. Tonelli, 'Il Canto 23 del *Paradiso*', *Convivium*, 5 (1932) 675–91; C. F. Goffis, *Lectura Dantis Scaligera* (Florence, 1968); P. P. Trompeo, *Letture Dantesche* (Florence, 1964); A. Scaglione, 'Imagery and thematic patterns in *Paradiso* XXIII', in *From Time to Eternity*, ed. T. G. Bergin (London, 1967); A. Pagliaro, *Ulisse* (Florence, 1967); U. Bosco, *Dante vicino* (Rome, 1972) pp. 342–68; L. Pertile, 'Stile e immagini in *Paradiso* XXIII', in *The Italianist*, 4 (1984), 7–34.
2. *De consolatione philosophiae*, II, 7.

3. Trivia is a name for the moon worshipped at a place where several roads met –
   cf. Hecate (Inferno), Diana (earth).
4. See B. Nardi, *Dante e la cultura medievale* (Bari, 1949) pp. 309–55 and
   P. Boyde, *Dante Philomythes and Philosopher* (Cambridge, 1981) p. 254.
5. T. S. Eliot (*Dante*, 1929) and C. S. Lewis (*Studies in Medieval and Renaissance
   Literature*, Cambridge, 1966) make similar points. For further discussions of
   the simile in Dante see I. Brandeis, *The Ladder of Vision* (1960) and
   R. Kirkpatrick, *Dante's 'Paradiso' and the Limitations of Modern Criticism*
   (Cambridge, 1978). For a sensitive analysis of the structure of the Canto
   XXIII similes see Pertile, 'Stile e immagini', pp. 8–11.
6. See L. Malagoli's comments on the 'slancio verso l'alto' of this canto in his
   commentary (Milan, 1966). See also his *Linguaggio e poesia nella Divina
   Commedia* (Genoa, 1949) p. 89.
7. See F. Squarcia, 'Il canto XXIII del *Paradiso*', in *Letture Dantesche* (Parma,
   1955); Boyde, *Dante Philomythes*, pp. 183–4.

3

Lectura Dantis: *Paradiso* XXVII

Uberto Limentani

Canto XXVII has been described by one critic as the most dramatic of
the whole *Paradiso*, and by another as the canto of invective *par
excellence*. While no one would quarrel with the first view, the second
should be treated with many reservations. It would, perhaps, be better to
stress the variety and the wide range of its subject-matter, the swiftness
with which the narrative moves, again and again, from Heaven to earth
and from earth to Heaven, from visions of Paradise to the contemplation
of human shortcomings. The frequent changes of register heighten the
contrast between the different scenes that follow each other in these very
full 148 lines.

What commentators have failed to notice, dazzled as they have been
by the never flagging interest of the narrative, is that Canto XXVII is also
a canto of transition. Its opening can be seen as the conclusion of the
three preceding cantos. These were aimed at intellectual enlightenment
and are all of a piece. Likewise, the cantos which follow it (from XXVIII
onwards) are fairly homogeneous. In them Dante's gaze will focus on
Heaven, a fitting prelude to the supreme vision of Canto XXXIII. By
contrast, here his eyes turn more than once towards the earth and
towards the perverted condition of mankind. And full vent is given once
again, through invective, to Dante's indignation at human failings,
especially within the Church. But after the two outbursts of Canto
XXVII invective, appropriately enough, will disappear and preoccupations with life on earth will never again come to the fore with such
prolonged intensity. The poet and his readers have other matters to
concentrate their minds on.

'Al Padre, al Figlio, a lo Spirito Santo',
cominciò, 'gloria!', tutto 'l paradiso,
sí che m'inebrïava il dolce canto.   3
    Ciò ch'io vedeva mi sembiava un riso
de l'universo; per che mia ebbrezza
intrava per l'udire e per lo viso.   6
    Oh gioia! oh ineffabile allegrezza!
oh vita intègra d'amore e di pace!
oh sanza brama sicura ricchezza![1]   9

It is doubtful whether one could find in the whole poem many more
joyful passages than the first nine lines of this canto. They express pure
delight, that undiluted inebriation with joy – indeed, with beatitude –
which one would associate with Paradise. The canto opens with a
'fortissimo', a hymn of glory and thanksgiving for Dante having successfully undergone his theological examination on faith, hope and charity
and for having had the benefit of his encounters with the souls of three
apostles, St Peter, St James and St John, and of the first man, Adam
(Cantos XXIV–XXVI). The effect is greatly enhanced by the posi-
tioning of the crucial word, 'Gloria!', in isolation. Syntactically, the first
line should follow the word 'Gloria!', but then the startling resonance of
the liturgical hymn intoned by the infinite number of blessed souls,
'tutto 'l paradiso', would be lost. Dante placed it instead immediately
after the pause forced on the reader's eye (or voice) by the verb
'cominciò': a verb preceding its subject and interrupting the opening
sentence of the hymn. In fact, these lines rely more on the reader's
imagination stimulating his ear than by any sound produced by the
human voice.
    If the canto opens with a climax, the next two terzine are no anticli-
max. The same feeling of bliss is sustained throughout them. Bliss seems
to pervade the whole universe (ll. 4 and 5). The expression 'riso del-
l'universo' is particularly felicitous, in so far as it conveys the notion of
the rejoicing of all that has been created in the presence of its Creator.
The rest of the terzina is an analysis of Dante's own reaction to what
surrounds him. It stems from an ingrained scholastic habit, which must
have become second nature, and draws the reader's attention to the fact
that Dante's rapture is experienced through both sight and hearing, the
two senses which are stressed throughout the poem as stimulating

Dante's own feelings and providing the raw material to be interpreted by his mind.

Lines 7–9 are an explosion of exultation, a celebration of that life full of love and peace (l. 8) which Dante has found in Paradise, but is so far from being achieved on earth. Line 9 implies that wealth acquired in this world is insecure. It is troubled both by fear of losing it and by the craving to increase it. Dante had dwelt at length on the subject of worldly riches in Book Four of the *Convivio*, and had explained how they are powerless to satisfy man's craving. But here he is concisely and poetically harking back to the final part of the quotation from Cicero (*Paradoxa*) which he had summoned to his aid in the *Convivio* (IV, xii, 6): 'When men have plenty they crave for more even more eagerly. For covetousness is never satisfied. And men torment themselves not only with desire to increase what they already possess but also with fear of losing what they have'.

> Dinanzi a li occhi miei le quattro face
> stavano accese, e quella che pria venne
> incominciò a farsi più vivace,   12
>   e tal ne la sembianza sua divenne,
> qual diverrebbe Iove, s'elli e Marte
> fossero augelli e cambiassersi penne.   15

Now Dante directs our attention to what is going on round him. The four torches of line 10 are St Peter, St James, St John and Adam, who hold the stage in the three preceding cantos. The light that grows brighter (l. 12) is St Peter's, and the colour it takes on is red. This is conveyed by means of a comparison (ll. 13–15) which may justifiably be thought somewhat bizarre and most unlikely to clarify the event it is meant to illustrate. If the planet Jupiter, which sheds a white light, and the planet Mars, which is red, were birds and exchanged plumage, the planet Jupiter would become red; and this is what happened to St Peter. The thought immediately springs to one's mind that planets are not even remotely like birds, and that birds do not exchange plumage. Some commentators explain such elaborate and far-fetched associations by pointing to the greater imagination of the medieval mind, and to its being more ready than ours to find analogies; but the link might well be via the eagle ('uccello di Giove') which dominated the whole of the presentation of events in the Heaven of Jupiter and is still fresh in the reader's mind.

Moreover, Dante had stressed the change of colour (fading of a blush) in Canto XVIII (ll. 64–6), in the ascent from Mars to Jupiter; and the intermediate role of Jupiter between Mars (hot) and Saturn (cold) is stressed in Canto XXII (ll. 145–7). By referring to the planets (which is the main point), Dante stresses the passage from the theme of justice (which requires calm and similar qualities and looms large in the Heaven of Jupiter) back to Mars (which stands for righteous anger, doing something, being active). But there is more. Dante may also deliberately wish to force us to make an intellectual effort. By exercising our mind we are made to appreciate more fully the import of what is being described. There are other, less obvious, examples of the same technique further on in this canto, and many more throughout the *Paradiso*.

> La providenza, che quivi comparte
> vice e officio, nel beato coro
> silenzio posto avea da ogne parte,　　　　　　　　　　18
> 　　quand' ïo udi': 'Se io mi trascoloro,
> non ti maravigliar, ché, dicend' io,
> vedrai trascolorar tutti costoro.　　　　　　　　　　21
> 　　Quelli ch'usurpa in terra il luogo mio,
> il luogo mio, il luogo mio che vaca
> ne la presenza del Figliuol di Dio,　　　　　　　　　　24
> 　　fatt' ha del cimitero mio cloaca
> del sangue e de la puzza; onde 'l perverso
> che cadde di qua sú, là, giú, si placa'.　　　　　　　　27

Lines 16–18 mark a pause. Silence intervenes between the resounding chorus of the opening stanzas and the thundering St Peter's voice; this alternation of opposites is, indeed, the stuff of which this canto is made. The 'quando' of line 19 breaks the silence imposed by Providence, that is, by God. The gloss 'che quivi comparte / vice ed officio' (ll. 16–17) is intended to specify in theological terms the nature of God's rule in Heaven.

The silence, then, is broken by the thundering voice of St Peter. His invective falls into two parts, with a descriptive passage in the middle to enhance its force. The first terzina (ll. 19–21) is, so to speak, introductory. The two following ones (ll. 22–7) are, perhaps, the most scathing indictment in the whole *Comedy* of one of the principal targets of the poet's wrath: Pope Boniface VIII, who was the reigning Pope in 1300, at the fictional time of Dante's journey. It was Boniface who had indirectly caused Dante's exile by engineering the revolution of 1301 in Florence and the ousting from power of the White faction of the Guelph party, to which Dante belonged. Moreover, this Pope had constantly used his office for the enrichment and aggrandisement of himself and his family, as Dante had loudly affirmed in Cantos XIX and XXVII of the *Inferno*. But this time his condemnation as a pope is even more awe-inspiring than the previous ones since it is pronounced by the very Apostle from whom the popes derived their authority. The violence of its substance is paralleled by the vehemence of its wording. St Peter even resorts to extremely coarse language ('cloaca / Del sangue e della puzza', ll. 25–6) to make his point more forcefully; and he scornfully avoids mentioning Boniface's name. Here, 'Quelli' (l. 22) has definitely derogatory overtones: *that* man!, and could be compared with the contemptuous, hostile 'quel d'Alagna' (the man from Anagni) used by Beatrice to describe the same Boniface in Canto XXX of the *Paradiso* (l. 148). The rhetorical device of lines 22–3 (threefold repetition of the words on which the main emphasis is meant to fall) has been shown to have precedents in the Scriptures (Jer. 7: 4–11). Its awful solemnity is in keeping with the indignation exhibited by St Peter and its impact is devastating. The exact meaning of lines 23–4 needs some clarification. It would be wrong to take them literally in the sense that Boniface had been illegitimately elected, as some of his contemporaries maintained, and that St Peter's throne was really empty. There is a passage in Canto XX of the *Purgatorio* (l. 87) in which Dante explicitly admits that Boniface was the Vicar of Christ. As far as his election was concerned, Dante clearly recognised it as valid. But he usurped St Peter's place 'in the sight of the Son of God' (l. 24), owing to his moral unworthiness. His misdeeds caused satisfaction to Lucifer ('il perverso', l. 26).

> Di quel color che per lo sole avverso
> nube dipigne da sera e da mane,
> vid' ïo allora tutto 'l ciel cosperso.   30
> E come donna onesta che permane
> di sé sicura, e per l'altrui fallanza,
> pur ascoltando, timida si fane,   33
> così Beatrice trasmutò sembianza;

e tale eclissi credo che 'n ciel fue
quando patí la supprema possanza.   36
    Poi procedetter le parole sue
con voce tanto da sé trasmutata,
che la sembianza non si mutò piúe: 39

Another interval of silence follows from line 28 to line 39, another
relaxation of tension. The allusion to the darkness at the Crucifixion
(ll. 35–6) is probably meant to stress that the whole Heaven grew
darker at the 'trascolorare' of the blessed souls. The imaginative and
precise description of red dawns and sunsets (ll. 28–30) and the comparison in lines 31–3 indicate that Beatrice's countenance changes
colour at the same time as that of St Peter and of the other blessed
souls. But she does not blush only with indignation. When Dante turns
his gaze to her, she appears to him like a chaste woman who is sure of
her virtue, yet feels put to shame when confronted with another woman
who has misbehaved. The passage should be seen in the light of what
Dante says about 'vergogna', in the sense of 'verecundia' (modesty), in
the *Convivio* (IV, xix, 8–9). It is, he explains, a good and praiseworthy
virtue in women and children. But Beatrice's show of modesty is also a
hint that even in her new role in Paradise she retains something of her
femininity.

'Non fu la sposa di Cristo allevata
del sangue mio, di Lin, di quel di Cleto,
per essere ad acquisto d'oro usata;   42
    ma per acquisto d'esto viver lieto
e Sisto e Pïo e Calisto e Urbano
sparser lo sangue dopo molto fleto.   45
    Non fu nostra intenzion ch'a destra mano
d'i nostri successor parte sedesse,
parte da l'altra del popol cristiano;   48
    né che le chiavi che mi fuor concesse,
divenisser signaculo in vessillo
che contra battezzati combattesse;   51
    né ch'io fossi figura di sigillo
a privilegi venduti e mendaci
ond' io sovente arrosso e disfavillo.   54

In vesta di pastor lupi rapaci
si veggion di qua sú per tutti i paschi:
o difesa di Dio, perché pur giaci?   57
Del sangue nostro Caorsini e Guaschi
s'apparecchian di bere: o buon principio,
a che vil fine convien che tu caschi!'   60

The second part of St Peter's invective (ll. 40–66) moves one step further
forward in a relentless progression. His denunciations are not directed
against just one pontiff, but against all the popes of Dante's time. St
Peter's eloquence is still in full flow and he finds ever new ways of
expressing his indignation, such as, for instance, the hammering effect of
the negative particles placed at the beginning of each terzina ('Non ...
ma'; 'non'; 'né'; 'né') which punctuate the first part of his speech. The
abundance of echoes from the two cantos of the *Inferno* (XIX and
XXVII) which express equally violent sentiments is also worth noting.
'Sposa di Cristo' (l. 40) harks back to 'la bella donna' (the beautiful lady)
of *Inferno* XIX, 57; 'le chiavi che mi fuor concesse' (l. 49) to 'son due le
chiavi' of *Inferno* XXVII, 104; 'che contra battezzati combattesse' (l. 51)
to 'ché ciascun suo nimico era Cristiano' of *Inferno* XXVII, 87; and
several more passages could be added. Likewise, St Peter resorts to the
Scriptures to impart greater cogency to his words. The ravening wolves
of line 55 come straight from St Matthew's Gospel (7: 15); and expressions inspired by the Old Testament will be found at the end of his
speech.

The metaphor in which the Church is the Bride of Christ nurtured with
the blood of early martyrs in order to gain possession of heavenly
beatitude and not to gain possession of gold (ll. 40–3) occurs more than
once in the *Paradiso*. It is set in contrast both with the image of the
contemporary Church represented as a prostitute in *Purgatorio* XXXII
(ll. 147 ff.) and with the metaphor a little further on in this same passage
(ll. 58–9) of popes preparing to drink that same blood that was shed by
those who gave their lives for the Church, that is, of popes who are about
to use her for their own advantage and thus to ravage her spiritual
heritage.

The popes named or, rather, bunched together by St Peter in lines 41
and 44 as having been his successors and having been martyred are, some
of them at least, nebulous figures with the exception of Calixtus, and

belong to somewhat different periods in the early history of the Church. Their existence is attested by distant sources, the most likely being the 'Liber Pontificalis'. Some of the earliest ones may have been Peter's supporters or close collaborators rather than popes, in the sense that the papacy as we now understand it, that is, as a claim to universal spiritual authority asserted by the Bishop of Rome, did not exist in their time. In the case of some of them death by martyrdom may have been a legend rather than historical fact. However, Dante's uncritical acceptance of what was common belief does not matter to his readers. Peter, the character in the *Paradiso*, wishes to make a point, and succeeds in making it strongly. Setting Boniface on one side, other popes, like those clearly referred to in line 58, Clement V of Gascony and John XXII of Cahors, had behaved no less reprehensibly in the first two decades of the fourteenth century. Both had pursued gain while sitting on their papal throne in Avignon and had disastrously interfered, as Dante saw it, in Italian politics. Hence, the reference in lines 46–8 to favours lavished on one part of Christ's people, the Guelphs, and to persecutions against the other, the Ghibellines and White Guelphs; hence, the other references to private wars waged by them instead of promoting crusades (ll. 49–51) and to sale of privileges under the seal bearing St Peter's own image (ll. 52–4).

The pope who waged private wars was clearly Boniface VIII, and the war Dante had in mind was the crusade he proclaimed in 1296–1297 against the powerful Roman family, Colonna, who opposed him. But there may be more. It is possible that when Dante wrote these lines (49–51) he was recalling a particular event which had taken place more than fifteen years earlier. On 19 June 1301 the Consiglio dei Cento met in Florence in order to decide upon a request from Boniface for continued support on a military expedition (again, for the purpose of dynastic aggrandisement) against Margherita Aldobrandeschi, whose vast domains he was eager to annex; or, more precisely, the Commune of Florence was asked not to withdraw the hundred horsemen whom they had sent to aid him. Two of those present moved that the Pope's request should be accepted. Dante alone, as witnessed by the official minutes of the meeting, which are extant, spoke against: 'Dante Alagherii consuluit quod de servitio faciendo d[omino] pape nichil fiat' (Dante Alighieri gave it as his opinion that in the matter of providing service to the Pope nothing should be done). This must have displeased Boniface, and may well have prompted him to single Dante out for special vengeance (as, indeed, he was singled out) when the White Guelphs, of whom Dante was one, were ousted from power less than five months later.

> 'Ma l'alta provedenza, che con Scipio
> difese a Roma la gloria del mondo,
> soccorrà tosto, sí com' io concipio;   63
>   e tu, figliuol, che per lo mortal pondo
>   ancor giú tornerai, apri la bocca,
>   e non asconder quel ch'io non ascondo'.   66

The last two terzine of St Peter's speech are quite different in substance as well as in tone. The change is heralded by the new and almost impatient appeal for divine help in line 57: a new appeal, because there had already been several earnest invocations to God both in the *Purgatorio* and in the *Paradiso*, echoing the words from the Psalms (43: 23) which every commentator quotes: 'Exsurge; quare obdormis, Domine?'. Be it as it may, in his final words St Peter seems to allude once again to those prophecies of the coming of a saviour of mankind, of a Veltro, as Virgil had called him in Canto I of the *Inferno* (l. 101), of one 'sent from God', as Beatrice described him in the last canto of the *Purgatorio* (ll. 43–4). It goes without saying that Dante had no idea of what kind of assistance God would send. All he knew, or firmly believed, was that it would be sent. When? 'Tosto', says line 63; but the adverb should not be read literally, but rather as an expression of optimistic faith, an expectation of fulfilment sooner or later of a cherished hope. The prophecy is followed almost in the same breath by a new solemn investiture. St Peter entrusts Dante with the mission of speaking out and telling what he had heard. Dante had a strong sense that he was performing a mission. This is why he had undertaken the immense task of writing the *Comedy*, and this is what had sustained him through his long years of labour. St Peter's final words (ll. 64–6) are a paraphrase of Cacciaguida's famous exhortation in Canto XVII of the *Paradiso* (l. 128): 'Tutta tua vision fa manifesta', and at the same time they are a translation of a passage from Jeremiah (50: 2): 'Praedicate et nolite celare'.

Scipio Africanus, the deliverer of Rome from Hannibal, who paved the way, in Dante's eye, for the establishment of the Roman Empire, and was thus another instrument of Providence, is brought in at the end of an invective against contemporary popes (l. 60). This allusion is meant to reinforce the warning that God will not allow his designs to be thwarted for much longer, in the same way as they were not thwarted when Hannibal threatened Rome.

> Sí come di vapor gelati fiocca
> in giuso l'aere nostro, quando 'l corno
> de la capra del ciel col sol si tocca, 69
> in sú vid' io cosí l'etera addorno
> farsi e fioccar di vapor trïunfanti
> che fatto avien con noi quivi soggiorno. 72
> Lo viso mio seguiva i suoi sembianti,
> e seguí fin che 'l mezzo, per lo molto,
> li tolse il trapassar del piú avanti. 75

And now, back from earth to Paradise. The transition is abrupt, deliberately abrupt, no doubt. Another moment of silence suddenly follows the echoing of St Peter's loud, indignant voice. The simile in lines 67–72 makes us prick up our ears before we take it in, because of the paradoxical nature of a snowfall (in which the flakes move downwards, ll. 67–8) being compared with the brightly shining flames of the blessed spirits (the 'triumphal vapours' of line 71) soaring upwards. But, if we succeed in disregarding the direction of the movement (upwards rather than downwards), we will find the image effective and apt to convey visually and pictorially the even, silent, slow movement of the almost unimaginable multitude of the souls filling and adorning the ether, that is, the Heaven (l. 70), with their splendour. And, by the way, the horn of the Heavenly Goat is touched by the sun (in other words, the sun is in the sign of the Capricorn, ll. 68–9) in the depth of winter, from 21 December to 21 January.

> Onde la donna, che mi vide assolto
> de l'attendere in sú mi disse: 'Adima
> il viso e guarda come tu se' vòlto'. 78
> Da l'ora ch'ïo avea guardato prima
> i' vidi mosso me per tutto l'arco
> che fa dal mezzo al fine il primo clima; 81
> sí ch'io vedea di là da Gade il varco

folle d'Ulisse, e di qua presso il lito
nel qual si fece Europa dolce carco.   84
    E piú mi fora discoverto il sito
di questa aiuola; ma 'l sol procedea
sotto i mie' piedi un segno e piú partito.   87

Dante has revolved (l. 80) together with the Heaven of Fixed Stars since
he looked down for the first time (l. 79). And he has revolved from the
middle to the end of the first clime (ll. 80–1) in the previous six hours
(that is, since he turned his eyes towards the earth at the end of Canto
XXII of the *Paradiso*). Now, each of the seven zones, or climes, into
which ancient geographers divided the earth fit for habitation extended
through 180 degrees of longitude, and Dante had therefore revolved
through half a clime, or ninety degrees. He is over Cadiz (l. 82), but can
see beyond it to the West, and make out the 'varco folle' of Ulysses, that
is, the vast expanse of the Ocean; if he looked towards the East, he could
see the shore of Phoenicia (the place where the nymph Europa was
carried off by Jupiter in the form of a bull, ll. 83–4). The astronomical
and geographical accuracy of lines 85–7 is disputed, and more than one
explanation has been put forward; these do not really matter for our
enjoyment and understanding of Dante's poetry. It is, perhaps, more
profitable to concentrate on the myths of Ulysses and Europa, to which
Dante resorts instead of describing in detail what he sees beneath him. In
this way he does more than impart to the reader the measure of his
westward movement; the two myths conjure up the idea of a fabulous
distance in time, and with it of a boundless perspective, of the immensity
of the space surrounding him and of his enormous distance from the
earth. Line 84, particularly the adjective 'dolce', is highly evocative. It
kindles in the reader's mind the strange fascination of the legend, and
leaves him with the impression of a soft, feminine form abandoning
herself to her abductor and becoming a sweet burden.

    The brief allusion to the legend of Ulysses, however, cropping up
again at this point, towards the end of the poem, is even more worthy of
attention. This story had haunted Dante from Canto XXVI of the
Inferno onwards. It is referred to twice in the *Purgatorio*, and now the
poet's mind turns to it again in the *Paradiso*. There is even a verbal echo
of *Inferno*, XXVI ('varco folle' – 'folle volo'). For Dante Ulysses is the
incarnation of thirst for knowledge. In some ways he identifies himself

with him, in other ways he makes a contrast. Ulysses had relinquished his
country and his dear ones – wife, son, parents – in order to pursue 'virtute
e conoscenza': a pursuit he regarded as a duty for man. Likewise, Dante
had left his native city and his family, and refused to seek readmission
into Florence at the cost of betraying his past and his principles. Both,
then, the imaginary hero and the real man, that is, Ulysses and Dante
had chosen to be consistent and to follow their lonely, heroic path rather
than be untrue to themselves. But the voyage of Ulysses had been a
defiance of reason, a 'folle volo', since he had dared to go beyond the
boundaries permitted to men; whereas Dante in his journey through life
had sought to acquire and disseminate knowledge and wisdom for the
benefit of his fellow men.

> La mente innamorata, che donnea
> con la mia donna sempre, di ridure
> ad essa li occhi piú che mai ardea;   90
>   e se natura o arte fé pasture
> da pigliare occhi, per aver la mente,
> in carne umana o ne le sue pitture,   93
>   tutte adunate, parrebber nïente
> ver' lo piacer divin che mi refulse,
> quando mi volsi al suo viso ridente.   96

Now Dante, after looking downwards at Beatrice's bidding (ll. 76–8),
yields to the urge of turning his eyes again from that puny threshing floor,
the earth (l. 86), to his lady. Line 88 sets the tone. The verb ('donneare'
comes straight from the Provençal courtly lyric; and in their commentary
to Dante's lyric poems Kenelm Foster and Patrick Boyde paraphrased its
meaning as 'to pay court to in its noblest sense'. These lines are, indeed,
pervaded by sentiments belonging to that tradition of courtly lyric which
was behind the development of lyric poetry in Italy in the thirteenth and
early fourteenth century. But at the same time the beauty of Beatrice and
her smile (l. 96) have undergone a subtle transformation. A heavenly
light surrounds this lady who has become a dispenser of divine knowledge, and her attributes are now meant to appeal to the mind rather than
to the senses. In fact, this is stated in so many words in lines 91–3: they
are lures (or images) to take the eyes so as to possess the mind. The
comparison, or implied comparison, is once again couched in a style and

language which demand some effort from the reader, and aim at concentrating his attention on the divine delight (1. 95) which Beatrice's smiling face has the power of imparting. Lines 91 and 93 should be set side by side: nature makes images in human flesh, art in its portraiture.

> E la virtú che lo sguardo m'indulse,
> del bel nido di Leda mi divelse
> e nel ciel velocissimo m'impulse.   99
>   Le parti sue vivissime ed eccelse
> sí uniforme son, ch'i' non so dire
> qual Bëatrice per loco mi scelse.   102
>   Ma ella, che vedëa 'l mio disire,
> incominciò, ridendo tanto lieta,
> che Dio parea nel suo volto gioire: 105

If, in the convention of courtly lyric, the lover experienced extraordinary effects from his lady's gaze, here the virtue that her look grants him (1. 97) is what draws Dante forth from the constellation of Gemini (the sons of Leda, who is mentioned in line 98): it makes him ascend from the eighth Heaven (the Heaven of Fixed Stars) to the ninth Heaven (the Crystalline Sphere, or Primum Mobile), described here as the swiftest of the Heavens (1. 99). As its names imply, it is the Heaven that imparts motion to all heavenly bodies. Unlike the other Heavens, the first to the eighth, the ninth Heaven has no planet or constellation in its substance: hence, the uniformity of all its parts and Dante's inability to tell which of these parts Beatrice chose for his place (ll. 100–2). They are in an invisible Heaven (invisible, because, as explained in the *Convivio* (II, iii, 7) it is diaphanous, that is, wholly transparent; hence, its description as the Crystalline Sphere). Beatrice immediately answers the unspoken question that has arisen in Dante's mind.

> 'La natura del mondo, che quiëta
> il mezzo e tutto l'altro intorno move,
> quinci comincia come da sua meta;   108
>   e questo cielo non ha altro dove
> che la mente divina, in che s'accende
> l'amor che 'l volge e la virtú ch'ei piove.   111
>   Luce e amor d'un cerchio lui comprende,

sí come questo li altri; e quel precinto
colui che 'l cinge solamente intende.   114
    Non è suo moto per altro distinto,
    ma li altri son mensurati da questo,
sí come diece da mezzo e da quinto;   117
    e come il tempo tegna in cotal testo
    le sue radici e ne li altri le fronde,
    omai a te può esser manifesto.'   120

Dante now explains with extreme economy of words and with remarkable lucidity what a lesser poet would have needed a hundred lines to
impart: the nature and function of the ninth Heaven, or Primum Mobile,
and the origin of motion and time within the structure of the universe.
Even in our days when talk of dark matter and black holes has become
commonplace, mastering these staggeringly vast themes with such assur-
ance seems to be an extraordinary *tour de force*. Dante and Beatrice are
at the starting point of the movement of everything that lies round the
earth (ll. 107–8), while the earth itself, lying at the centre ('il mezzo'), is
kept still by the force which gives life to the universe ('la natura del
mondo', l. 106). This Heaven has no other *where* but the Divine Mind
(ll. 109–10); in other words, it is not in space, but it is in the Empyrean
Heaven or (as others will have it) in the same condition as the Empyrean
Heaven. It is the pure medium through which the light of God is
communicated to the whole universe. Only the Empyrean encloses it,
which is pure light and love, boundless, motionless. It is a perfect
manifestation of the unity of God, and it is understood only by God in its
essence and its operation (ll. 112–14).

    There is no term of reference for the movement of the Primum Mobile
apart from itself, the origin of all motion, in the same way as the number
ten is understood by means of the numbers that make it up, that is, by
means of its factors, two and five (ll. 115–17).

    But the Primum Mobile is the origin of time as well as of motion, for
time is measured by the rotation of the Heavens which we experience
every day. This is conveyed by a brilliant metaphor; time is like a tree
growing upside down (ll. 118–20). It has its roots in that vessel, the
Primum Mobile. Thus, its roots are invisible, just as the rotation of the
Crystalline Sphere is invisible. The visible part of the tree, its leaves, can
be seen in the other Heavens where motion is visible, that motion by

which we measure time. In other words, our idea of time is based on the motion of the planets, which we can see; and this motion has the invisible motion of the Primum Mobile for its cause.

Lines 106–20 are a good example of a certain kind of poetry at its best: the poetry of the *Paradiso* which deals with doctrinal or philosophical matters. Far from suppressing inspiration, these subjects stimulate it in Dante's mind, which delights in the discovery of truth. And they also stimulate his imagination. His very enthusiasm is a source of poetry in itself – that fresh excitement at the beauty of discovered truth which is so well described in a passage of the *Convivio* (III, xv, 2) where Dante discusses the truths persuasively demonstrated by wisdom, and says: 'In this demonstration and in this persuasion that extreme pleasure of blessedness is felt, which is the greatest good of Paradise'. The discovery of truth is equivalent to that 'luce intellettual' (*Paradiso* XXX, 40) described as part of the bliss experienced in the Empyrean, indeed, as part of the Empyrean itself. Surely, the import of line 112 of Canto XXVII is the same.

> 'Oh cupidigia, che i mortali affonde
> sí sotto te, che nessuno ha podere
> di trarre li occhi fuor de le tue onde!   123
> Ben fiorisce ne li uomini il volere;
> ma la pioggia continüa converte
> in bozzacchioni le sosine vere.   126
> Fede e innocenza son reperte
> solo ne' parvoletti; poi ciascuna
> pria fugge che le guance sian coperte.   129
> Tale, balbuzïendo ancor, digiuna,
> che poi divora, con la lingua sciolta,
> qualunque cibo per qualunque luna;   132
> e tal, balbuzïendo, ama e ascolta
> la madre sua, che, con loquela intera,
> disïa poi di vederla sepolta.'   135

The canto ends with a pendant to St Peter's discourse, but with some important differences. Peter, the first Vicar of Christ, concentrates on the corruption of the popes and speaks, as it were, *ex cathedra*. Beatrice, who is not a saint of the Catholic Church, uses a different tone; but her invective still marks a relentless progression. Its target is mankind in general, although she does link the deviation of men from the path described by Providence to the vacuum of power caused by the neglect of their duties by both popes and emperors (ll. 139–41). Both invectives culminate in the same prophecy.

The transition from scientific truths and theological matters to the passionate castigation of the moral decadence of mankind may appear to be a little sudden, but it has a logic of its own: men pursue 'cupidigia' (l. 121), and in their spiritual blindness neglect the contemplation of the perfection of the universe. They fix their gaze on worldly preoccupations and become incapable of lifting themselves from the morass of covetousness. This final passage of the canto shows how close, in Dante's eyes, was the link between the order of the universe and the system ordained by Providence for the happiness of men; or, to put it in other words, between his conception of the cosmos and his outlook on politics.

Lines 125–6 may cause mild astonishment at first, as the down-to-earth image of plums and withered fruits undoubtedly marks a temporary lowering of stylistic register which contrasts with the rest of Beatrice's speech. However, the metaphor of rain corrupting the flowers and making the fruits wither stems almost naturally from the metaphor in the previous line (124) of men's will initially blossoming well. The word 'fiorisce' supplies the link.

The 'good will' of line 124 will be seen from the examples which follow to be an innate tendency towards what is good, manifesting itself in many ways, such as innocence, inability to harm, willingness to make sacrifices, obedience to precepts, love for one's parents and submission to them; while the continual rain of line 125 is likely to be the moral climate prevailing on earth, and chiefly the bad example given by those who ought to govern, but fail to do so, thus allowing men's innate tendencies to become corrupted.

As for the two examples themselves (ll. 130–5) – neglect of fasts by adults, and immoderate wish of possessing even the wealth of one's own mother to the point of hoping for her early death – they both stem from the dominant theme of men's covetousness, more obviously in the case of the second one (a monstrous desire for acquiring wealth); but the first one, too, a craving for food, could be accepted as belonging to the same category.

'Cosí si fa la pelle bianca nera
nel primo aspetto de la bella figlia
di quel ch'apporta mane e lascia sera.   138
    Tu, perché non ti facci maraviglia,
pensa che 'n terra non è chi governi;
onde sí svïa l'umana famiglia.   141
    Ma prima che gennaio tutto si sverni
per la centesma ch'è là giú negletta,
raggeran sí questi cerchi superni,   144
    che la fortuna che tanto s'aspetta,
le poppe volgerà u' son le prore,
sí che la classe correrà diretta;
    e vero frutto verrà dopo 'l fiore'.   148

No one has given a convincing explanation up till now of lines 136–8. Line 138 is plain enough: it refers to the sun, which Dante could take to symbolise God. If, out of the many partly plausible and partly implausible interpretations which have been excogitated, one was to choose an interpretation which seems to fit fairly closely into the general context, the meaning would roughly be: thus the skin of the fair daughter of the sun (that is, of human nature) grows darker as the day progresses. The simile would then run as follows: in the same way as that never satisfactorily explained fair daughter of the sun grows black, so do men, who are born with an innate disposition to be good, degenerate as they grow up.

The concept of mankind as a human family referred to in line 141 is significant. Dante attached importance to it. It meant for him that men are all citizens of a vast city, an ideal city destined to be ruled by an Emperor and to be spiritually guided by the Pope. This concept can be found first in the *Convivio* (IV, iv, 1): 'umana civilitade che a uno fine è ordinata cioè a vita felice' (where the key word is 'civilitade'); and several years later in the *Monarchia* (I, ii, 8) in almost the same words: 'universalis civilitas humani generis'. It is an ideal which he conceived in terms of the medieval society of his time; but it has retained its appeal even now as a general concept, albeit in different terms.

The last seven lines of the canto (142–8) reiterate once more the solemn promise of the coming of a saviour of mankind. The complex astronomical circumlocution (ll. 142–3) signifying 'before too long' is another example of the ways devised by Dante to concentrate his readers' minds on what follows: this time, the momentous prophecy Beatrice is about to utter. A loose paraphrase will, perhaps, make it plainer: 'before the whole of January leaves the winter' alludes to the error in the calendar which was gradually making January a spring month. The Julian calendar, dating from the time of Julius Caesar, was based on a year consisting of 365 days and a quarter, with every fourth year being a leap year. But the year is slightly shorter, by a little less than one hundredth part of a day ('la centesma' of line 143). In Dante's time the error had already accumulated to more than eight days. It was corrected in 1582 by Gregory XIII. Consequently, in the Gregorian calendar currently in use a leap year is abolished at the end of three out of four centuries.

'Fortuna' (l. 145) can be taken to have in the first place the archaic meaning of 'storm', in keeping with the image of the fleet which follows; but the associate meaning of 'fortunate event' cannot be discarded. The 'good fruit' of the last line is, of course, in direct contrast with the withered plums of line 126. And, finally, it should be noted that in the first two lines of the immediately following canto (XXVIII) the nature of Beatrice's discourse is defined: it is intended to speak out against the present life of wretched mortals and to declare the truth.

A list of the ingredients of this canto – invective against corruption, prophecy of the coming of a redeemer, Dante's acceptance of the task of preaching truth to the world, doctrinal matters concerning the universe – is enough to vindicate the assertion made at the very beginning of this *Lectura*, and to show how many and how momentous are the themes the poet has succeeded in dealing within its various sections.

Notes

1. The edition used is by G. Petrocchi, *La Commedia, secondo l'antica vulgata* (Milan, 1967). I should like to thank Professor Patrick Boyde for his many invaluable suggestions.

4

Benvenuto da Imola on Fact and Fiction in the *Comedy*

Pamela Williams

Among many references to texts in the *Comedy* two illustrate a familiar textual problem in the fourteenth century and two different kinds of solution. The problem in each case is how to square what a text says with what is accepted as the truth. When in the early canti of *Purgatorio* events seem to contradict a line in Virgil (*Aeneid* VI, 376) on the inefficacy of the prayers of the living for the dead the character Dante asks Virgil to explain (*Purgatorio* VI, 25–48). The character Dante has a similar problem in the Heaven of the Moon when Plato's doctrine of transmigration is apparently confirmed by the appearance there of the souls of the blessed (*Paradiso* IV, 22–4). Beatrice explains, and thereby confirms what most educated Christians of Dante's time held as an article of faith, that the Empyrean is the abode of the blessed souls, in which case the *Timaeus* text seems dangerously misleading. Both episodes are indicative of a general concern with textual issues of this kind and they illustrate two of the most common ways of dealing with them. The character Virgil solves the problem of prayer by appealing to the pagan context in which he was writing; Beatrice suggests that Plato might have been speaking figuratively about the influence of the heavens on human nature in which case his text is acceptable to Christian belief.   ·

For Benvenuto da Imola writing his commentary on Dante *c.* 1380 the most difficult passage in the whole poem is Pier della Vigna's declaration that the souls of the suicides will not be clothed with their cast-off flesh at the Last Judgement (*Inferno* XIII, 103–4); the most difficult because the letter of the text was plainly heretical, just as the literal sense of Plato's text had been condemned as heresy by the Council of Constantinople. Beatrice does after all deal with Plato first, because that particular problem has 'piú di felle' than another one concerning the will. Later in his commentary on *Paradiso* XXIV Benvenuto will claim that Dante included his profession of faith precisely to forestall a charge of heresy in reference to the *Inferno* XIII passage.[1] In his commentary on the Pier della Vigna episode itself he discusses a figurative interpretation of the problematic lines and finally appeals to the demands of character realism. He rejects the figurative interpretation because it violates the letter of the text (if the resurrection of the body means a moral resurrection, what does it mean to say, as it does in *Inferno* XIII, 103, that the souls will come to the Valley of Jehosaphat?). On this occasion Benvenuto, like Virgil in the *Purgatorio* episode, seeks a solution in the context itself: Pier della Vigna says what he believed. He obviously did not believe in the resurrection of the flesh, for if he had, he would not have killed himself (*Comentum* I, 449). Other Trecento commentators find the passage equally difficult. Boccaccio makes a distinction – following St Thomas's advice in *Paradiso* XIII – between two kinds of punishment for suicide, of person and of property. Pier della Vigna has no property, he would therefore imagine that divine justice will punish his body.[2] This explanation is qualified by a general remark which prefaces this section of the commentary and restricts the poetic licence of Christian writers: while pagans may be forgiven their errors in matters of religion, Christians, and of course Dante is included, ought not to make statements which, if only in a literal sense, are contrary to the Christian faith.

Figurative explanations are naturally enough very common in solving textual problems of this kind, since poets are expected to use figurative language. While rejecting the figurative interpretation of *Inferno* XIII, 103–4, Benvenuto naturally finds it perfectly acceptable that the author might be speaking 'poetically and figuratively' ('poetice et figurate' – the two terms here are virtually synonymous) because 'he would not be a poet if he spoke literally' ('aperte', *Comentum* I, 449). Commenting on Beatrice's figurative interpretation of the *Timaeus* text in *Paradiso* IV, Benvenuto reminds his readers that what she says is after all quite possible because Plato was a poet, and poets use figurative language (*Comentum* IV, 390).

The commonplace identification of poetry and figurative language was strengthened by the terms in which the value of poetry was discussed in the fourteenth century. Poets, particularly classical poets who referred to pagan gods, were accused by Christian theologians, among others, of being liars.[3] The traditional line of defence was that these pagan writers did not literally mean what they said, they were speaking figuratively. And even if they did intend literally what they said their texts could nevertheless be interpreted figuratively and be shown to convey truths about the physical world or human nature.

The distinction so often made was that poets do write fiction, but they do not lie, they make things up, but they do not intend to deceive. As it happens the most important poems were considered to be a mixture of fact and fiction, and generally only the fictional parts were interpreted figuratively.[4] The major interpretative problem was in fact to determine which parts were which. St Augustine advised readers of the Bible to find out first if the writer used literal or figurative language (*De doctrina christiana* III, x, 14) and this was the standard practice of many commentators on major poems in the fourteenth century, as important to their reading of those texts as it would be in a debate on fundamentalism today. It was all too easy to confuse fiction with fact, or figurative with literal language. St Augustine had warned readers of Virgil not to take the fiction of *Aeneid* VI too seriously.[5] Boccaccio who defended classical poetry so eloquently nevertheless advised Christians to be careful when reading pagan poetry in case they were unwittingly misled by untruth (*Genealogia* XIV, xviii). On several occasions Benvenuto reminds his educated audience that parts of Dante's fiction are based on ridiculous popular beliefs: the angels did not fight one another with shields and lances (*Inferno* III, 37–9; I, 112); there was no real battle between St Francis and the Devil for Guido da Montefeltro's soul (*Inferno* XXVII, 112–27, *Comentum* II, 328).[6] The popular confusion between fact and fiction made it easy for Fra Cipolla to dupe the credulous people of Certaldo with stories of the finger of the Holy Ghost and other reliquaries shown to him by the venerable Nonmiblasmete Sevoipiace (*Decameron* vi, 10). Apparently there are many people today who think the fiction of their favourite soap opera is fact and of course there are obvious mistakes about the status of texts which can be more dangerous than that.

Texts considered to be mixtures of fact and fiction ranged from one extreme to the other. Benvenuto describes the *Metamorphoses* as a compilation of fables and fictions (*Comentum* I, 152), yet thinks a great deal of Ovid is literally true. For the most part the stories are considered to be historical fact, generally only the metamorphoses are judged incredible, on St Augustine's authority (*De civitate Dei*, xviii, 18; *Comentum* III, 380), and so are interpreted figuratively. Lucan at the other extreme seems more like a historian than a poet because of the great deal of fact in his poem. Such was his credibility on historical fact of the *Pharsalia* that there are doubts about the status and authority of this text on natural history. Benvenuto thinks Dante treats the metamorphoses of Lucan as fiction (*Inferno* XXV, 94–6), yet cites several authorities who claimed there was a snake whose bite produced a swelling which festered with the hideous effects that Nasidius, according to Lucan, experienced (*Pharsalia* IX, 789–804; *Comentum* II, 246).[7]

Virgil's text is thought to be historical for the most part. When the character Virgil refers to the 'veltro' who will save that Italy for which Camilla, Euryalus, Turnus and Nisus died (*Inferno* II, 106–8), Benvenuto describes nearly the whole of Virgil's subject-matter as history, as the record of actual events. Only that part about the Amazon woman Camilla could be poetic fiction in Benvenuto's view and therefore might need interpreting (*Comentum* I, 67). The hyperbole was perhaps obvious at the end of *Aeneid* VII (*Esposizioni*, p. 49), but a modern example, a certain Maria of Priverno, suggests to Benvenuto that the account of Camilla's exploits in war in *Aeneid* IX is true. Just as Christian writers, like Dante, could be criticised in matters of faith, poets, like Virgil, who mixed historical fact with fiction could be criticised for deliberately distorting the known facts. The well-known story about Dido in *Aeneid* IV was a famous example. Many 'documentary dramas' are criticised for the same reason today. According to St Augustine the meeting between Aeneas and Dido was anachronistic; more important, St Jerome considered the story to be a defamation of a good woman's character. Whatever Virgil's poetic purpose, that was not sufficient justification for Benvenuto, and he criticises Dante for following his source (*Comentum* I, 200).[8]

The importance of the distinction between fact and fiction within a poem cannot be overestimated in reading a Trecento commentary on the *Comedy*, for the two kinds of writing are treated and evaluated in different ways. Fact elicits extra information; in the Trecento context it requires confirmation or refutation because then the truth or falsity of the text was a point at issue. Generally fiction has to be interpreted or explained, whereas factual details may be included simply because they are worthy of note, the criteria for inclusion being similar, if the subject is history, to works such as Valerius Maximus's, *De dictis et factis memorabilibus* or Petrarch's *Rerum memorandarum libri*. An extreme example to illustrate the point is Benvenuto's commentary on the hero of Petrarch's *Affrica*. Dante's allusion to Scipio in Virgil's address to the giant Antaeus (*Inferno* XXXI, 115–17) elicits in the modern printed edition of the *Comentum* eight pages on Scipio's great victories in Africa, and Benvenuto still excuses his brevity (*Comentum* II, 481).

Logically speaking, an account of fact and fiction cannot be evaluated in the same way. Dante cannot be criticised for getting his facts wrong if what he writes is fiction and he cannot be praised for his fiction if what he writes is factual. Benvenuto's comments on Ugolino's dream indirectly illustrate this logical distinction. If Ugolino actually had the dream to which the text refers then it was an amazing occurrence; if not, then the author wrote a beautiful fiction which was very appropriate to subsequent events. If the reader thinks of Dante as a reporter, the story is truly pitiful (*Inferno* XXXIII, 42); but Benvenuto actually believes the story is Dante's invention and therefore praises the poet's skill (*Comentum* II, 539).

Benvenuto states in the introduction to his commentary that the *Comedy* contains 'historica et poetica', which I would translate as 'fact and fiction'; any accurate reading of the *Comentum* would necessarily involve determining, as far as the subject allows, his attitude to the particular blend of fact and fiction in Dante's poem. Benvenuto did not of course think the story of a journey to the realms of the dead was fact. Pietro di Dante's well-known statement about his father's poem – who in their right mind ('sani intellectus') would believe he had literally been to Hell[9] – was the plainly stated reply to all those literal-minded people who, according to Boccaccio's anecdote (*Vita di Dante* XX), pointed Dante out in the streets as the man who had been to Hell.

Benvenuto's judgement of Dante as a historian best illustrates his attitude to fact in the poem, for his commentary includes more historical information, both ancient and modern, than any other Trecento commentary. Dante is described as a 'bonus historicus' (*Comentum* IV, 426) on ancient history and as a 'curiosissimus investigator rerum memorandarum' (*Comentum* III, 526) on the modern period. Benvenuto disagrees with Dante's judgement rarely and confirms that for the most part Dante has set down the truth as Cacciaguida commands (*Paradiso* XVII, 128) following as it were the laws of history boldly to set down the truth and nothing but the truth without partiality or malice (Cicero, *De oratore* II, xv, 62).

Benvenuto judges historians good by virtue of their accuracy, but accurate knowledge of the distant past was limited; the ancient historians provided the material for his study and his method of enquiry was a process of selection and compilation. His own methods were in fact very similar to those of Livy, 'che non erra' (*Inferno* XXVIII, 12), whom Benvenuto thought recorded faithfully what others had said, keeping as close as possible to the truth and leaving doubts to the judgement of his readers (*Comentum* II, 341). Benvenuto uses documents if they are available, or else follows common sense and reason when they are not. In many cases he argues by analogy (as in the case of Camilla and Maria of Priverno), guided by his own experience or his reading, or the reports of other people, first-hand if possible.

Benvenuto was something of a specialist in Roman history. His historical works include the *Romuleon*, a compendium of Roman history from the destruction of Troy to the Emperor Diocletian, the *Libellus Augustalis*, lives of the Caesars, and a commentary on Valerius Maximus. In his long commentary on Roman history in *Paradiso* VI his specialist knowledge is most in evidence and it is in this context that he calls Dante a good historian. In a reading of this canto, J. H. Whitfield, defining the historian as 'one who looks back patiently to find, by sifting the evidence, what really happened', declares that Dante is no historian and that the providential sequence of Justinian's survey of the victories won under the Roman standard is 'Dante's invention, not a historic fact'.[10] To judge by Benvenuto's standards, however, Dante has scrupulously kept to the historical facts. Benvenuto notes the omission of the First Punic War, but for the most part commends Dante's accuracy and his wondrous brevity commenting at some length because here he treats the text as an abridged account of fact.[11]

The *Comedy* seemed much more like history to Benvenuto not only because his methods of ascertaining the facts were different from those of a modern historian. In discussions about the value of poetry in the Trecento poetry was often defended by comparing it to philosophy or theology, never to history, presumably because such a comparison would not have suited the argument in poetry's defence or persuaded anyone of poetry's value, yet the similarities as they appeared at that time between

Dante's poem and history must have been very striking. Like history Dante's poem recorded the deeds of great men and women, and by doing so, furnished examples for moral guidance. Cacciaguida's words in *Paradiso* XVII, 136–42 in fact state the medieval view of history: history as the biography of great men and women and history as a series of moral lessons. The similarity between works such as Petrarch's *Rerum memorandarum libri* and Boccaccio's *De claris mulieribus* and the *Comedy* must have been evident to Benvenuto. What has been pointed out as a novelty in these works – as regards their classical models, the inclusion of men and women from the modern world, is in fact a novelty in Dante to which Benvenuto often draws his reader's attention.[12]

Benvenuto shared Dante's Christian view of history as 'a story with a divine plot' and agrees with the general principle demonstrated in the poem that 'everything is going to the dogs'.[13] His opinion of Dante as a historian extends to his judgements in the afterlife as well. Giovanni Villani's aim was apparently different from that of Dante: not to show that our fate in the next world corresponded to our merits in this one, but that even in this life, divine justice manifested itself in the actual resolution of earthly conflicts and the actual consequences of human action,[14] but the difference was not apparent to Benvenuto. He believes that God's justice as demonstrated in the poem is based on Dante's historical judgement: his damning of Boniface VIII is based on his knowledge of that Pope's depraved life and violent death (*Comentum* II, 41). A notable exception proves the general rule. According to Benvenuto some of Dante's early readers believed, on the poet's authority, that Manfred had repented at the end of his life. Benvenuto admits that there were letters which proved that Manfred wanted to be reconciled with the Church, but in his opinion the poet has invented the fiction of last minute repentance to show that the Pope is powerless when God forgives; no one, however horrible their sins, is denied salvation if they repent *in articulo mortis*. History, however, according to Benvenuto, following Villani, without acknowledging his source, teaches a different lesson: 'Whoever sets himself against the Church is punished in this world' (*Comentum* III, 111). The house of Swabia is a memorable example, for in the untimely deaths of so many of its members the judgement of God can be clearly seen. As Benvenuto astutely points out the very discrepancy between fact and fiction in this particular case greatly enhances the moral lesson.

Commenting on the fiction of the poem Benvenuto is careful to distinguish between the fictions of other poets which Dante has used in his poem and fictions which the poet himself has invented. This distinction is another important one; without it Benvenuto's interpretation and evaluation of the *Comedy* cannot be properly understood. Logically speaking, when Dante includes the fictions of other poets in his poem, he can be praised only for the appropriate way in which he does so. The creativity of his imagination can be praised when he invents new fictions, and Benvenuto will use 'inventio' in the sense of creating something new, as well as in the rhetorical sense. In fact the emphasis throughout the *Comentum* is on the novelty of Dante's fiction, which is perhaps its most original feature.

Naturally enough traditional interpretations of other texts provide the key to understanding Dante's borrowed fictions. The 'intelletti sani' of the author's address in *Inferno* IX are considered to be those readers who have knowledge of the fictions of poets. And in this respect Benvenuto calls Boccaccio's *Genealogia deorum gentilium* a very useful handbook (*Comentum* V, 154). Boccaccio's commentary, too, would be a useful, general guide:[15] his 'esposizione allegorica' is full of detailed explanations of the fictions of other poets together with the interpretative principles he follows. Dante's use of other fictions is nearly always described as appropriate, only on rare occasions does Boccaccio find in his author a daring, but still appropriate, departure from his model.[16] Benvenuto makes the general point that Dante is very good at selecting what is to his purpose ('circumspectissimus'), which is declared, on the authority of Horace (*Ars Poetica*, 128), to be a difficult thing to do in the Cacciaguida episode in connection with *Aeneid* VI. But quite rightly he prefers to stress the novelty of Dante's fiction in relation to his classical models. This general point appears in the *Paradiso* when the character Dante marvels at the eagle formed of many blessed souls, which opens its beak and speaks with one voice, though it speaks for many (*Paradiso* XIX, 7–9). Dante addresses his reader as a poet who is in the process of writing to tell them that no one ever spoke about what he saw, or wrote about it, or even imagined it. Benvenuto states that the author is here praising the subtlety of his own imagination and commending his artificial fiction, his reordering of natural images in artificial arrangements (*Comentum* V, 233). And he thinks that what Dante himself says in this context can be said in general about the whole work. Thinking of

Dante's classical models, Homer and Virgil, Benvenuto not only has the *Purgatorio* and the *Paradiso* in mind, but the *Inferno* as well. In his comments on the novelty of Dante's poem at the beginning of the *Paradiso*, it is for the invention of so many new punishments in the *Inferno*, not found in Virgil's Hell, that Benvenuto particularly admires Dante's art (*Comentum* IV, 336–7).

Many studies in recent years have analysed the self-consciousness of poems; Benvenuto's commentary is of particular interest in this respect. He consistently interprets the story of the journey as a poetic journey, but not in the way in which Gianfranco Contini has written of Dante's 'personaggio-poeta' and of episodes in the poem as representing earlier stages in Dante's poetic development.[17] For Benvenuto the fiction represents the actual process of the poem's composition, from the very first line of the poem, which indicates the time Dante first began to write his poem, to the last canto of the *Paradiso*. Dante's doubts and fears along the way are interpreted as a poet's doubts as to whether he is good enough to continue his poem and the difficulty of the journey is always interpreted as that of poetic subject-matter.[18]

Concerning the fiction which Dante invents, a further distinction has to be made. There are those parts of the poem's fiction which are wondrous and strange, with images never imagined before and not found in the natural world, such as the eagle image in *Paradiso* XIX, and other fictional parts which can be described as lifelike. In the seventh 'bolgia' Dante invents an incredible, unnatural fiction. Benvenuto's literary interpretation will seem appropriate to modern readers in this section of the poem where Dante claims a poetic victory over Lucan and Ovid because his metamorphoses outdo theirs (*Inferno* XXV, 94–9). Benvenuto interprets the entire episode in this way, however, beginning with the gesture of the character Dante who puts his fingers to his lips to silence Virgil (*Inferno* XXV, 44–5). For Benvenuto this indicates a poetic challenge to Virgil as well as to Lucan and Ovid later in the episode as if the poet were saying 'see if you ever wrote a fiction like this' (*Comentum* II, 235). The literary interpretation continues right through to the end of the episode when Dante returns to the novelty of what he has written. If he has bungled or botched a little let the novelty of the metamorphoses be his excuse (*Inferno* XXV, 143–4). Benvenuto compares Dante at this point, appropriately enough, to a soldier in Caesar's army who fought with great courage against the English, and then asked

Caesar to forgive him. Likewise Dante asks for forgiveness when he actually deserves great praise. In Benvenuto's opinion such marvellous and unheard-of fictions deserved the laurel crown (*Comentum* II, 257).

In other parts of the poem the fiction is closer to a reflection of the natural world. An important distinction in this connection is made between Dante's description of Hell, Purgatory and Paradise whether 'essentialiter' or 'moraliter'. The former term does not, as might be supposed, refer to what the text actually says about the state of souls after death, but rather to those parts of the text which, when read literally, tell the reader something about the three realms of the dead as they were conceived by educated Christians. Thus lines in the *Inferno* which refer to the eternal duration of the punishments are literally true of 'Infernus essentialis', and they are also true of 'Infernus moralis' in that they describe the state of the souls of obstinate sinners in this world (*Comentum* II, 169).[19] In Boccaccio's commentary there are three Hells: upper Hell, the poetical Hell of Dante, as well as Homer and Virgil, which describes the human heart, middle Hell which corresponds to Limbo, and lower Hell which is the place where damned souls are actually punished (*Esposizioni*, pp. 11–14). This alternative view of Dante's fiction as a description of a drama in the human heart produces many abstractions. Benvenuto's concept of Hell, Purgatory and Paradise 'moralis', however, as the 'outside', not 'inside' world of human life, produces a more lively and at times very literal reading of the poem, especially in his commentary on the first *cantica* simply because there are more people who 'live' in Hell and therefore greater diversity for the poet to portray and for the commentator to respond to.

A great deal of the new fiction perceived by Benvenuto in the *Comedy*, which comes under the heading of 'Infernus moralis', is interpreted literally. The punishments in Dante's Hell often correspond literally to punishments received on Earth: sodomites are burnt alive (*Comentum* I, 550) and panders and seducers are whipped (*Comentum* II, 8). Where they are thought to describe the consequences of sin, Benvenuto's literal reading of the text may verge on the grotesque. The punishment of the 'cattivi' describes the miserable state sinners such as these are reduced to in this world: they lie in hospice beds or ditches, no one visits them except flies and wasps, and the flies breed worms in the dirt and putrefaction in their rotting limbs (*Inferno* III, 66–9; *Comentum* I, 121). Some punishments literally describe the conduct of sinners. Dante's fiction of the hypocrites – walking slowly and weeping (*Inferno* XXIII, 58–60) – bring scenes in 'Infernus moralis' to Benvenuto's mind. Hypocrites often affect a slow walk so as to appear wise and Benvenuto remembers one hypocrite who drank a great deal of Malmsey wine to make him weep as he preached a sermon on the Passion of Christ in order to move the congregation deeply and so cheat them of their money.

In the *Genealogia deorum gentilium* XIX, ix Boccaccio describes three kinds of fiction worthy of consideration and the distinctions are useful for understanding Benvenuto's attitude to Dante's fiction. One kind has no appearance of truth at all, another is a mixture of fact and fiction, and the third is verisimilar. Of course a Trecento notion of verisimilitude may be very different from our own; for Dante's fiction to appear 'truthlike' it must give the illusion of truth as it seems to his reader. Dante's fiction of the giants may well have seemed truthlike to Benvenuto. Antaeus's colossal height of some seventy feet (*Inferno* XXXI, 113) was not incredible; giants did exist once on the authority of Hebrew, Greek and Roman historians, and St Augustine had found some evidence in the kingdom of Antaeus, a huge tooth a hundred times bigger than human size (*De civitate Dei*, xv, 9; *Comentum* II, 473).

Boccaccio's examples of the kind of fiction which is totally incredible by accepted standards of truth are Aesop's fables and the parable of the conference of the trees in Judges 9: 8–15. Benvenuto would have *Inferno* XXV and *Paradiso* XIX in mind. The second kind is a blend of fact and fiction. The examples are Ovid's stories about the daughters of Minyas and the mates of the sailor Acestes (*Metamorphoses* IV, 31–415; III, 582–686). Benvenuto's treatment of Ovid might explain what Boccaccio means: that the stories themselves were historical fact, only the incredible metamorphoses were fiction. Boccaccio's biblical example is nearly the whole of the Old Testament with intermittent events which are beyond belief.

The kind of fiction which has the appearance of truth is more like fact than fiction; the events described did not actually take place, but they could occur. Here Boccaccio makes a distinction between fictions such as Aeneas in the storm or Ulysses bound to the ship's mast to escape the lure of the Sirens and fictions which literally mean what they say and give lessons in moral conduct. The first can be interpreted figuratively to convey a truth beneath the veil of fiction as in the commentaries of Fulgentius or Bernard Silvester. Examples of the second kind are the

comedies of Terence and Plautus which Quintilian recommended for the
study of characters and emotions (*Institutio oratoria* I, 8).

Benvenuto treats a good deal of the *Comedy* as fiction of the latter
kind. The best example is his commentary on the barratry canti. This is a
new fiction which some of Dante's early readers according to Benvenuto
judged to be frivolous nonsense. The main thrust of Benvenuto's
remarks on the episode is to show those critics how well Dante has
described the conduct of barrators. Obviously some parts are interpreted
figuratively, the pitch, the devils etc., but much of the fiction evokes
memories of Benvenuto's own experience at the papal court in Avignon
and the court of the pope's legate in Bologna. When the alchemist
Capocchio boasts how good an ape of nature he was (*Inferno* XXIX)
Benvenuto uses those words to describe Dante: he is a poet who knew
human nature so well he was able to invent a fiction both to delight and
inform us (*Ars Poetica*, 333–7; *Comentum* I, 9) with its lifelike imitation
(*Comentum* II, 414).

With reference to the theory of the *Genealogia deorum gentilium*,
Francesco Tateo suggests Boccaccio may have had a similar view of his
'novelle'[20] and though Benvenuto seems to treat the *Decameron* stories
as fact and not fiction (he describes Boccaccio as a 'curiosus investigator
omnium delectabilium historiarum', *Comentum* III, 392), he must have
seen the similarity, too. For twentieth-century readers this is I think a
refreshingly straightforward reading of the poem's fiction from one of
Dante's early commentators who as a group have a reputation for
allegorising everything.

Benvenuto was greatly indebted to both Petrarch and Boccaccio on
points of poetic theory; his commentary also makes clear how their
historical works on the one hand and the *Decameron* on the other
influenced his reading of the *Comedy*, or perhaps, to make a more bold
connection, how the *Comedy* influenced in part the factual and the
creative writing of Petrarch and Boccaccio. Of course in Dante it was the
combination of fact and fiction that Benvenuto so admired, just as
Horace admired the skilful blend of fact and fiction in Homer (*Ars
Poetica*, 150).

Notes

1. *Comentum super Dantis Comoediam*, ed. G. F. Lacaita, 5 vols (Florence, 1887) V, 340.
2. *Esposizioni sopra la Comedia di Dante*, ed. G. Padoan (Verona, 1965) pp. 621–2.
3. Boccaccio, *Genealogia deorum gentilium* XIV, xiii.
4. When a text is interpreted according to the so-called 'allegory of theologians' the story, which is historical fact, is interpreted literally and can also be interpreted figuratively. Also, on the authority of St Augustine, not all fiction needs interpreting (*De civitate Dei* XVI, ii, cf. *De monarchia* III, iv). Nevertheless in most cases when a text is being read as a mixture of fact and fiction this general statement holds true.
5. C. T. Davis, *Dante and the Idea of Rome* (Oxford, 1957) p. 53.
6. Cf. *Comentum* II, 551, Benvenuto's comments on Dante's description of the Devil with a cross reference to *Paradiso* IV where the text evidently in Dante's mind is St Thomas's warning to readers of the Bible not to take the figurative language used to describe God and the angels literally (*Summa theologica*, I, q. I, a. 10).
7. Lucan is always an interesting test case for distinctions between poetry and history. See *Genealogia deorum gentilium* XIV, xiii (cf. Macrobius, *Saturnalia*, V, ii, 9); C. G. Osgood, *Boccaccio on Poetry* (Princeton, 1956) pp. 173–4; G. Martellotti, 'La difesa della poesia nel Boccaccio e un giudizio su Lucano', *Studi sul Boccaccio*, 4 (1967) 265–74.
8. Petrarch, *Seniles* iv, 5; Boccaccio, *Esposizioni*, pp. 295–300; *Genealogia deorum gentilium* xiv, 13; *Comentum* IV, 481; V, 18.
9. *Commentarium*, ed. R. Della Vedova and M. T. Silvotti (Florence, 1978) p. 7.
10. *Dante Commentaries*, ed. D. Nolan (Dublin, 1977) p. 147.
11. When poets and historians write about the same thing the distinguishing feature of the poetic account is *prolixitas*, where fiction is mixed in with fact; the historian's account is admired for being *brevis* (see Benvenuto on Cacus, *Inferno* XXV, 17–34; *Comentum* II, 229). Sallust, 'nobilis et veridicus historicus' (*Comentum* II, 228) was the most illustrious example of *brevitas* (Macrobius, *Saturnalia* V, i, 6). Geoffrey of Vinsauf recommended brevity for the narration of fact (*Poetria nova*, 704–5).
12. See T. G. Bergin, *Petrarch* (New York, 1970) p. 117. Benvenuto raises the question in connection with Guido da Montefeltro (*Inferno* XXVII, 22–3, *Comentum* II, 300) expecting Dante to be criticised for including moderns, who are not so illustrious as the ancients, in his poem. His reply, on the authority of St Augustine (*De civitate Dei* XVIII, ii), is that perhaps the famous of the past were not so magnificent after all until writers made them so.
13. C. S. Lewis, *The Discarded Image* (Cambridge, 1964) p. 176.
14. Louis Green, *Chronicle into History: an essay on the interpretation of history in Florentine fourteenth-century chronicles* (Cambridge, 1972) p. 18.

15. Benvenuto was present at Boccaccio's *lecturae Dantis* in Santo Stefano (*Comentum* V, 145). Cf. L. M. La Favia, 'Benvenuto da Imola's Dependence on Boccaccio's Studies on Dante', *Dante Studies*, 43 (1975) 161–75, which demonstrates that the biographical details which Benvenuto includes in the *Comentum* derive from the *Vita di Dante* and not Boccaccio's Dante commentary.

16. See *Esposizioni*, pp. 469–70 (in Virgil, Phlegyas represents 'pride', in Dante, 'anger'). The same borrowed fiction can have different meanings (Cerberus represents 'gluttony' in *Inferno* VI, 'avarice' in *Inferno* VII), the ambiguity is justified by reference, as in other cases to the Bible and to the diametrically opposed interpretations of the serpent (the Devil) in the Garden of Eden and the brass serpent (Christ) of Moses (*Esposizioni*, pp. 415–18).

17. Gianfranco Contini, 'Dante come personaggio-poeta della *Commedia*', *Un'idea di Dante: saggi danteschi* (Turin, 1976) pp. 33–62.

18. See Louis M. La Favia, *Benvenuto Rambaldi da Imola: Dantista* (Madrid, 1977) pp. 141–3; Louis R. Rossi, 'Dante and the Poetic Tradition in the Commentary of Benvenuto da Imola', *Italica*, 32 (1955) 219–21; Pamela Williams, 'Benvenuto da Imola's commentary: a Trecento reading of Dante' (Cambridge University Ph.D., 1984) pp. 210–23.

19. In most cases when Benvenuto refers to 'Infernus essentialis' the meaning of the text is said to be true of 'Infernus moralis' as well; one notable exception is the description of the Harrowing of Hell (*Comentum* I, 146).

20. '*Retorica*' *e* '*poetica*' *fra medioevo e rinascimento* (Rome, 1960) pp. 160 and 198.

5

Le *Piacevoli notti* di Giovan Francesco Straparola e le 'commedie elegiache' latine medievali*

Simona Rizzardi

Manlio Pastore Stocchi, nell'introduzione alla sua edizione delle *Piacevoli notti*, a proposito della brutta novella XIII 3, tradotta alla lettera dal latino di Gerolamo Morlini, pur denunciando il plagio e l'"infedeltà alla memoria di quel suo Boccaccio tanto lodato', notava che lo Straparola conosceva assai bene quella lingua, di cui 'poteva essere buono e fine traduttore'.[1] Non è dunque illegittimo presupporre che nella sua ricerca di materiale egli, come si serví della raccolta del Morlini, abbia utilizzato anche testi latini medievali.[2] In questo articolo vorrei segnalare appunto tra le probabili fonti le cosiddette 'commedie elegiache' del XII e XIII secolo[3] e una raccolta di *exempla* disponibile nell'edizione ottocentesca di Thomas Wright.[4]

Col nome di 'commedie elegiache'[5] ci si riferisce a una serie di componimenti poetici latini databili dal XII al XIII secolo, in versi elegiaci (esametri e pentametri alternati); alcune di esse si presume siano state scritte per essere rappresentate mentre altre, la maggioranza, dall'andamento decisamente narrativo, si pensa siano state concepite come dotte esercitazioni letterarie da leggersi davanti a un pubblico scelto di chierici, studenti o cortigiani ancora in grado di capire il latino; in questo caso sarebbero 'commedie' solo secondo l'accezione medievale del termine codificata nell'*Epistola a Can Grande della Scala* (XIII 10), e cioè componimenti letterari caratterizzati da un inizio tragico e un lieto fine, scritti in stile dimesso.[6] Esse condividono, oltre al metro, alcuni elementi caratteristici, e precisamente l'imitazione di Ovidio, lo sviluppo del tema dell'amore, l'atteggiamento misogino e infine la presenza degli

* Ringrazio sentitamente il Prof. Ferruccio Bertini dell'Università di Genova per aver letto questo articolo e per avermi dato preziosi suggerimenti.

schiavi.[7] Se ne contano una ventina,[8] alcune delle quali, a giudicare dal numero dei manoscritti (piú di 60 nel caso del *Geta* di Vitale di Blois, che fu l'archetipo del nuovo genere letterario) e delle citazioni in svariati florilegi, furono molto diffuse in tutta Europa. Che fossero note al Boccaccio è ormai appurato: egli ne aveva trascritte alcune in una sua antologia personale di autori latini classici e medievali,[9] le aveva utilizzate come fonti delle novelle III 10 e VII 9 del *Decameron*[10] e infine, come è stato recentemente dimostrato, per la stesura dell'*Elegia di Madonna Fiammetta*[11] e del *Ninfale Fiesolano*.[12] Ma l'influenza di questi componimenti si sarebbe estesa, ben oltre il Medioevo, fino al tardo Rinascimento se è vero, come cercherò di dimostrare, che furono utilizzati dallo Straparola.

La novella delle *Piacevoli notti* da cui vorrei cominciare è la quarta della IV notte: un giovane studente confessa ad un medico con cui ha fatto amicizia a Padova che nessuna donna per lui può superare in bellezza ed eleganza la madre. Il medico, per smentirlo, fa in modo che incontri piú volte la propria bellissima moglie, senza pensare ai potenziali rischi della sua macchinazione. Lo studente, infatti, si invaghisce della donna e, di fronte al rifiuto del medico di rivelargliene l'identità, la segue segretamente, scopre dove abita, penetra in casa sua e riesce a piegarla ai suoi desideri. Il giorno dopo incontra il medico e gli racconta ingenuamente la sua avventura dicendogli che andrà a trovare la donna anche la sera seguente. Il marito, pensando di svergognare gli adulteri e porre fine allo scherzo già durato troppo a lungo, quella sera piomba inaspettato in casa sua, ma la moglie nasconde lo studente nel letto a baldacchino e nega ogni accusa. Per altre due mattine il giovane racconta le sue prodezze al medico, che anche le due notti seguenti rientra all'improvviso ma è sempre ingannato dalla moglie, che nasconde l'amante la seconda notte in una cassa e la terza in uno 'scrigno', introducendosi nel quale egli riesce perfino a scampare a un incendio scatenato dal marito nel vano tentativo di snidarlo. Il medico allora invita lo studente a una cena insieme ai parenti suoi e della moglie, con l'intenzione di ubriacarlo e farlo confessare davanti a tutti. Alla moglie ordina di non farsi vedere. Un servo fedele, però, la informa che lo studente sta per rivelare tutto davanti ai parenti e lei astutamente gli ordina di portare all'amante un boccale in cui fa scivolare un anello che lui stesso le aveva regalato. Il giovane, riconosciuto l'anello, comprende finalmente che l'amante non è altri che la moglie del medico, interrompe la sua storia dicendo che è stato tutto un sogno e in questo modo si salva.

Giuseppe Rua individua la fonte principale di questa novella nella I 2 del *Pecorone* di Ser Giovanni da Prato,[13] ma E. Gorra[14] (seguito da Letterio Di Francia)[15] ha rilevato in modo convincente che il debito dello Straparola per quanto riguarda questa novella è piuttosto dalla 'commedia elegiaca' *Miles gloriosus*:[16] oltre allo stesso tipo di intreccio, lo Straparola vi avrebbe desunto i motivi dell'incendio, della cena, dell'ubriachezza, dell'occultamento della moglie, della presenza di spirito della donna e del sogno. Le varianti che avrebbe apportato riguardano l'incendio, nella sua versione provocato dall'ira del marito e concepito per svelare il nascondiglio dell'amante e non certo per fornirgli un'occasione di fuga, il particolare della moglie che non viene mascherata ma è costretta dal marito a nascondersi in cucina con l'ordine di non farsi vedere, e infine il segnale che svela l'identità della donna al giovane, non piú la leggera pressione del piede, ma il ritrovamento dell'anello nel fondo del bicchiere. A sostegno delle osservazioni del Gorra (che sono a livello esclusivamente contenutistico) aggiungo i due riscontri testuali seguenti:

Miles gloriosus	*Le piacevoli notti*[17]
(1)	
Condita vicinam mutuat archa domum.	. . . gli fece traere di casa *lo scrigno* e ponerlo in *casa* della vicina
Tempore freta bono, cum sciret abesse periclum,	vecchiarella; e celatamente lo aprí, che niuno se n'avide, e
Ad loca nota redit; clave iubente patet. (222–4)	ritornossene a casa. (p. 194)
(2)	
'Sis conviva meus – orat – , mea mensa peroret;	. . . maestro Raimondo *pregò* Nerino che si dignasse d'*andare* il
Se polit ad festum regia nostra tuum'.	giorno seguente *a desinar seco*; ed il giovane *accettò* volentieri l'invito.
Paret eques civi; . . . (251–3)	(p. 195)

Ma la novella dello Straparola differisce dalla versione del *Pecorone* anche in un altro particolare che finora è stato trascurato dagli studiosi: e cioè il fatto che il giovane protagonista Nerino sia arrivato fino al diciottesimo anno di età senza aver visto altre donne che la madre e la balia. Ho buon motivo di credere che per questa caratteristica lo

Straparola si sia ispirato a un'altra 'commedia elegiaca', e precisamente
l'*Alda* di Guglielmo di Blois, che compare in almeno tre dei manoscritti
in cui ci è pervenuto il *Miles gloriosus*[18] e quindi avrebbe potuto
facilmente essere letta dallo Straparola: è la storia di Alda, una giovi-
netta bellissima la cui madre è morta nel darla alla luce; ella è stata
allevata dal padre con grande rigore; vive quasi sempre in casa e non
conosce uomini. Il giovane Pirro, però, attirato dalla fama della sua
bellezza, si innamora di lei e riesce ad avvicinarla grazie alla straordinaria somiglianza con la propria sorella gemella, amica di Alda, i cui
panni riveste. Riesce cosí a sedurre Alda, anche grazie alla sua estrema
ignoranza delle cose del mondo, facendole credere che, compiendo
l'atto sessuale, diventerà immortale. La giovane però rimane incinta e il
padre accusa la sorella di Pirro di essere ermafrodita. Allora Pirro
rivela la verità e sposa Alda, salvando insieme l'onore proprio e quello
della sorella. Dall'*Alda* lo Straparola avrebbe desunto e addattato in
versione maschile il motivo della giovane cresciuta senza vedere
uomini, facendo cosí del personaggio di Nerino un ingenuo, ben diverso
dallo smaliziato protagonista della novella di Ser Giovanni. Di Alda si
legge: '*Hanc pater a cunis custos devotus ab omni / Aspectu prohibet
colloquioque viri*' (vv. 137–8) e '*Nec preter patrem viderat Alda virum*'
(v. 152).[19] Allo stesso modo il padre di Nerino 'in tal maniera il fece
nudrire, che egli, sino a tanto che non pervenisse al decim'ottavo anno
della sua età, non potesse vedere donna alcuna, se non la madre e la
balia che lo nodricava' (*Le piacevoli notti*, p. 189). Quella che il Rua
definiva la 'incredibile ingenuità di Nerino' (*Tra antiche fiabe*, p. 70)
avrebbe dunque una spiegazione. Ora, è vero che il motivo del giovane
che non ha mai visto donne è molto diffuso negli *exempla* medievali, ma
vi è sempre sfruttato in modo ben diverso, cioè in senso misogino/
cristiano: vedi gli *exempla* 3 e 78 della raccolta del Wright in cui le
donne, finalmente apparse per la prima volta rispettivamente a un
principe e a un giovane eremita, vengono definite nel primo caso come
'*daemones homines seducentes*' e nel secondo come '*anseres*' (oche!).
Nell'*Alda* figura anche un intermediario (il servo Spurio), che trova
riscontro nella 'vecchiarella' dello Straparola (ma che era già presente
nel *Pecorone* nei panni della 'merciaiuola') e, infine, è interessante
notare come la figura dell'ermafrodito appaia in un'altra novella delle
Piacevoli notti, la XIII 9.

La seconda novella che vorrei esaminare è la V della terza giornata. 'In questa favola si narra che Lucaferro, geloso del favore accordato da suo fratello Emiliano al vaccaro Travaglino, uomo leale e veritiero, scommette con lui che lo farà mentire. A tale scopo Isotta, moglie di Lucaferro, seduce co' suoi vezzi il buon vaccaro, e come prezzo de' suoi favori ne ottiene il capo d'un toro dalle corna d'oro prediletto da Emiliano. Travaglino, ucciso il toro, pensa lungamente al modo di giustificarne la morte presso il padrone: ma alla fine gli confessa il suo peccato, e gli fa vincere la scommessa'.[20] Letterio Di Francia afferma che questa novella è stata 'attinta sicuramente dalla tradizione orale' (*Novellistica*, I, 720), ma cita ugualmente le fonti proposte dal Rua, e cioè una novella turca tratta dal libro dei *Quaranta Viziri*, in cui però si parla del cuore e del fegato di un cavallo invece che delle corna di un toro, e un *exemplum* dei *Gesta Romanorum* (cap. CXI)[21] in cui, 'sotto una veste intessuta di reminiscenze classiche troviamo il nostro racconto, tal quale: non vi manca il soliloquio del custode pentito, e v'è di piú vicino, invece del cavallo, la vacca dalle corna d'oro' (Rua, *Tra antiche fiabe*, p. 27). In realtà questo racconto differisce dalla versione dello Straparola non solo nell'ambientazione classica ma anche in altri particolari non secondari: la vacca, pur essendo piú vicina al toro di un cavallo, è pur sempre una vacca (tant'è vero che si insiste sul particolare che era particolarmente generosa nella sua produzione di latte) e manca completamente la figura della seduttrice, la cui funzione viene incorporata dall'ingannatore stesso che, abilissimo nell'arte musicale, incanta e addormenta con le sue canzoni il vaccaro, e gli sottrae la vacca. Il racconto dei *Gesta Romanorum* finisce qui e manca dunque tutta la parte finale della novella dello Straparola.

Molto piú numerosi e significativi sono invece i punti di contatto con la prima delle 'Latin Stories' raccolte da Thomas Wright che ho citato all'inizio. Il titolo è *De Mauro bubulco* ed è contenuta nel MS. Corp. Chr. Coll. Cambridge No. 633. Nella nota che dedica a questo racconto, il Wright riporta l'*exemplum* dei *Gesta Romanorum* integralmente, giudicandolo, con una certa superficialità, 'a brief story, identical with the one given here' (*A Selection of Latin Stories*, p. 215) e, alla fine, afferma che il manoscritto di Cambridge risale al XIII secolo (e che quindi il racconto in esso contenuto sarebbe piú antico di quello dei *Gesta Romanorum* che risalgono al XIV), ma aggiunge anche alquanto confusamente che 'the name *Maurus* (quello del manoscritto di Cambridge)

may be itself a corruption of *Argus'* (il nome mitologico del guardiano
nell'*exemplum*). Ma in fondo stabilire quale dei due racconti sia il piú
antico non ci interessa, in quanto sono entrambi precedenti alle *Piacevoli
notti* e, da un esame del contenuto, risulta chiaramente che lo Straparola
elaborò il racconto di Mauro piuttosto che quello di Argo! I punti in
comune sono i seguenti: il toro dalle corna d'oro, la sfida dell'invidioso a
far mentire il vaccaro e il conseguente patto col re, l'iniziativa della
moglie dell'invidioso, la seduzione del vaccaro, la richiesta da parte della
donna delle corna o della testa del toro come compenso dei suoi favori,
l'uccisione del toro, il sollievo dell'invidioso all'apparente riuscita del-
l'inganno della moglie (senza però che ella gli abbia rivelato come si è
procurata le corna/la testa del toro con cui ricatterà la sua vittima), l'im-
barazzo tardivo del vaccaro resosi conto del suo 'tradimento', la curiosa
'prova generale', davanti a un bastone incappucciato, del suo discorso
giustificativo davanti al padrone/re con la stessa identica prima bugia (i
lupi hanno divorato il toro) e infine la decisione di confessare tutta la
verità e la punizione dell'invidioso. Ecco la serie dei passi paralleli:

De Mauro bubulco, ed. T. Wright	*Le piacevoli notti*
(1) ... *quin Maurum quem tuum* [sic] *laudas in tua presentia et audientia facerem mentiri.* (p. 2)	– *Tu lodi* tanto cotesto tuo vaccaro ... e mi offero di fartelo vedere ed udire, che *in tua presenza egli ti dirà la bugia.* – (p. 151)
(2) *Propositus abiit, domum suam adiit, et contristatus cogitare coepit quod stultam finationem fecisset, si perderet.* (p. 2)	*Partitosi* l'uno dall'altro, ... Lucaferro *cominciò* pentirsi *del pegno che egli aveva messo* (p. 151)
(3) *'Nisi,'* inquit, *'pro eo quod fruitus es concubitu, mihi dederis aurea cornua quae gerit taurus domini tui, accusabo te apud dominum meum, ...'* (p. 3)	– Altro da te non voglio, – disse Isotta, – se non *il capo del toro dalle corna d'oro*; e tu disponi poi di me come ti piace. – (p. 153)

(4)

[*Maurus*] ... *cogitare coepit* ... *et quod eum ante regem* ... *de armentis regis quae multa diu custodierat, et maxime de tauro cujus aurea cornua dederat, reddere rationem oporteret,* ... (p. 4)

Travaglino ... *cominciò pensare* molto *come fare dovesse per iscusarsi* della perdita *del toro dalle corna d'oro* ... (p. 153)

(5)

Et valide baculum suum in terra percutiens, et firmiter figens, pileum suum de capite suo sumit et super baculum ponit. ... *Et abiens retro quantum jactus lapidis, iterum revertitur ad baculum* ... *et inclinans se adoravit eum* ... *dicens, 'Salve, rex! salve, rex!' Et respondens pro baculo sibimet ipsi dixit, 'Salveris* ... *Et quomodo se habet* ... *taurus meus aureis cornibus?'* (p. 4)

Acconciato adunque *il ramo d'albero* in una camera *con la beretta in* testa ... usciva Travaglino *fuori* dell'uscio della camera, *e dopo* dentro ritornava, e quel ramo salutava, dicendo: – Bon giorno, patrone. – *Ed a sé stesso* rispondendo diceva: – Ben venga, Travaglino ... *E come sta il toro dalle dorate corna*? – (pp. 153–4)

(6)

'Nudius tertius,' ait Maurus, 'divertit a collegio pecorum, et veniens turba luporum jugulavit eum, et comedit.' Et respondens pro baculo suo, ait 'Male custodisti taurum meum; verumptamen redde mihi cornua eius, ... *'* (pp. 4–5)

– Signore, il toro *è stato* nel bosco *da' lupi divorato. – E dove è* la pelle ed *il capo con le corna dorate*? – (p. 154)

(7)

... *cuncta quae gesserat* ... *coram baculo quasi coram rege staret, replevit* (p. 5)

Travaglino, avendo fatte piú proposte e risposte *con l'uomo* di legno, non altrimenti che se *stato fusse il propio* patrone ... (p. 154)

(8)

Quid plura? non est mentitus Maurus, et ideo non imputavit ei rex peccatum, quia non est inventus dolus in ore ejus. (p. 6)

Onde, *per aver* Travaglino *detta la verità, fu tenuto uomo veritiero* e di buona estimazione (p. 155).

Dall'esame dei passi paralleli sopra riportati risulteranno anche chiari i punti in cui lo Straparola ha mutato il testo originario: dal passo (3) si vede che la donna in *De Mauro bubulco* fa la sua scellerata richiesta *dopo* aver concesso al vaccaro i suoi favori, e sotto pena di far scoppiare uno scandalo, mentre nelle *Piacevoli notti* la richiesta è formulata *prima* dell'adulterio, e da (4) si vede come il proprietario del toro in *De Mauro bubulco* sia addirittura il re. In effetti il racconto latino ha un'ambientazione piú generica e vaga e, almeno per la parte iniziale, una certa aura di favola. L'inizio è tipicamente favolistico (*'Fertur fuisse quidam rex nobilis, potens, et dives, qui habuit principes multos, comites, barones, ...'* ecc.) e il toro è una creatura meravigliosa nata con le corna d'oro (mentre nelle *Piacevoli notti* le corna sono solo dipinte!). Si direbbe quasi che lo Straparola, vincendo la sua consueta tendenza al favolistico e al miracoloso, per questo racconto abbia deciso di mantenersi nell'ambito della novella tradizionale, scegliendo personaggi e situazioni perfettamente realistici e credibili. L'ambientazione, infatti, è bergamasca, e per tutta la novella si respira l'aria di sicura prosperità dei ricchi proprietari terrieri lombardi (forse ebrei, a giudicare dai nomi dei due poderi Ghorèm e Pedrènch).[22] Tipicamente novellistica è anche l'introduzione del motivo delle corna fatte dalla moglie al marito, per cui il prezzo delle corna d'oro sono le corna che lei fa a lui (*Le piacevoli notti*, p. 154). La figura dell'invidioso, infine, un subalterno del re in *De Mauro bubulco*, è qui impersonata da Lucaferro, fratello del proprietario del toro (Emiliano), indispettito dalla confidenza e dalla fiducia accordata da quest'ultimo a un semplice mandriano. Sembrerebbe trattarsi dunque di una ripicca di tipo classista a difesa dello *status quo* favorevole ai padroni, e l'intera novella potrebbe essere letta in chiave sociale, con la quasi totalità dei personaggi negativi appartenenti alla classe dominante e il trionfo finale del semplice e onesto mandriano, se non fosse stato provato che parlare di una coscienza sociale nello Straparola è fuori luogo, perché la fortuna cieca nelle sue novelle favorisce ora il ricco ora il povero, senza alcuna logica o moralità.[23]

Il motivo dello sposo incantato, liberato dall'incantesimo che gli conferisce un aspetto animalesco o mostruoso grazie all'amore di una fanciulla, è sempre stato uno dei piú sfruttati nelle fiabe. Di origine antichissima, probabilmente orientale, in Europa trova il suo avallo letterario piú noto in Apuleio, nella 'favola di Amore e Psiche' (*Metamorphoses* IV–VI) ma, secondo S. Thompson,[24] questa non sarebbe che

una delle numerosissime versioni del tema. Già il Di Francia aveva messo
in guardia dal cercare di individuare fonti letterarie per le 'fiabe' dello
Straparola che, secondo lui, egli dovette cogliere direttamente 'dalle
labbra del popolo' (*Novellistica*, p. 716) ma lo studioso faceva un'ecce-
zione per la novella/fiaba II 3 (p. 721)[25] e questo mi incoraggia a proporre,
sebbene con cautela, il confronto tra la prima novella della II notte dello
Straparola (la prima che si possa definire propriamente una 'fiaba') e la
'commedia elegiaca' *Asinarius*, l'una basata sulla trasformazione di un
porco e l'altra di un asino in uomo.[26] Entrambe le storie prendono le
mosse dalla sterilità di una regina, si discostano brevemente quando lo
Straparola introduce l'intervento di tre fate (l'ultima delle quali responsa-
bile del parto mostruoso) e si riavvicinano nella descrizione delle reazioni
di re e regina alla nascita dei due principi animali: in entrambi i casi il re o
la regina ordinano o pensano di buttare a mare il figlio:

Asinarius[27]	*Le piacevoli notti*
(1)	
Ergo non esse mater quam mater aselli	. . . il re piú fiate ebbe
Mallet et ut detur piscibus esca iubet.	animo di farlo uccidere e
(29–30)	gettarlo nel mare. (p. 64)

(2) Il crudele proposito viene però a cadere in seguito alla considerazione che, in fondo, per mostruoso che sia, il piccolo è sempre figlio
di un re:

Utpote qui regis nobile pignus erat.	. . . era generato da lui ed
(40)	era il sangue suo (ibid.)

(3) In entrambi i racconti si insiste sul fatto che il principino viene
allevato e nutrito in maniera adeguata al suo stato:

Tunc iussu patris nimio nutritur honore	. . . il re . . . volse al tutto,
(39)	non come bestia, ma come
	animal razionale allevato e
	nodrito fusse. Il bambino
	adunque, diligentemente
	nodrito . . . (ibid.)

(4) Cresciuto, il principino comincia ad andare in giro per la/le città da
solo:

Oppida iam girat, iam regni circuit urbes,	. . . cominciò umanamente
(45)	parlare e andarsene per la
	città (ibid.)

(5) Le due versioni differiscono per il numero delle spose: nel-
l'*Asinarius* ce n'è una sola, mentre in Straparola le spose sono tre, e
solo la terza riuscirà a liberare il marito dall'incantesimo. La
reazione della prima sposa alla richiesta di matrimonio del principe-
porco è però identica a quella della fanciulla nella commedia latina:

Virgo suo more faciem suffusa rubore	La figliuola, queste parole
Patris ad hanc vocem lumina flectit	udendo, molto si turbò: e
humo. (277)	venuta rossa come mattu-
	tina rosa, disse . . . (p. 65)

(6) Il momento della trasformazione in uomo è quasi identico nelle due
versioni:

Extemplo sponsus asininum ponit	. . . si trasse la puzzolente e
amictum;	sporca pelle, e un vago e
Exposita veteri pelle novus fit homo.	bellissimo giovane rimase
(309–10)	(p. 68)

(7) L'indomani però, col sorgere del sole i due sposi-animali devono
riprendere le loro sembianze mostruose:

Inde revestitur asinino rursus amictu	. . . presa la sua spoglia
Et fit asellus item sicut et ante fuit.	porcina, alle immondizie,
(325–6)	sí come per l'addietro fatto
	aveva, si diede. (ibid.)

(8) Nell'*Asinarius* è un servo a raccontare al re della trasformazione;
nelle *Piacevoli notti* la sposa stessa (e alla regina), ma uguale è
l'invito a penetrare nella stanza nuziale e ad assistere coi propri
occhi al prodigio:

Nunc age, mi domine, si vis, quod	– Verrete questa notte su'l
suggero, nosse,	primo sonno alla camera
En, ea ventura nocte probare potes.	mia, e trovarete aperto
Hac igitur nocte thalamum secretius intra,	l'uscio, e vederete ciò che
(359–61)	io vi dico, essere il vero. –
	(p. 69)

(9) È curioso che in entrambi i racconti sia presente l'elemento dei
'torchi' (*lumina* nell'*Asinarius*):

Ergo subit thalamum dilecte virginis, in	. . . la reina fece accendere
quo	i torchi, e con il re se
Lumina sunt posita, rege iubente, duo.	n'andò alla camera del
(303–4)	figliuolo (p. 69)

(10) Nell'*Asinarius* è il re, nelle *Piacevoli notti* la regina a guardare
    stupefatta le nuove meravigliose sembianze del genero:

Leniter accedens rex appropiansque	. . . e accostatasi la madre
cubili,	al letto, vide il suo figliuolo
Formosum cernit accubitare virum.	essere un bellissimo
(373–4)	giovane (ibid.)

(11) Alla fine della narrazione, le pelli di animale vengono distrutte per
    ordine dei due re:

Fornacemque iubet accendi fomite multo	. . . e ordinò il re che,
In qua fit pellis rege iubente cinis.	avanti alcuno indi si
(377–8)	partisse, la pelle fusse tutta
	minutamente stracciata
	(ibid.)

(12) I due racconti si concludono con l'incoronazione dei principi, di cui
    in entrambi i casi è specificato un nuovo nome: *Neoptolemos*[28] nel-
    l'*Asinarius* e 're porco' nelle *Piacevoli notti*:

Tuncque Neoptolomus regni monarcha	. . . con grandissimo trionfo
creatur; (399)	fu coronato il figliuolo . . .
	chiamato re porco (ibid.)

(13) Infine, è curioso come, proprio alla fine della novella delle *Piacevoli
    notti* si faccia menzione del 'diadema e il manto regale' (ibidem),
    entrambi nominati nell'*Asinarius* in uno stesso passo. Particolar-
    mente significativa mi sembra la scelta del primo vocabolo, prefe-
    rito al piú ovvio 'corona' e apparentemente preso di pari passo dalla
    commedia latina: *Absit ut hanc asini frontem **diadema** coronet*
    (*Asin.* 99) e *Nec setas asini **purpura munda** tegat.* (*Asin.* 102).

Tenuto conto del modesto valore letterario sia delle 'commedie
elegiache' sia, soprattutto, degli *exempla* citati, non si può negare che lo
Straparola, in genere criticato senza pietà per il modo in cui ha trattato i
suoi modelli migliori (il Boccaccio innanzitutto), abbia utilizzato queste
fonti piú modeste (almeno per quanto riguarda il primo volume delle
Piacevoli notti) con un certo successo. Non c'è dubbio che la lenta e
monotona novella I 2 del *Pecorone*, tagliata e snellita in grazia dell'ag-
giunta del nuovo finale abbia acquistato in vivacità. Peccato che lo
Straparola, secondo il suo consueto gusto per il macabro, abbia voluto
aggiungere il particolare infelice (un vero anti-climax, assente nella

'commedia elegiaca') della disperazione e della morte del medico in seguito alla fuga della moglie. Della novella III 5, in cui lo Straparola avrebbe insolitamente eliminato gli elementi fiabeschi in favore di quelli novellistici, abbiamo già parlato. Per la novella II 1, invece, il nostro autore avrebbe sfruttato al massimo, e anzi potenziato, il carattere favolistico della fonte latina (anche se nella sua maniera limitata, caratterizzata dalla assenza di ogni senso di meraviglia nella descrizione di eventi straordinari).[29] Ancora una volta, però, la scelta stessa dell'animale (un porco invece di un asino, con le continue insistenze sulla sua sporcizia e ripugnanza) e l'introduzione delle uccisioni cruente delle prime due mogli appesantiscono il tono lieve e da letteratura cortese che caratterizzava l'*Asinarius*, col suo protagonista gentile, la cui natura umana si poteva intuire dalla sua passione per la musica e dai suoi modi cavallereschi! La favola, però, ebbe fortuna, e Calvino la incluse nella sua raccolta, in una versione del Pitré.[30]

Note

1. G. F. Straparola, *Le piacevoli notti*, a cura di Manlio Pastore Stocchi, 2 voll. (Bari, 1979) I, p. xiv. È da questa edizione che saranno tratte tutte le citazioni dell'articolo. Cfr. anche M. Guglielminetti, *La cornice e il furto, Studi sulla novella del '500* (Bologna, 1984) pp. 79–99, il cap. 'Il plagiatore plagiato (lo Straparola fra il Morlini e il Basile)', dove è detto che 'la non comprensione del testo latino rimane un fatto piuttosto raro per lo Straparola' (p. 90), e si esamina il metodo con cui egli elaborava il testo del Morlini.
2. Cfr. G. Mazzacurati, *Conflitti di culture nel Cinquecento* (Napoli, 1977), il cap. 'Rapporto su alcuni materiali in opera nelle *Piacevoli Notti* di G. F. Straparola', pp. 83–117 sullo Straparola scrittore di consumo, che scriveva (o meglio trascriveva!) in modo 'parassitario' (p. 110), 'assorbito ... dai ritmi produttivi della fascia media del mercato letterario' (p. 98) del '500, e accumulando 'detriti d'ogni sperimentazione e d'ogni modello' (p. 111). Questo capitolo si può trovare (sostanzialmente identico) già in G. Mazzacurati, *Società e strutture narrative (dal Trecento al Cinquecento)* (Napoli, 1971) pp. 73–130.
3. L'ultima e più completa edizione di queste 'commedie' è quella curata da Ferruccio Bertini e da un'*équipe* dei suoi collaboratori per l'Istituto di Filologia Classica e Medievale dell'Università di Genova, *Commedie latine del XII e XIII secolo*, di cui sono usciti i primi cinque volumi, rispettivamente negli anni 1976, 1980 (aprile), 1980 (novembre), 1983 e 1986, e il sesto ed ultimo è di imminente pubblicazione. Questo *corpus* è stato concepito come aggiornamento e miglioramento della raccolta a cura di Gustave Cohen, *La*

'*comédie*' *latine en France au XIIe siècle*, 2 voll. (Paris, 1931). Per una bibliografia esauriente sulle 'commedie elegiache' rimando a quelle che si trovano alla fine di ogni volume del *corpus* del Bertini, e a quella di Alison Goddard Elliott in *Seven Medieval Latin Comedies* (New York & London, 1984) pp. LII–LXIII; questo volume contiene anche la traduzione di sette delle commedie e una introduzione generale molto chiara e informativa sull'argomento.

4. *A Selection of Latin Stories from Manuscripts of the Thirteenth and Fourteenth Centuries*, vol. VIII della raccolta *Early English Poetry, Ballads, and Popular Literature of the Middle Ages* (Percy Society, London, 1843) Gli *exempla* a cui mi riferirò occupano la prima parte del volume, pp. 1–136. Le note esplicative del Wright sono alle pp. 215–44.

5. La definizione di 'commedie elegiache' fu proposta da E. Müllenbach alla fine del secolo scorso (*Comoediae elegiacae*, Bonn, 1885) e subito accolta dalla maggior parte dei medievalisti.

6. Il problema del genere letterario di questi componimenti è forse il piú spinoso, e gli studiosi che se ne sono occupati hanno sostenuto le opinioni piú disparate: E. Faral ('Le fabliau latin au moyen âge', *Romania*, 50 (1924) p. 385) le riteneva dei *fabliaux*, da cui sarebbero derivati quelli francesi; I. Thomson ('Latin "Elegiac Comedy" of the Twelfth Century', *Versions of Medieval Comedy*, University of Oklahoma Press, 1977, p. 53) racconti comici: D. Bianchi ('Per la commedia latina del sec. XII', *Aevum*, 29 (1955) p. 178) 'novelle in versi o poemetti'; P. Dronke ('The Rise of the Medieval Fabliau: Latin and Vernacular Evidence', *Romanische Forschungen*, 85 (1973) p. 291) dei 'fabliaux in classicizing and dramatic forms'; P. O. Bröndsted ('The Medieval "Comedia": Choice of Form', *Classica et Mediaevalia*, 31 (1970 ma pubblicato nel 1976) p. 268) come 'the vehicle of lyrical complaint whether blended with amorous material or not'.

7. Queste caratteristiche sono state messe in luce da F. Bertini, 'La commedia latina del XII secolo', in AA.VV., *L'eredità classica nel Medioevo: il linguaggio comico*, Atti del III Convegno di Studio (Viterbo, 26–28 maggio 1978) (Viterbo, 1979) pp. 63–80.

8. Sono 20 nella collana del Bertini, anche tenendo conto delle 'commedie' non ancora uscite al momento della stesura di questo articolo. Eccone l'elenco: *Aulularia* e *Geta* di Vitale di Blois, *De Afra et Milone* di Matteo di Vendôme, *De tribus sociis* di Goffredo di Vinsauf, *Miles gloriosus* e *Lidia* attribuiti ad Arnolfo di Orléans, *De Paulino et Polla* di Riccardo da Venosa, *Alda* di Guglielmo di Blois, *De uxore cerdonis* di Jacopo da Benevento, e le anonime *Pamphilus, Gliscerium et Birria, De tribus puellis, De nuntio sagaci, Babio, De clericis et rustico, Pamphilus, Baucis et Traso, De mercatore, De Lombardo et lumaca, Asinarius, Rapularius*.

9. Si tratta del cod. Laurenziano XXXIII 31, su cui cfr. B. M. Da Rif, 'La Miscellanea Laur. XXXIII 31', *Studi sul Boccaccio*, 7 (1973) pp. 59–124.

10. Per *Decameron* III 10 cfr. F. Bertini, 'Una novella del Boccaccio e l'*Alda* di Guglielmo di Blois', *Maia*, 29–30 (1977–78) pp. 135–41. Per *Decameron* VII 9 cfr. V. Branca (ed.), *Decameron*, vol. IV della serie *Tutte le opere di*

Giovanni Boccaccio (Milano, 1976) pp. 1390–1: 'È una delle poche novelle di cui sia chiara e sicura la fonte: cioè la *Comoedia Lydiae*, mediocre poemetto già attribuito a Matteo di Vendôme, trascritto di proprio pugno dal B. nel cod. Laurenziano XXXIII 31, cc. 71 ss'. Il Branca (p. 1312) accetta inoltre l'ipotesi di M. Pastore Stocchi ('Un antecedente latino-medievale di Pietro di Vinciolo', *Studi sul Boccaccio*, 1 (1963) pp. 349–62) che anche la novella V 10 derivi da una 'commedia elegiaca', il *De Cavichiolo*, ma probabilmente fu la novella boccacciana ad influenzare quella, che d'altronde, per ragioni stilistiche, è da annoverare tra le commedie umanistiche piuttosto che tra le 'commedie elegiache' (cfr. A. Stäuble, *La commedia umanistica*, Firenze, 1968, pp. 36–7 e A. Perosa, *Teatro umanistico*, Milano, 1965, p. 29).

11. Cfr. Paola Navone, 'Fiammetta tra classici e medievali: appunti sulla fortuna di letteratura ovidiana e pseudo-ovidiana nell'"Elegia" ', *Studi di filologia e letteratura*, 6 (Istituto di Letteratura Italiana della Facoltà di Lettere e Filosofia di Genova, Genova 1984) pp. 45–64.

12. Cfr. Susanna Calliero Amorino, 'L'"Alda" di Guglielmo di Blois ed il "Ninfale Fiesolano" del Boccaccio', *Sandalion*, 3 (1980) pp. 335–43.

13. Cfr. G. Rua, *Tra antiche fiabe e novelle, I. Le 'Piacevoli notti' di Messer Gian Francesco Straparola* (Roma, 1898) pp. 68–9.

14. Cfr. E. Gorra, 'Una *commedia elegiaca* nella novellistica occidentale', *Raccolta di studi critici dedicata ad Alessandro d'Ancona* (Firenze, 1901) pp. 165–74.

15. Cfr. L. Di Francia, *Novellistica* (Milano, 1924) vol. I, p. 724. Il Di Francia però attribuiva il *Miles gloriosus* a Matteo di Vendôme e lo definiva una 'elegia latina'.

16. Il titolo di questa 'commedia', come quello di due altre 'commedie elegiache' (*Aulularia* e *Asinarius*) è plautino, ma in nessuna di esse si può riscontrare la minima traccia dell'inconfondibile lessico dell'autore latino, nel Medioevo probabilmente conosciuto solo attraverso citazioni e cattive imitazioni. Si veda per esempio il prologo dell'*Aulularia*, in cui Vitale di Blois si vanta di essere superiore a Plauto (vv. 25–28) sia perché crede che il suo modello (oggi individuato nel *Querolus* di anonimo databile fra il III e il VII secolo d.C.) sia veramente una commedia plautina (cfr. F. Bertini ed., *Aulularia*, in *Commedie latine del XII e XIII secolo*, cit., vol. I, pp. 35–43) e le citazioni dalle *Piacevoli notti* dal primo volume dell'edizione di Manlio Pastore Stocchi (cfr. nota 1).

17. Traggo tutte le citazioni dal *Miles gloriosus* dall'edizione di Silvana Pareto, nel vol. IV della collana di *Commedie latine* del Bertini, pp. 11–93.

18. Si tratta dei mss. Vindobonensis 312, Bodleianus Misc. Lat. D 15 e Vindobonensis 303; cfr. ibidem, pp. 41, 47 e 48.

19. Cito dall'edizione di M. Wintzweiller, contenuta nella citata raccolta del Cohen, vol. I, pp. 131–51.

20. Riporto per comodità il riassunto del Rua, *Tra antiche fiabe*, p. 27 n. 1.

21. Esso è riportato in Wright, pp. 215–16.

22. È curioso come già in *De Mauro bubulco* esista un riferimento agli Ebrei: il re

inizia il suo colloquio finale con Mauro con le parole '*Tune es . . . verax et veridicus servus meus Maurus, bonus, prudens, et fidelis, e t v e r e I s r a e l i t a, in quo dolus non est?*'.

23. Cfr. G. Bàrberi Squarotti, 'Problemi di tecnica narrativa cinquecentesca: lo Straparola', *Sigma*, 5 (1965), vedi soprattutto le pp. 92–3 e 95.

24. S. Thompson, *The Folktale* (New York, 1946) p. 99.

25. Egli individuava la fonte della novella II 3 ('Carlo d'Arimino ama Teodosia, ed ella non ama lui, perciò che aveva a Dio la verginità promessa; e credendosi Carlo con violenza abbracciarla, in vece di lei abbraccia pentole, caldaie, schidoni e scovigli: e tutto di nero tinto, da' propri servi viene fieramente battuto') nel cap. VII della *Legenda aurea* di Iacopo da Voragine; F. Bertini, però, ha recentemente dimostrato che la novella sarebbe piuttosto il frutto di una contaminazione tra la *Legenda aurea* e il *Dulcitius* di Rosvita di Gandersheim (cfr. l'articolo di F. Bertini, 'La *Legenda aurea*, Rosvita e lo Straparola', *Atti del I congresso su Iacopo da Voragine* tenutosi a Varazze nel 1984, pp. 107–13, attualmente in corso di stampa e una copia del quale mi è stata gentilmente fornita dallo stesso autore).

26. Cfr. S. Thompson, *Motif-Index of Folk-Literature* (Copenhagen, 1955–58) 6 voll., i motivi E 611.3 e D 114.3 per l'uomo reincarnato o trasformato in porco, D 136 e M 313 per la trasformazione opposta porco-uomo. Quanto al matrimonio con un porco, l'unico esempio sembra essere quello dello Straparola (B 601.8), come risulta anche dall'indice di D. P. Rotunda, *Motif-Index of the Italian Novella in Prose* (New York: Haskell House Publishers, 1973, reprint of 1942 edition, Indiana University Press), motivo D 733.2. Sulla particolare natura fiabesca che distingue l'*Asinarius* dalle altre 'commedie elegiache' cfr. Simona Rizzardi (ed.), *Asinarius*, in *Commedie latine del XII e XIII secolo*, cit., vol. IV, pp. 140–7.

27. Traggo tutte le citazioni dell'*Asinarius* dalla mia edizione (cfr. nota 26).

28. Cfr. la nota al v. 399, p. 251 della mia edizione.

29. Cfr. Bàrberi Squarotti, 'Problemi di tecnica narrativa', p. 100.

30. Si tratta della n. 19 delle sue *Fiabe italiane: Re Crin*.

6

Topographical Aberrations in the Cycle of the Miracles of the Cross from the Scuola di San Giovanni Evangelista, Venice*

John G. Bernasconi

The paintings of the Cycle of the Miracles of the Cross in the Accademia, Venice, are unique among the great surviving narrative cycles of the Venetian Scuole in that the events depicted are all set in Venice itself.[1] They have long been celebrated for their detailed and accurate representation of fifteenth-century Venice: 'pictures of street architecture with various more or less interesting transactions going on in the streets. Large Canalettos, in fact' was Ruskin's description.[2] Gentile Bellini's 'Procession in the Piazza' and 'Miracle at the Ponte San Lorenzo', like Carpaccio's 'Miracle of the Relic of the Cross' set at the Rialto, provide what are probably the best known and most reproduced early images of Venice.

The accuracy of the representations has made them a valuable source of topographical evidence. Gentile's vast depiction of the Piazza shows it as it was before its rearrangement by Sansovino and others, and the precision of the detail is such that the painting provides, for example, our best source for the thirteenth-century mosaics on the façade of San Marco which were replaced in the seventeenth and eighteenth centuries. This is not to say that these paintings are without an element of 'artistic licence' in the rendering of their real locations. Writers have frequently discussed the extent to which Gentile manipulated the viewpoint(s) of his

* Brian Moloney has been a good friend for many years but we have only once coincided in Venice, in 1980. On that occasion Brian's major contribution to my research was his introduction of me to *grappa* as a reviver of academic morale and the guarantee of a good night's sleep in an Italian city. I am particularly grateful to Jennifer Fletcher for her advice and support for many years. I am also grateful to Pat Brown, Peter Humphrey and Jürg Meyer zur Capellen for the exchange of information and opinion and to the staff of the Venetian State Archives. Part of my research has been carried out on a fellowship from the Gladys Krieble Delmas Foundation.

painting to show both the basilica frontally and the entrance to the Doge's Palace unobscured by the Campanile.[3] Lazzaro Bastiani, for example, in his representation of the Scuola's own buildings in his 'Presentation of the Cross' reverses the 1481 entrance arch by Pietro Lombardo so that its better side with the impressive carved eagle of St John should be seen in the painting.

Two paintings in the cycle, however, depart much more radically from topographical accuracy. These are Mansueti's 'Miracle at Campo San Lio' and Gentile Bellini's 'Miraculous Cure of Pietro de' Ludovici'. It is surprising that this aspect of them has essentially been ignored, particularly since in both cases drawings provide us with some evidence about the artists' intentions.

The subject of Mansueti's painting (Plate I) is described in two printed accounts of the miracles worked by their Cross that the Scuola produced: an *incunabulum* of the late fifteenth century[4] and a pamphlet of 1590.[5] Though much later, the Pamphlet is particularly valuable as it also gives us the date of the painting as 1494. The event happened, not in 1474, as is usually said but sometime between 1389 and 1414.[6] The Miraculous Cross was being brought to the church of San Lio to accompany the body of a deceased member to the grave. The individual, however, had lived a dissolute life and had once said that he had no intention of accompanying the Cross during his life and could not care less if it accompanied him when he was dead. The Cross, it seems, took him at his word and when it got to the bridge leading into the campo, by a miracle, it could be moved no further and a cross from the church of San Lio had to be substituted. The miracle would have seemed a particularly topical one to the authorities of the Scuola in the 1490s as it showed the consequence (the active displeasure of the Cross) of failing to attend processions of the Scuola. Poor attendance at the frequent funeral processions was a major problem in the 1490s, which the Scuola tried to meet by making them compulsory for regular recipients of the Scuola's charity.[7] The painting shows the members of the Scuola fulfilling their duties and carrying the accessories employed for a funeral, including special black candle-holders.[8]

There exists in the Uffizi a drawing that is clearly a detailed study for the painting.[9] It is generally ascribed to Gentile Bellini rather than to Mansueti himself. The drawing is much more topographically accurate than the painting. It shows, particularly, the bridge leading into the campo on the far left, some way from the well and the centre of the campo as it appears in Jacopo de' Barbari's bird's-eye-view map of 1500 and as indeed remains the general layout today. In the painting, on the other hand, the *rio* (with the bridge) appears running through the heart of the campo itself. Writers discussing the painting, where they have concerned themselves with this at all, have tended to attribute the loss of topographical accuracy to Mansueti's limitations'as an artist, though sometimes at the same time noting his concern with authenticity in his very detailed rendering of architectural features.[10] It seems more plausible to seek some positive reason for the artist having abandoned the realistic representation of the campo shown in the drawing.

One benefit of the manipulation of topography found in the painting is that by placing the bridge parallel to the picture plane, with the *rio* in the foreground below, the variations in the levels and groupings of the figures now possible, provide greater opportunities for portraiture with, in effect, two close tiers of figures that run virtually across the full width of the painting. But this in itself would hardly justify the less realistic treatment of the location.

It is worth examining the role of the bridge itself in the narrative. The accounts in the *incunabulum* and in the 1590 Pamphlet are very close and both stress that the bridge was the point at which the miracle occurred. The crucial role of the bridge is also clear from the ceremonial practice of the Scuola. In 1474 the Scuola successfully petitioned the Council of Ten to be allowed to commemorate the miracle with a procession to the church of San Lio on that saint's feast day (20 April).[11] The earliest account of the procession I have found that gives any detail about its form is not until 1570 where it is described in the surviving book of the then *Guardian da Mattin*. By that time the procession was no longer observed but the earlier practice is recorded and it seems probable that the procession was an annual event in the 1490s, though by 1552 it had died out, having been forgotten, and had to be revived.[12] After High Mass in the Scuola San Giovanni Evangelista, the Scuola processed with the Cross to San Lio. It was at the bridge of San Lio that the Scuola stopped to sing a *laude* in commemoration of the miracle before proceeding to the church for a service.[13] Indeed, it is noted elsewhere in the book that whenever the Scuola, in procession, passed over the bridge the special hymn was to be sung.

The drawing, in preserving the correct spatial relationship between the

Giovanni Mansueti: 'Miracle at Campo San Lio'; Accademia, Venice (photo Böhm).

Gentile Bellini's 'Miraculous Cure of Pietro de' Ludovici'; Accademia, Venice
(photo Böhm).

two important locations of the narrative – the bridge and the church – pushes the main events out to the very edges of the picture. The main incident of members of the Scuola trying to move the Cross on its *mazza* across the bridge is barely visible in the middle ground on the far left while the substitute cross is somewhat more prominent, being brought out of the church on the far right of the drawing.

Given the importance of the bridge in the narrative, it is not hard to see why topographical accuracy should have been abandoned to some extent in the final painting. If the Cross could not be dragged across the bridge into the campo then the only solution was to move the bridge itself into the campo; thus placing the site of the miraculous event in the centre of the painting. In fact it is now the Cross being entrusted to the parish priest of San Lio (probably a portrait of the parish priest of the time of the painting, one Nadal Colona, who was a member of the Scuola)[14] that is shown while the substitute one is fitted to the *mazza*. This was both easier to depict and allowed the Miraculous Cross to be depicted in a more visible and dignified upright position.

Gentile Bellini's 'Miraculous Cure of Pietro de' Ludovici' of 1500 (Plate II) is a more puzzling case, since it presents a completely fictionalised representation of what should be the specific Venetian location. The *incunabulum* has a fuller account than the 1590 Pamphlet of the miracle depicted; though the Pamphlet's text is a first-person account by Pietro de' Ludovici, a member of the Scuola. He described how he had suffered from malaria which first struck him on 15 August 1447. The next January, being in Venice and due for another attack of the fever, on the first Sunday of the month he went to the Scuola and prayed before the Miraculous Cross. He then retired to bed taking with him a candle that had been in contact with the Cross and, praying continuously to the Cross, his fever completely disappeared.

The account suggests two possible settings for a painting of the miracle: Ludovici's bedroom or his encounter with the Cross. However, two other miracles depicted in the Cycle were set in bedrooms. Mansueti's 'Miraculous Healing of Benvegnudo's Daughter' shows such a scene and a painting mentioned by the 1590 Pamphlet as by Perugino but later destroyed by fire, probably showed Andrea Vendramin invoking the Cross in his bedroom.[15] Gentile's painting shows the Cross exposed on an altar in a church and since the miracle occurred on the first Sunday of the month, the Cross would have been in the church of San Giovanni Evangelista.

The problem is that the church is not that of San Giovanni Evangelista. As many commentators have noted,[16] it does not resemble the church of San Giovanni depicted in Lazzaro Bastiani's 'Presentation of the Relic to the Scuola'. Bastiani's representation of the Scuola's own buildings on the left of the painting is very precise, even including contemporary work on the large upstairs *Sala*, in the form of heightening it by two metres,[17] and there is little reason to suppose that the church is not an equally true representation. The church as it exists today has been largely remodeled but recent discoveries and research tend to confirm the accuracy of Bastiani's representation.[18] Far from showing a Gothic building Gentile's painting employs the vocabulary of contemporary Renaissance architecture in its use of classicised columns and pilasters, with inset polychromatic tondi, articulating the domed cubic space. It has echoes of the façades of San Zaccaria and the Scuola San Marco but there is also a strong fantasy element to it. It has been related to drawings in Jacopo Bellini's sketchbooks[19] though any connections are not very close. What seems clear is that Gentile is not depicting an existing structure but exercising his imagination in a way closer to Carpaccio's architectural inventions in his St Ursula Cycle. This is borne out by surviving drawings for the painting.

It was Baumeister in 1934 who first identified a group of drawings in Munich as preparatory sketches by Gentile Bellini for the San Giovanni picture.[20] The drawings are concerned with working out the architectural environment and though the reliquary that appears in two of the sketches is not drawn as a cross the association with Gentile's painting seems convincing both because of similar (largely unchanging) actions of the figures, where shown, and echoes in the architecture of the forms of the eventual painting. Baumeister argued that the drawings showed a coherent development, from a composition similar to Bastiani's 'Presentation of the Cross' towards the eventual painting.[21] More recently Jürg Meyer zur Capellen has suggested a somewhat modified evolution through the drawings to the final painting[22] but their differences do not affect the argument here. The changing architectural forms in the sketches make it clear that the artist was not trying to reproduce a specific existing location of the events but to create an imaginary idealised setting.

The problem then, which writers on the Cycle or Gentile have not tackled, is why Gentile should have abandoned the topographical accuracy of his two earlier paintings for the Cycle (and indeed of his fellow contributors to it) when the location for the narrative was the very building which actually stood directly opposite the windows between which the painting was to hang.

A possible explanation lies in the relationship between the Scuola and the priory who possessed the church of San Giovanni Evangelista. Like other Scuole, San Giovanni Evangelista made use of a nearby church and its priests for their religious ceremonies. Hence they used the church of San Giovanni Evangelista, for example, for their regular Mass, preceded by a procession, on the first Sunday of each month; the event at which Pietro de' Ludovici obtained his candle.[23] The Scuola San Marco similarly made use of the church adjacent to their Scuola, San Giovanni e Paolo, for their mass on the first Sunday of each month.[24] It was not uncommon for relationships between Scuole and their host churches to become very strained at times. The church of San Giovanni Evangelista from its foundation (by tradition in about 970) until 1582 was under the patronage of the Badoer family who appointed the secular prior who ran it and the attached hospital for the poor.[25] The appointment was made for life and the occupant was usually a member of the Badoer family. Under Alvise Badoer, who became Prior in 1489, relationships between church and Scuola became particularly bad.

Prior and Scuola were constantly in dispute through the 1490s, invoking in their fight the various authorities of the Patriarch of Venice, the Patriarch of Constantinople, the Council of Ten and the Holy See.[26] The Scuola accused the Prior of obstructing their rights of access to the church and its facilities and to the cemetery in front of it which was used by the Scuola for the burial of their members (on payment of a fee). They cited agreements going back to 1340 and the large sums they had spent on the embellishment of the church in support of their claims. The Prior further sought to prevent them saying low mass or the office of the dead in the Scuola itself.[27]

This background of dispute alone might perhaps explain why the Scuola should not wish a second representation of the actual church of San Giovanni Evangelista to feature in the Cycle. The painting by Bastiani does, of course, show the church very prominently but it was recording a very specific and important event – the presentation of the miraculous cross to the Scuola in 1349. In any case the scene also allowed the artist to include the Scuola's own building alongside the church. It may be argued that Gentile's work concerns a miracle for which the church was not essential as the location of the miracle but merely provided the opportunity for the exposition of the Cross and the provision of the candle that led to the miracle. In that case, however, it is puzzling that the setting for the painting should be a church even if it is not an accurate representation of San Giovanni as it then was. It seems, though, that the Scuola were planning to replace that church.

A petition of the Scuola to the Council of Ten in 1491, after referring to the dispute with the Prior, sought permission to build a new church from the Scuola's own funds, under the dedication of St John of the Flagellants, after which they should be free of all payments to, or obstructions by, the Prior.[28] The new church was never built and the Scuola seems soon to have had to become less ambitious in its plans.[29] But the aspiration for a new church may provide the explanation for the imaginative architecture of Gentile's painting. Not that the drawings or painting probably represent any actual design for a new building but rather that the proposal of a new church inspired or justified the exercise of the artist's imagination.

An objection to this hypothesis is, of course, the chronology. Gentile's painting is dated 1501 by the Pamphlet of 1590 and there is no reason to dispute this as the date of completion.[30] At that time there was a new Prior, Alberto Badoer, who had succeeded Alvise in 1499, and, after arbitration, a settlement had been reached between Prior and Scuola in 1500.[31] However there is reason to suppose that the conception of Gentile's painting including its architecture dates from well before the date of its completion.

It has not been appreciated that the Munich drawings provide evidence about the date of conception of Gentile's painting. Several of the drawings are in horizontal or 'landscape' format rather than the vertical or 'portrait' format of the others and the eventual painting. That the painting was being designed in a horizontal form means that it was almost certainly being planned before 1494 at the latest. This is because the paintings were to decorate a specific room in the Scuola – the Sala della Croce. The dimensions of the paintings of the Cycle relate closely to the available hanging spaces in the room, the length and width of which has not changed since the fifteenth century. This and Sansovino's account of the paintings in the room in the late sixteenth century allow a clear reconstruction of the original placing of the paintings.[32] On the evidence of the 1590 Pamphlet, by 1494 only two possible sites for paintings of a horizontal format existed – the ones to be occupied by Gentile's 'Procession in the Piazza' in 1496 and his 'Miracle at the Ponte San Lorenzo'. The unique size and subject matter of the first make it inconceivable that any other painting could have been intended for its site, the entrance (west) wall opposite the altar on which were Carpaccio's and Perugino's works of 1494. The miracle at the Ponte San Lorenzo was the most celebrated miracle of the Cross and it is therefore highly probable that it would have been among the first commissioned and its subject would seem to demand a landscape format.[33] This means that the Munich drawings belong to an early planning stage of the Cycle before the allocation of sites to the paintings completed in 1494. The Scuola's petitions to the Council of Ten make it clear that work on the Sala della Croce (or *Albergo* as it was then more usually named) was being undertaken by 1491 with a major part of this, a ceiling, having been completed by 1493.[34] A further reason for supposing the miracle of the healing of Pietro de' Ludovici to have been among the first considered as subjects for the paintings is that, as Pat Brown has noted, Pietro's son and namesake was a leading figure in the Scuola at the time and indeed on the *Banca*, or governing body of the Scuola, as *scrivano* from August 1490 to August 1491.[35] The late date of Gentile's 'Healing of Ludovici' is not so surprising when one recalls that his 'Procession' and 'San Lorenzo' paintings would presumably also have been commissioned at the time of the ones completed in 1494 but were themselves completed only in 1496 and 1500 respectively. Gentile at this time had many demands on his time, especially at the Doge's Palace and we know, for example, that his progress with work for the Scuola San Marco was extremely slow.[36]

The events depicted in the Cycle of the Miracles of the Cross are portrayed in specific Venetian locations because that is where the miracles happened. The detail and accuracy of the representation of the locations was not simply for its own sake but, as Pat Brown has rightly argued, a means of attesting to the authenticity of the miracles.[37] A significant departure from topographical accuracy was not likely to be for any capricious reason or a sign of artistic failure but rather for a specific purpose, to better express the concerns of the Scuola commissioning the painting.

86 Moving in Measure

Notes

1. The paintings are: Gentile Bellini, 'Procession in the Piazza San Marco', 'Miracle at the Ponte San Lorenzo' and 'The Miraculous Cure of Pietro de' Ludovici'; Vittore Carpaccio, 'Miracle of the Relic of the Cross'; Giovanni Mansueti, 'Miracle in the Campo San Lio' and 'Miraculous Cure of the Daughter of Benvegnudo of San Polo'; Lazzaro Bastiani, 'Presentation of the Relic of the Cross'; Benedetto Diana, 'Miracle of the Cross'. See the relevant entries in S. Moschini Marconi, *Gallerie dell'Accademia di Venezia* (Rome, 1955) vol. I.
2. John Ruskin, *Guide to the Principal Pictures in the Academy of Fine Arts at Venice* (first published 1877) (London, 1906) vol. III, p. 162.
3. See, for example, J. G. Links, *Townscape Painting and Drawing* (London, 1972) pp. 74–5; J. Meyer zur Capellen, *Gentile Bellini* (Stuttgart, 1985) pp. 74–6.
4. Museo Civico Correr, Venice, Inc. H222 bis., entitled *Questi sono imiracoli delasantissima croce delascola demiser san zuane evangelista*. On this see P. Brown, 'An Incunabulum of the Miracles of the True Cross of the Scuola Grande di San Giovanni Evangelista', *Bollettino dei Musei Civici Veneziani*, N.S. 27 (1982) 5–8.
5. *Miracoli della Croce Santissima della Scuola de San Giovanni Evangelista* (Venice, 1590). See J. G. Bernasconi, 'The Dating of the Cycle of the Miracles of the Cross from the Scuola Grande di S. Giovanni Evangelista, Venice', *Arte Veneta*, 35 (1981) 198–202.
6. Both the Incunabulum and the Pamphlet of 1590 give the miracles in the same, chronological, order. 1474 is the date of a Council of Ten decree, which is reprinted in the 1590 Pamphlet, authorising a commemorative procession for the miracle.
7. Archivio di Stato Venice, Consiglio dei Dieci, Parti Miste (abbreviated as A.S.V., C.X., p.m. hereafter), filza 4, f. 44; Registro 24, f. 143 (27 March 1490); A.S.V., Scuola Grande San Giovanni Evangelista (abbreviated as S.G.S.G.E. hereafter), 140, 192–3. See also B. Pullan, *Rich and Poor in Renaissance Venice* (Oxford, 1971) pp. 77–8.
8. An inventory of 1462 lists 'dopieri de legno negri' (A.S.V., S.G.S.G.E., 72, f. 12v) and 'Doppieri negre' for funerals and Good Friday are listed in an inventory of 16 February 1537 (A.S.V., S.G.S.G.E., 76, f. 64).
9. Florence, Uffizi 1293, pen and ink, 44.2 x 59.1 cm.
10. See, for example, D. von Hadeln, *Venezianische Zeichnungen des Quattrocento* (Berlin, 1925) p. 45; S. Miller, 'Giovanni Mansueti: A Little Master of the Venetian Quattrocento', *Revue Roumaine d'Histoire de l'Art*, Série Beaux-Arts, 15 (1978) 81–4.
11. A.S.V., C.X., p.m., Registro 18, f. 69; A.S.V., S.G.S.G.E., 140, f. 140, f. 182v (11 May 1474). The text of the Council's decree is also included in the 1590 Pamphlet, incorrectly dated 2 May.
12. A.S.V., S.G.S.G.E., 38, ff. 415–16 (24 February 1553). For some reason the permission of the Council of Ten had failed to be written into the Scuola's *Mariegola*.

13. A.S.V., S.G.S.G.E., 16, n.p., 'feste'.
14. A.S.V., S.G.S.G.E., Registro 13, f. 41. Colona died in 1502.
15. The date of the fire is probably established by a payment for repairs of 4 January 1566 (A.S.V., S.G.S.G.E., 32) and some idea of Perugino's painting is provided by the description of Andrea Vicentino's replacement of it in 1588 in Giovanni Dionisi Capitanio, *Sommario di memorie, ossia Descrizione succincta delli quadri esistenti nella Veneranda Scuola Grande di S. Giovanni Evangelista* ... (Venice, 1787) pp. 20–1; discussed in my M.A. dissertation at the Courtauld Institute, University of London, 'The Cycle of the Relic of the Cross from the Scuola Grande di San Giovanni Evangelista', 1972, pp. 7–8.
16. Most recently, Meyer zur Capellen, *Gentile Bellini*, p. 80.
17. Bernasconi, 'The Dating of the Miracles of the Cross', p. 199.
18. Piero Pazzi, *La Chiesa di San Giovanni Evangelista a Venezia* (Venice, 1985) pp. 16–17, 39.
19. The closest is probably f. 69a in the British Museum Sketchbook (V. Goboulew, *Les Dessins de Jacopo Bellini au Louvre et au British Museum* (Brussels, 1912) vol. I, plate LXXXIII). See Meyer zur Capellen, *Gentile Bellini*, p. 136.
20. E. Baumeister, 'Studienblätter zur Kreuzesreliquie', *Münchner Jahrbuch der Bildenden Kunst*, 11 (1934) pp. 36ff. The drawings are Munich, Staatliche Graphische Sammlung, Nos 12552, 12553, 12554, 14644, 14647, 14648; recto and verso in each case. The attribution to Gentile has (with a couple of dissenting voices giving them to Carpaccio) generally been accepted; see Meyer zur Capellen, *Gentile Bellini*, pp. 165–6 (illustrated, plates 69–80).
21. Baumeister, 'Studienblätter', pp. 39–40.
22. Meyer zur Capellen, *Gentile Bellini*, p. 166.
23. A.S.V., S.G.S.G.E., 16, n.p., 'feste'.
24. They attended High Mass after a procession round the campo with the Friars. A.S.V., Scuola Grande di San Marco, 17 (Notatorio, 1498–1530), f. 60 (11 August 1515).
25. The status of the Badoer family in relation to church, hospital and the property occupied by the Scuola is summarised in F. Corner, *Notizie storiche delle chiese e monasteri di Venezia* ... (Padua, 1758) pp. 371ff.
26. A.S.V., S.G.S.G.E., 75 (Chiesa), *passim*; 140 (Notatorio I) ff. 193ff; Cattastico Generale, vol. I, pp. 35–8 and *passim*.
27. A.S.V., S.G.S.G.E., Cattastico Generale, vol. II, pp. 31–2 (28 May 1491), in the first instance.
28. '... licentia de poder far e construer una giexa a spexe di fradeli de la scuola predita. Intitulando quella giexia de Missier San Zuane di Batudi ...' A.S.V., S.G.S.G.E., 72 (among items bound in at the back) and another copy in Registro 140 (Notatorie I), ff. 194–5v. Urbani de Gheltorf referred to the latter but his date of 27 March 1490 relates to the previous entry in 140 (G. M. Urbani de Gheltorf, *Guida storico-artistica della Scuola di S. Giovanni Evangelista in Venezia* (Venice, 1895) p. 35). The petition in question is not dated more precisely than 1491. The Scuole Grandi were often referred

to as 'Scuole dei Battudi' (of the beaten) from their practice of public flagellation, a practice on the wane by this period (see Pullan, *Rich and Poor*, pp. 34–40, 50–2 and *passim*).

29. On 22 February 1492 the Scuola obtained a papal bull from Alexander VI granting permission to institute a chapel or oratory, with several altars, for the celebration of mass and other divine offices (A.S.V., S.G.S.G.E., 74, ff. 46r–v). It would seem that some progress was made on this as on 5 March 1493 the Patriarch of Venice granted a forty-day indulgence for contributions towards the completion and decoration of the Oratory of San Giovanni Evangelista (A.S.V., S.G.S.G.E., Cattastico Generale, vol. II, p. 132). However, the Patriarch of Constantinople, giving judgment between the Scuola and Prior Badoer on 24 May 1494, decreed that the Scuola could not make a new chapel but have private masses with only members present, at the altars in the Scuola itself. It appears that the new oratory or chapel was to be on the ground floor, or in a place near to the chapel, of the *Ospitale* adjacent to the Scuola (A.S.V., S.G.S.G.E., 37, p. 422; Cattastico Generale, vol. I, p. 36).

30. Bernasconi, 'The Dating of the Miracles of the Cross', pp. 200–1. Contrary to the reading of this in G. Nepi Sciré and F. Valcanover, *Accademia Galleries of Venice* (Milan, 1985) p. 87, the chronology is such that Gentile's painting can hardly have been commissioned or executed following a grant of funds to the Scuola for the paintings of the Cycle by the Council of Ten in late February 1502 (1501 m.v.) though, of course, they may have been used to pay for it.

31. A.S.V., S.G.S.G.E., 140, ff. 198r–v (19 February 1500). This, however, was by no means the end of disputes between Prior and Scuola.

32. The reconstruction of the original arrangement of the Cycle is discussed at tedious length in Bernasconi, 'The Cycle of the Relic of the Cross', pp. 19–40.

33. See Bernasconi, 'The Dating of the Miracles of the Cross', p. 200 and p. 202 n. 31.

34. Ibid., pp. 199–200.

35. P. F. Brown, 'The Painted Histories of the Scuole Grandi of Venice, *c.* 1494–*c.*1534' (University of California at Berkeley Ph.D., 1983) p. 161.

36. The Mantuan Ambassador described the extent of Gentile's commitments at this time to Francesco Gonzaga in a letter of 22 October 1493 (A. Luzio, 'Disegni topografici e pitture di Bellini', *Archivio Storico dell'Arte* (1888) p. 276). For the Scuola San Marco see P. Paoletti, *Raccolta di documenti inediti per servire alla storia della pittura veneziana nei secoli XV e XVI* (Padua, 1894) vol. I, pp. 17–19 and *La Scuola Grande di San Marco* (Venice, 1929) *passim*.

37. P. Brown, 'Painting and History in Renaissance Venice', *Art History*, vol. 7, no. 3 (September 1984) pp. 263–6.

7

Richecourt's Inheritance: Administration and Economy under the Last of the Medici*

Doug Thompson

Charles Fane, the British Resident in Florence prior to the much more celebrated Horace Mann, was an assiduous correspondent, as behoved his office, and the year 1737 certainly gave him a great deal to write home about! From the very first days of that eventful year he kept his superior, the Duke of Newcastle, fully informed about the delicate negotiations, troop movements and various comings and goings of important personages as well as the rumours, tittle-tattle and gaffes which led up to the death (on 9 July) of the last of the Medici line, the Grand Duke Gian Gastone, and the transfer of the Grand Duchy of Tuscany to the Habsburg-Lorraine dynasty.[1]

On 16 July, a week after the demise of the Grand Duke, Fane wrote: 'On the twelfth instant Prince Craon took formal possession of this government and received the oath of Fidelity and Obedience to the Duke of Lorrain from the Senate and Council of Two Hundred which represents the whole State of Florence' (PRO: SP 98, 40/133), while a couple of weeks later (and this is an early indication of what was to follow) Fane informed Newcastle that 'the Prince Craon pursuant to his instructions

---

* I met up with Brian Moloney again, after several years of moving in different orbits, at an ATI conference in Norwich in 1979. He was at once enthusiastic about my own recently awakened interest in the Tuscan eighteenth century, wistful perhaps at seeing an old love in the arms of another! The following summer we coincided in Florence, he chuckling endlessly over Sacchetti in the Biblioteca Nazionale and I struggling with the social and economic ills of eighteenth-century Tuscany, though meeting up in the long warm evenings to do our bit to help keep the Chianti industry afloat. In the intervening years different interests have from time to time taken me away from these questions but now, at last, that projected study is taking shape. It seems wholly fitting, therefore, that this essay, an abbreviated version of the first chapter of *Economy and Society in Tuscany, 1700–1765* should be dedicated to Brian.

has ordered the suspension of the survivancy of all such employments as were granted in the deceased Grand Duke's reign, and may become vacant by the death of the respective persons in those posts: He has abolished likewise several supernumerary pensions that were a burthen to the State' (PRO: SP 98, 40/159).

However, it is in Fane's letter of 3 September that we read that 'On the 29th Mons.r de Richecourt, the Duke of Lorraine's Minister and Counsellor of State arrived here from Vienna to assist Prince Craon in the administration of the government here'.[2]

Count Diodato Emanuele de Richecourt, like his superior Craon, plunged immediately and with an energy which certainly dismayed his Florentine subordinates, into the complex task of analysing and evaluating the State administrative machinery and its various institutions. Only a week after his arrival in Florence Craon was writing to tell the Grand Duke in Vienna that with every day that passed Richecourt was making some new and startling discovery (ASF: *Reg.*, F171, 10/9/1737) and as if to corroborate this information Fane, on the very same day, was busy telling *his* superior that 'M. de Richecourt agreeable to his instructions is examining at the respective publick banks the particulars and nature of these (aforementioned) debts, an exact plan whereof is to be sent to Vienna. Orders have been given to these banks to suspend the payment of all such superfluous pensions as are judg'd to be a burthen to the State revenues' (PRO: SP 98, 40/191).

Strangely, Rodolico insists that 'il Richecourt non affrettò giudizi' ('Emanuele de Richecourt etc.', p. 365) and yet less than three weeks after his arrival in Florence he was writing in the following terms to the new Grand Duke, a letter which has become a *locus classicus* in any evaluation of the efficiency of the late Medicean State:

Le gouvernement de ce pays est un cahos presque impossible a debrouiller, c'est un melange d'aristocratie, de democratie et de monarchie. Il semble que l'on ait pris plaisir à entremeler les affaires de façon qu'on ne puisse jamais les voir au clair ... Le seul expedient pour demesler ce noeud qu'on peut appeler gordien sera de le couper et de prendre un nouveau sisteme, mais cela ne peut se faire qu'avec bien du temps, du travail et de la patience, d'autant plus que nous trouvons tous les ministres et gens en place convenir du mal, mai nul ne veut parler pour proposer le remède. Il y a icj bien d'honnêtes gens, mais ils sont craintifs et le plus grand nombre pense à son interêt particulier sans s'embarasser du bien public. L'on trouvera tout le mond convenir sur la necessité d'une reforme, et tout le mond s'y opposer de lorsque ce la regardera un tribunal où il est, ou quelqu'un de ses parents, ou de ses creatures. Tell'est la situation general de ce pays jetté dans la mollesse et l'oisivité par l'exemple et la faiblaisse du gouvernment passé. Pour y apporter du remède il faudra necessairement de la fermeté et y avoir d'abord des troupes pour s'y assurer de l'obeisance et y etoufler les murmures aux quels on doit s'attendre.[3]

As we shall see, Richecourt's assessment of the situation was far from exaggerated. Since the times of Cosimo I the power of the formerly Republican State Assemblies and of the Magistracy had been gradually concentrating in the hands of the Grand Dukes and a small oligarchy of aristocratic state counsellors and the balance of power had swung back decisively in favour of the patrician class. This administrative centralisation had encouraged the older Republican tendency to concentrate economic activity in the capital so that by the beginning of the eighteenth century a huge imbalance existed between the wealth and privilege of Florence (truly 'la Dominante') and the various provinces.

However, the system was only as effective as the will or ability of the despot allowed it to be and in the cases of Cosimo III and Gian Gastone, the religious bigotry of the one and the indolence of the other coupled with the instinctive and extreme conservatism of both served to impose a general stagnation and to stifle all initiative in administrative and economic affairs. In such circumstances as these all that seemed to flourish was corruption and self-interest on the part of officials, a consequence which was not lost on Richecourt who commented:

Tout le mond pillent, ils [the administrative officials] estoient sûres qu'ils ny avoit personne en état de l'attaquer et de leurs faire rendre compte sans risquer lui meme à son tour ... L'officier general, le governeur de place, le provvediteur, le ministre, tous *mangent*, pour me servir des termes du pays; ils mangent sur tout, sur les choses les plus viles, sur les gens les plus miserables.

(ASF: *Reg.*, F13. Letter 2/11/1738)

The key to future change lay in the possession of land in the provinces. Medicean clientelism had effectively re-established the *latifondia*, much land having been granted to those families or institutions which had faithfully served the prince's interests, thus adding a new layer of aristocratic landowners to the older nobility who had gained their wealth from manufacture and commerce in Republican times. In either case, however, the possession of land ensured an income and continuing privilege and status at a time when commercial and industrial activity had reached its lowest ebb in Tuscany as well as (in Quazza's words) 'la presenza dominante di un gruppo, il quale ... esercita in città, negli organi politici e amministrativi, la potenza acquisita e mantenuta col predominio economico posseduto in campagna'.[4]

Exaggerated claims were made by some early historians about the changes in the direction of a greater degree of liberalisation during the reign of Gian Gastone, but the evidence suggests that the composition and style of his government remained much the same as before. While it is true he banished from court circles the numerous churchmen, religious bigots and other hangers-on encouraged and protected by his father and abolished the dubious pensions many of these laid claim to, the most noticeable (but politically insignificant) change was in the tenor of court life in which a gloomy pietism gave way to an excessive, at times glittering hedonism, itself probably induced by the acute sense of time running out for the dynasty.

The Tuscan economy continued to be dominated by the same classes and in many cases families which had been prevalent in the State's commercial and manufacturing heyday. It was their defence of the generally uneconomical, certainly unjust *sistema annonario* which, by keeping down principally grain prices at an artificially low level, ensured that the vast majority of smaller landowners and tenant farmers were never able to challenge their hold on the food supply market nor yet find sufficient surplus cash to break into the monopoly class themselves by buying more land. This monopoly was in any case further safeguarded and reinforced by the *fidecommesso* and *manomorta* laws which prohibited the division of large land holdings into smaller units. It was this consequent concentration of wealth in few hands coupled with the fact that these landowners were themselves generally resident either in Florence or Siena which largely accounted for the economic and political dominance of *città* over *campagna*, particularly in the century leading up to the extinction of the Medici, a dominance which was greatly reinforced by laws which, in many areas of trade and industry, effectively dictated a monopoly in favour of the capital over the provinces.

It was in these circumstances that many small proprietors[5] or tenant farmers (*locatari*), unable to make ends meet, had no alternative but to sell out to those who were better off,[6] sometimes to the *grossi terrieri* but sometimes too to more modest landowners who, with their subsequently increased production capacity, were better able to hold their own with the dominant class. Sometimes too, medium-sized areas of land were leased, usually on relatively short-term contracts, from the *grossi terrieri* but were then sublet among small farmers at rents which ensured a comfortable lifestyle for the major tenant who also thus joined the ranks of this newly emerging rural bourgeoisie.[7]

Yet another route into this new class was via agricultural 'speculation' by city-based manufacturers or merchants but also many *fattori*, the often powerful intermediaries who stood between the absentee landlords and their tenants. Indeed, the Medici themselves had provided the model, having profited enormously over almost three centuries from precisely this kind of activity.

However, land was purchased, or more frequently rented, with the aid of loans granted by the *Scrittoio di Possessioni* or by bodies such as the *Religione di Santo Stefano*. In order that the borrower should not fall behind with his repayments he had to ensure that his own sub-tenants, in their turn, produced the crops whose sale would either pay their rents to him directly or a part of which he claimed in part or full payment of the lease, and in these precarious circumstances (as in the cases of short lease) this intermediate class, at very least, injected a sense of urgency into production, at worst became tyrannical, exploitative, even rapacious in its dealings with the peasantry whose lot was unenviable. In these circumstances and with these very particular pressures operating on the agrarian economy, Anzilotti rightly perceived the creation of 'una gerarchia di dipendenti, sottoposti a svariate condizioni e sacrificati all'interesse dell'imprenditore' ('L'economia toscana', cit. p. 105).

The closed, inflexible system within which they were constrained to operate, a system controlled (as has been shown) by the large, essentially conservative landowning aristocracy, paradoxically infused a new, energetic entrepreneurial spirit into this middle class which, in order to survive, tended (as Quazza has suggested) to cut through 'la ristretta cerchia del rapporto locale di lavoro e di produzione, ampliando i rischi e l'entità degli investimenti di capitale, migliorando alquanto la tecnica delle culture, ottenendo maggiori possibilità d'esportazione per tipi particolari di prodotti' (p. 194).

This mentality was not surprisingly (given the social or geographical origins of many of this incipient rural bourgeoisie) more typical of that found in commerce than in agriculture, vigorous, calculating, yet essentially seeking to break into the circle of privilege and prosperity rather than to break out of its highly restrictive system by supplanting it with a more flexible alternative.

As a distinct class, certainly by the end of the Medici dynasty at very latest, it had released new energies and revealed potentially new economic directions but, for the moment at least, chose to remain within the limits established by the Medici style of government over the preceding three centuries.

This system of economic exploitation in the interests of the dominant classes was. enforced through a harsh code of law which had reached a new peak of severity and cruelty with Cosimo III's *Ruota criminale* which was introduced in 1680 to deal with the most serious crimes. Robiony's observation seems rather to understate the case: 'In tutti gli angoli del granducato imperversava la piú cruda miseria, a cui faceva strano contrasto il lusso sfacciato della corte e de' nobili . . . La delinquenza, fedele seguace del pauperismo, aumentava rapidamente senza lasciarsi intimorire dalla feroce legislazione penale del Granduca, assumendo proporzioni davvero spaventose, e moltiplicando i delitti atroci'.[8]

The government's response was to intensify repression rather than to deal with the social and economic ills which lay at the root of the increased lawlessness. 'Il Gran Duca', as Galluzzi rightly commented, 'era inesorabile con i miserabili, voleva nei processi la celerità, e nei supplizi tutto l'apparato per incutere dello spavento',[9] yet even though the *Ruota criminale* was renewed annually it had made no significant headway in curbing serious crime and was finally abolished in 1699. The problem was not only that continuing privation continued to breed crime but also that the administration of the law was as corrupt and inefficient as that in other areas of public life, a fact which Richecourt himself observed during those early weeks following his arrival in Florence in 1737 (ASF: *Reg.*, F12. Letter 29/10/1737). Indeed, the first proposals for a radical reform of the law came from Richecourt himself; its inefficiency and indeed much of the injustice it engendered derived from the multiplicity of tribunals with overlapping mandates, the confusion they created in contesting the right to try certain cases, and the slowness with which they operated.

A whole area of this brutal legal system was designed to protect the *sistema annonario* which was managed by the *Magistrature dell'Abbondanza e della Grascia* and the *appalto* system in which the collection of taxes due on the movement and/or sale of all manner of goods and materials was farmed out to the highest bidder by the government or prince. These two institutions formed the corner stone of the rigid economic system known as *vincolismo*. This system had been further strengthened during the reign of Cosimo III with the introduction of more frequent and more efficient checks on the amounts of grain being produced by individual farmers and the prices it was fetching in local markets; but also with the introduction of laws such as that which decreed that grain destined for Siena could only be transported from Florence and other specified areas provided a licence sanctioning such movement had been obtained from the *Rettore* of the place from which the *estratto* was to be made. The result, as with almost all of the legislation governing the economy, was delay, frustration and a loss of profits for the producer.

Towards the end of the reign of Cosimo III, a general reform of the *Abbondanza* was carried out and a new or rather revised set of regulations governing the provision of basic foodstuffs was published on 30 July 1697. In reality, this was not so much a reform as a co-ordination of the great number of regulations and provisions which had been accumulated over several centuries, aimed at eliminating contradictions and superfluities but above all else at closing loopholes which had hitherto resulted in loss of revenue for the State or the Grand Duke. In other words, it represented one more turn of the screw in an already heavily oppressive system in which 'spietate sanzioni erano dirette contro i trasgressori, e vessazioni di ogni genere permesse a impedire l'evasione delle disposizioni stabilite'.[10]

In the sixteenth and seventeenth centuries the system of *privative* and *appalti* had become ever more prevalent as a means of raising revenue and from about the middle of the seventeenth century to the end of the Medici dynasty there was hardly a commodity which was not subject to taxation in this way.[11] However, as we learn from a group of merchants

from Livorno in 1737, it was not only the direct financial loss which made
the system unpopular:

> Si pone in considerazione, che non avendo altra mira l'appaltatore
> protempore, che di beneficiare il proprio interesse, ad altro non pensa,
> che a procacciarsi dei vantaggi, li quali poi tutti ridondano in pregiudi-
> zio del commercio, giacchè non è la sola sperduta libertà che abbia
> molto danneggiato questo traffico, ma le stranezze ancora state sempre
> usate contro del medesimo dalli appaltatori.
>
> (ASF: *Misc. di Finanza*, A290C)

It is to these 'stranezze' (by which is clearly meant the arbitrary, often
whimsical and contradictory instructions given by the *appaltatori*, whose
powers were extensive) that the Livornesi merchants directly attribute
the loss by the port of most of the lucrative tobacco trade to the rival port
of Genova, the direct cause of which was, in their opinion:

> il pretendersi la fede d'immissione dai compratori dei medesimi, o sia
> il responsale da quei Paesi addove venivano spediti (i tabacchi); il che
> non poteva in conto alcuno accordarsi dai detti compratori, mentre
> venendo da questi mandati in Paesi forestieri, ed in contrabbando, gli
> era impossibile di poter ricavare il detto Responsale, e soddisfare a
> quell'obbligo a cui pretendevano di sottoporli gli appaltatori.
>
> (ASF: *Misc. Fin.*, A290C)

Needless to say, none of these complications born, as the merchants
make clear, of excessive greed, was to be found in Genova and foreign
merchants dealing in tobacco, losing time, money and patience found
they obtained a much better service in the latter port, and (the merchants
continue) 'abbenechè dopo qualche tempo sia stato sospeso l'obbligo di
far venire li detti Responsali, con tutto ciò, si è fin qui reso impossibile di
poter nuovamente acquistare il deviato negozio' (ASF: *Misc. Fin.*,
A290C).
After a long and detailed series of complaints about the many negative
ways in which they are affected by the multiplicity of *appalti*, the hapless
merchants conclude with the plea, 'Peraltro sembra necessariamente che
SAR si degni di riflettere che non vi è cosa piú contraria, piú nociva, e piú
incomoda ad un Portofranco, che li appalti' (ASF: *Misc. Fin.*, A290C).

Dal Pane was certainly correct in his observation that 'la pratica delle privative e degli appalti rende esattamente le finalità della politica economica e finanziaria del principato', aiming, as it did, 'di assicurare un'entrata fissa, e magari anticipata, alle pubbliche casse'. Unfortunately, the system was wide open to abuse for 'l'arbitrio illimitato conduceva spesso alla contraddizione di alienare le regalie, di concedere ad altri funzioni e prerogativi statali, di ridurre lo Stato ad un percettore di canoni di affitto e di concessioni' (*Finanza*, p. 31).

The great complexity of the Grand Duchy in seemingly every facet of its public life was owed to the acquisition of several different territories over the centuries together with their social, economic and cultural practices, some of which had been assimilated as a part of the general Tuscan cultural heritage whereas others had continued only at a local level in those formerly independent territories, side by side with 'national' laws and customs, frequently contradicting these latter either wholly or in part. Indeed, as Pompeo Neri was to point out in his report on the state of the judicial system, delivered to the Consiglio di Reggenza in mid-August 1745:

Dall'anno 1415 in poi, in cui fu compilato lo Statuto fiorentino, non è stata mai fatta alcuna altra compilazione metodica e generale; ma che sempre, non ostante tutte le rivoluzioni che sono seguite, si è proceduto con aggiungere, secondo il bisogno, leggi nuove, senza abolire però le vecchie, le quali nelle cose non riformate si sono sempre lasciate sussistere e tuttavia sussistono. (ASF: *Reg.*, F51)

This theme is taken up by Dal Pane at the outset of his monumental study of the finances and financial institutions of Tuscany, when he observes that:

Il sistema finanziario toscano dei primi decenni del Settecento rispecchia fedelmente la composizione strutturale dello Stato, formatosi per successive aggregazioni di territori, che, attraverso le capitolazioni, avevano conservato gran parte delle loro vecchie istituzioni economiche e finanziarie. Il Granducato aveva in tal modo assunto la figura di un mosaico composto di parti non omogenee, riunite in tempi diversi, separate ancora di barriere economiche, e tenute insieme da un comune vincolo politico che non sopprimeva le autonomie e le istituzioni locali in quanto non contrastassero con il rapporto di soggezione. Di qui i privilegi dei luoghi, che naturalmente si riflettevano nel campo finanziario, ponendo i sudditi del medesimo principe in condizioni diverse secondo le varie circoscrizioni territoriali cui appartenevano. Di qui anche una peculiare suddivisione di funzioni pubbliche fra il potere centrale e i poteri locali, gli ostacoli al costituirsi di una finanza statale ben ordinata.   (*Finanza*, p. 11)

This was precisely that state of affairs which Richecourt had referred to as 'ce noeud qu'on peut appeller gordien'.

In addition to the financial and other restrictions imposed by the *sistema annonario* and the various *appalti*, Tuscans were weighed down with direct taxes such as the *decima*, the *estimo*, the *catasto fiorentino* and frequent *collette straordinarie* as well as with a wide range of indirect taxes such as internal customs tariffs and other *gabelle*. These various systems and taxes were applied erratically according to class and geographical location but in general it tended to be the lower classes, especially in the countryside, who bore a disproportionate burden of taxation.

According to Francesco Maria Gianni, there were no fewer than 166 different customs barriers throughout the Grand Duchy towards the end of the Medici dynasty (ASF: *Gianni*, F36, 516/c.449), which itself testifies to the economic fragmentation of the state noted by Dal Pane. Bellucci exemplifies this confusion when he observes: 'Alla dogana di Firenze si percepivano undici diritti particolari, alle porte della stessa Firenze altre sette tasse speciali. Cinque tasse locali erano dovute alla dogana di Pisa (alle porte di Pisa altre quattro tasse); ancora tasse locali alle dogane di Siena, Pistoia e in quelle suburbane fiorentine, pisane e senesi'.[12]

Five provinces, the *contadi* of Florence, Pisa and Arezzo, the State of Siena and the Pistoiese, were all subjected to a great number of *gabelle regie*, and each of these areas tended to have an outer (at its borders) and an inner (between city and *contado*) circle of customs barriers; Pistoia had a third intermediate barrier between the countryside (up to a mile outside the city walls) and the *contado* proper. Furthermore, each different customs zone had its own individual *gabelle* and list of prohibited goods, its own different rates for *introduzione*, *estrazione* and *transito*, its own system of weights and measures as well as rules and procedures of operation and penalties for infringement. If the immediate purpose was the collection of revenue, a second, equally important intention was that of protecting the industries of the provincial capitals at the centres of these customs zones, and none more so than Florence itself. Ironically, it was thus the movement of the commonest and most necessary raw materials and foodstuffs which was most hindered and frustrated by this closed local protectionist policy. Parenti underlines the point in his discussion of the provisioning of the city of Siena in years when local harvests were insufficient to cater for its needs:

> basti pensare, a questo proposito, che verso la metà del '700 si valutava nella misura di una lira lo staio (circa un terzo del prezzo medio corrente) la spesa necessaria per importare grano da Livorno, e che una somma quasi uguale – se non superiore, data la distanza e le difficoltà del trasporto – doveva spendersi per portare in città il grano prodotto in certe zone della Maremma.[13]

Other *gabelle* which brought in substantial revenues for the State were the salt monopoly (in addition to those relating to tobacco and iron), the *macinato* (which covered every kind of flour, including chestnut), the taxes on meat and wine; newly born foals, asses and mules (the revenues from which were earmarked for the maintenance of rivers and dykes), and on all legally registered contracts such as those covering the buying and selling of real estate and personal property, inheritances and dowries.

These then were the principal forms and sources of tax revenue by which the State, the prince and many *comuni* were funded and which, conversely, were in large measure responsible for the sluggish character of the Tuscan economy by the end of the Medici dynasty. Yet, despite the enormous sums collected, the general quality of life in the state was poor and because the very source of revenue bled the economy so severely that it was continuously short of capital for self-renewal, especially technological improvement, the public debt increased inexorably until it had reached grotesque proportions during the first decade of the eighteenth century. Indeed, by the end of Cosimo III's reign (1723) it stood at around 20 million *scudi*, which seems excessively high for a state with a population of substantially below one million. True enough, Gian Gastone did address himself to this pressing problem with perhaps greater vigour than he habitually displayed for affairs of state and his administration did succeed in reducing the deficit; nevertheless, it still represented a serious financial crisis for the incoming Lorenese administration.

In the industrial sector, as Paolo Malanima has shown, principally through his detailed analyses of the woollen and silk industries, between the mid-sixteenth and early eighteenth centuries the general trend in industrial output for Florence and the rest of the Grand Duchy was downwards.[14] This was most marked in the woollen industry where, for example, a steady drop in the number of companies operating in the capital from the end of the sixteenth to the middle of the seventeenth centuries (100 in 1596 to 41 in 1646) became a veritable landslide from then until the 1730s (1662 – 22; 1723 – 15). The dangerously low level of production of woollen goods reached in the capital by the end of the Medici dynasty gradually began to be offset by the increase in production of *località minori* between 1739 and 1766, as a direct result of the liberalising legislation enacted by Richecourt's government with the *motuproprio* of 27 February 1738, which broke the stranglehold the capital had on the industry, though without quite removing all its privileges. The Commission set up to examine the state of the industry discovered that despite strict laws to the contrary, reaffirmed as recently as 1725 (for Florence) and 1732 (for Siena), the current huge influx of foreign woollen goods was having a very serious adverse effect on home production. Tuscan goods remained unsold with the consequent, inevitable reduction in the size of the work force and the increase in poverty and unrest which unemployment and the threat of unemployment brought to the workers and their dependants. The new legislation, when enacted, aimed at the maximum production and circulation of woollen goods within the state while offering protection for the internal market from foreign competition by prohibiting the import of almost every type of woollen goods. In practice, because of the strong protests from the powerful Florentine *case mercantili*, particularly in respect of high quality foreign manufactures, the government was forced to make substantial concessions over the last point.

By 1766, Florence had in fact lost the lead in the production of this commodity to the neighbouring city of Prato, itself perhaps an indicator of the release of long pent-up energies and abilities. However, despite a slight improvement in the fortunes of the industry during the period of the Regency, it was not sustained in the long term and the decline resumed towards the end of the century. However, the decline of the woollen industry was to a great extent compensated for by the expansion in silk production, even though the overall trend for these two manufacturing industries, taken together, was downward.

As Malanima makes plain, statistics relating to the number of companies operating in the capital between 1472 and 1775 are not very reliable indicators of the health of the industry if taken alone (p. 306). For one thing, the sources differ over such a long period, while the number of companies never seems to take into account 'la scala delle operazioni di ogni singola bottega' (p. 307). A much more persuasive indicator of performance is the statistical data on production and export, the former of which show a steadily downwards movement between 1721 and 1757, while for the same period the value by weight of *drappi di seta* exported shows a slight increase (p. 316). Indeed, from about the middle of the 1730s, with the general increase in agricultural prices in the international markets, the export and monetary value of Florentine silk products also increased, so much so that by 1773 the Florentine Chamber of Commerce was able to report that 'da quaranta anni in qua questa manifattura piuttosto può dirsi accresciuta che diminuita' (cit. Malanima p. 317). In fact, we know that even in 1757, 63 per cent of the total value of all exports from the Grand Duchy came from manufactured goods and that *drappi di seta* accounted for 55 per cent of that total;[15] these figures, however, should not be allowed to obscure the fact of the overall decline of manufacturing industries in the capital during the reigns of the last two Medici Grand Dukes. One further indicator of this decline is the population figures, for despite the many inducements and privileges enjoyed by the capital and generally withheld from the rest of the state, the population, which seems to have increased steadily to about 76,000 by 1622, then fell away to approximately 60,000 by 1649, at which figure 'il pessimo governo di Cosimo III tenne la popolazione nell'intiero corso del suo regno'.[16] During the reign of Gian Gastone the number of inhabitants began to rise again steadily, but it was only during the second half of the eighteenth century that it once again safely passed the 1622 levels.

The whole economic system, a variant of mercantilism, was designed and regulated in such a way as to maintain the domination of the city-based industries and commerce, but particularly during the reigns of

the last two Medici Grand Dukes the concentration of wealth in fewer
hands together with the many crippling fiscal restrictions placed on both
industrial and agrarian related commerce had the effect of steadily and
inexorably reducing the amounts of capital available for investment in
the cities, and although, as Di Nola points out, 'l'oppressione delle
campagne valse per qualche tempo ad alimentare il lusso, le manifatture e i commerci cittadini . . . li trasse poi nella propria rovina' (*Politica
economica* etc., p. 7). This undermining of industry and commerce was
in part a direct concomitant of that intensifying oppression, for 'venivano a mancare infatti le materie greggie che l'agricoltura preparava
per l'industria' (ibid.) so that more and more such materials had to be
imported, thereby greatly increasing production costs. The consequent
rise in prices gradually put most manufactured goods beyond the reach
of the vast majority of the population, while on the international
markets, where competition was extremely fierce, Tuscan goods, which
were often of inferior quality or, as we have intimated, very costly to
produce, fared badly on the whole.

One further long term deleterious effect of the economic dominance
of city-based activities was that only those infrastructures which directly
benefited them tended to be maintained in reasonable working order,
with the result that many roads and bridges were allowed to deteriorate
to the point at which they became unsafe or impassable, while many
waterways, notably though by no means exclusively in the Maremma,
were allowed to silt up and stagnate. This wholesale neglect of second-
ary highways was to increase the sense of social dislocation in the
countryside in general but especially in those areas which did not lie
along the main trade routes or which did not themselves contribute in
some way towards the industrial or commercial activities of the principal cities. A deteriorating network of communications and their generally poor state of repair meant that journeys were slower than they
need otherwise have been, which in its turn contributed to the overall
inefficiency but high costs of all economic activity. Alessandra Borgi
argues:

Il sistema delle infrastrutture sarebbe stato probabilmente l'unico
modo di avvicinare la redditività dell'agricoltura a quelle del commercio e dell'attività manifatturiera, permettendo nuovi e piú economici sbocchi ai prodotti agricoli e il miglioramento delle condizioni

sociali dei contadini col venir meno del loro isolamento: ma i Medici non riuscirono a realizzare tale disegno.[17]

At the heart of Tuscany's many problems lay the legally enforced exploitation of the great majority of the population in the state in the political and economic interests of the traditional ruling groups, whether landed noble families with commercial interests in the capital or city merchants or manufacturers who, within the period under scrutiny, saw their long term security and continuing privilege and prosperity lying in the purchase of land. Though things were beginning to change, even before the end of the Medici dynasty, nevertheless, that system of exploitation was to persist, albeit with changing characteristics, throughout the period of the Regency. According to Paolini – and with his analysis Bandini had earlier shown himself to be in substantial agreement, 'era nell'interesse pubblico l'invigilare sui bassi prezzi delle manifatture. Per conseguire questo fine era necessario di tener bassi i prezzi dei viveri, onde la sussistenza degli Artefici essendo di poco dispendio, si potessero tener bassi i salari pagati loro dai mercanti'.[18]

It was the enforced stagnation and poverty of the food-producing countryside coupled with the ever-deepening decline of the urban manufacturing industries and commerce which, throughout the whole of the Seicento, had largely been responsible for steadily pushing up the costs of production in the increasingly uneconomical manufacturing sector. That industry had notably not made the transition from a predominantly home-based to a factory-centred mode of production, mainly because of the enormous powers and privileges of the extremely conservative Florentine *Arti*, while in the countryside, the characteristic system of land tenure remained that of the semi-feudal *mezzadria*, many of whose participants provided the casual and therefore cheap labour force for the *lavoro a domicilio* in the woollen and silk industries. By the end of the Medici dynasty, this whole repressive system, while still continuing to damage and retard agricultural development was no longer able to sustain the manufacturing industries which were being left further and further behind by technical and organisational developments in the more advanced northern nations such as Britain, Holland and France. As the European movement towards free trade gathered momentum in the middle and later decades of the eighteenth century, the Grand Duchy of Tuscany, despite the urgings of many of its *lumi*, cautiously opted for a compromise solution in which admittedly free trade played a part, but in which the *mezzadria* system, with all its deficiencies, was extended so as to dominate completely most of the Tuscan countryside. This solution was itself in part the typical expression of a strong and persistent rearguard action by the ruling classes who, although they owned the land, were not generally themselves involved in working it; but also, it has to be said, it was in part the result of constant pressure from Vienna to maintain an assured flow of revenue to pay for its interminable wars.

In the end, it has to be acknowledged, though the vision, ability and will for far-reaching reforms which would benefit the whole of the state, were abundantly in evidence in Richecourt's Tuscany, in general only those reforms were permitted which were thought likely to increase revenue or at very least, which did not carry the risk of reducing it.

In this essay we have concentrated exclusively on the economic and financial aspects of the grave situation which awaited Craon and Riche-court when they took over the government of Tuscany in mid-1737, but it should be remembered also that the internal and external political situations were equally unpropitious. The popularity of the Spanish Bourbon Prince Carlos, especially in Florence and particularly among the most powerful families, and the sudden thwarting of the projected Spanish succession in the Grand Duchy as a result of international political agreement, did nothing to endear the Lorenesi to their new subjects. Pro-Spanish plots and factions were to persist, with the very real threat of invasion in 1738, and even many of those who did not favour the Spaniards had hoped for a return to some form of republican autonomy. Dissatisfaction and unrest were rife and in these circum-stances, together with the administrative, financial and economic con-straints more fully described in the foregoing pages, the achievements of the *Reggenza* under Richecourt's guidance were not inconsiderable and certainly were far higher than has generally been acknowledged. The inheritance ('quest'ombra di stato', Venturi calls it) was indeed a tangle of thorns, yet despite the many attendant limitations, Richecourt's patient, far-sighted government was to prepare the ground in which Pietro Leopoldo's reforming state could flourish and bear such remark-able fruits.

Notes

1. Fane's letters are to be found in the Public Record Office, London (PRO) in SP (State Papers) 98, file number 40.
2. PRO: SP98/40 doc. 188. Certainly, it appears from Craon's correspondence with Vienna in those early weeks that he was indeed in need of assistance in the administration of the state. The pro-Spanish faction at the Florentine court, led by Rinuccini, Tornaquinci and Padre Ascanio, the Spanish Resident, was very active organising at very least passive resistance to all attempts at reform by Craon. There seems to have been a widespread and firm conviction that the newly installed Lorenese government would be shortlived. A key to Craon's difficulties is offered, perhaps, by the Venetian consul in Tuscany, who wrote of him, 'Egli è un soggetto di un naturale assai dolce. I Signori Fiorentini se ne approfittano lusingandosi che gli affari devino continuare a correre come in passato [e] essi fanno non poco girare la testa al signor principe di Craon' (Archivio di Stato di Venezia, Dispacci del Console veneziano in Livorno, Sebastiano Bechi, Busta 1ª, dispaccio del 16 agosto 1737), cited in N. Rodolico, 'Emanuele de Richecourt, iniziatore delle riforme lorenesi in Toscana' in *Saggi di storia medievale e moderna* (Florence, 1963) pp. 362–78 (p. 364). For Craon's correspondence see Archivio di Stato di Firenze (ASF), *Reggenza*, Filza 171.
3. ASF: *Reg.*, F12, Letter of 17/9/1737. The bulk of Richecourt's early Tuscan correspondence is contained in this *filza*.
4. G. Quazza, *La decadenza italiana nella storia europea* (Turin, 1971) p. 189.
5. Patterns of land tenure varied greatly from one place to another and in some parts, notably Valdinievole, the Mugello, the Empolese, the upper Arno region near Florence and the countryside around Siena, the tradition of small landholdings still persisted strongly in the early years of the eighteenth century. See Quazza, *Decadenza*, p. 193.
6. In his discussion of the situation in the Sienese Maremma, Baker points out that 'i costi della produzione agricola erano tanto alti che era possibile coprirli solo negli anni in cui i prezzi erano particolarmente vantaggiosi. Nella Maremma senese, dove non c'era mezzadria, un agricoltore che per piú anni non fosse riuscito a coprire i costi, era costretto ad abbandonare la terra', G. F. R. Baker, *Sallustio Bandini* (Florence, 1978) p. 12.
7. A. Anzilotti, 'L'economia toscana e l'origine del movimento riformatore del secolo XVIII', in *Archivio storico italiano*, 1915, pp. 82–118 (p. 96 passim).
8. E. Robiony, *Gli ultimi dei Medici e la successione del Granducato di Toscana* (Florence, 1905) pp. 37–8.
9. J. R. Galluzzi, *Istoria del granducato di Toscana sotto il governo della casa Medici* (Leghorn, 1781) VII, p. 262.
10. C. Di Nola, *Politica economica e agricoltura in Toscana nei secoli XV–XIX* (Città di Castello, 1948) p. 6.
11. Luigi Dal Pane lists no fewer than 25 different *appalti* or *privilegi*, illustrating the point that 'Già nel secolo XVI e nella prima metà del XVII il sistema delle privative e degli appalti aveva trovato larga applicazione. A partire

dalla seconda metà di quest'ultimo secolo fino all'estinguersi della dinastia medicea, sembra che il sistema penetri sempre piú nell'uso, diventi la norma piú seguita e piú accreditata'. See *La finanza toscana dagli inizi del secolo XVIII alla caduta del Granducato* (Milan, 1965) pp. 31–2 & fn. 1, p. 32.

12. P. Bellucci, *I Lorena in Toscana: Gli uomini e le opere* (Florence, 1984) p. 16. A comprehensive list of tariffs, on what kind of goods and in which places, is shown in V. Mugnai, *Tariffa delle gabelle toscane* (Florence, 1781); see also Dal Pane, *Finanza*, pp. 22–7, and R. Mori, *Le riforme leopoldine nel pensiero degli economisti toscani del '700* (Florence, 1951) pp. 29–31.

13. G. Parenti, *Prezzi e mercato del grano a Siena* (1546–1765) (Florence, 1942) p. 128.

14. P. Malanima, *La decadenza di un'economia cittadina: L'industria di Firenze nei secoli XVI–XVIII* (Bologna, 1982).

15. G. R. Carli, 'Saggio politico ed economico sopra la Toscana fatto nell'anno MDCCLVII' in *Opere*, I (Milan, 1784) p. 337.

16. A. Zuccagni Orlandini, *Ricerche statistiche sul Granducato di Toscana* (Florence, 1848–54, 5 volumes) I, p. 434.

17. A. Borgi, 'La rete stradale della Toscana nei suoi caratteri attuali, nella sua evoluzione storica, nelle sue esigenze di sviluppo' in *L'universo*, anno LVII, n. 2, 1977, pp. 327–400 (pp. 346–7).

18. G. B. Paolini, *Della legittima libertà del Commercio* (Florence, 1785) II, p. 17.

8

Victorian Verecundity: d'Annunzio's Prudish Public

J. R. Woodhouse

If we disregard the *Appeal to Europe*, a propaganda pamphlet published in London in 1920, but in fact issued that year by d'Annunzio from Fiume, only one work of d'Annunzio's written after 1900 has been translated into English and published in Britain. The work concerned was the slight and obscure play written first in French, and published in 1914, *La Chèvrefeuille*. With those two eccentric exceptions, nothing d'Annunzio wrote after the age of thirty-five has been translated and published in Britain, yet his writings, in the massive tomes of the Edizione Nazionale, run to 47 volumes. And before 1902 eight major works had in fact been translated: five novels, *Il piacere, Il trionfo della morte, Le vergini delle rocce, L'innocente* and *Il fuoco*, and three plays, *La città morta, La Gioconda* and *Francesca da Rimini*. As far as the great British public was concerned, those were enough. In 1906 Henry St Ives translated *La figlia di Iorio* (his typescript still lies in Harvard's manuscript collection) but this play, arguably d'Annunzio's best, had to wait another twenty years before W. H. Woodward (of Renaissance educationists fame) privately printed a hundred copies of his own elegant translation. The only other work translated was a very selective anthology of *Le novelle della Pescara*, which seems to have been published as a socialist ploy to illustrate d'Annunzio's awareness of the plight of the socially underprivileged in 1920. Joseph Hergesheimer's preface to Mantellini's translation suggests that d'Annunzio's Renaissance sensitivity 'is troubled by modern apprehensions, a social conscience unavoidable now to any fineness of perception'.[1] The notion of a d'Annunzio with a social conscience is not one which readily springs to mind today. Hergesheimer goes on:

His tales . . . possess our own vastly more burdened spirit. In this, as
well, they are as English as they are Italian; the crimes and beggars and
misery of Pescara, the problems and hopes of one, belong to the other;
the bonds of need and sympathy are complete.   (pp. 15–16)

D'Annunzio did hate what he called the *grassa borghesia*, and I believe
that those tales did show a deep understanding, if not actually sympathy,
for the poor and beggars of his native town, but he is equally concerned
with deliberately shocking his readers with realistic descriptions of the
physical deformities of these creatures and the often harrowing details of
their fate. Harrowing reality has never been overtly popular with the
British reading public, and the volume achieved little critical success
here. In common with most other translations from d'Annunzio it failed
to achieve a reprint. Mantellini did not flinch from the worst excesses of
d'Annunzio's realism; he accurately translates, for instance, the sadistic
horror of *L'eroe*, but even here the several lacunae in his text of the
Novelle are significant; *Il cerusico di mare* and *La madia*, for example,
are omitted.

An unusual kind of vicious circle operates where d'Annunzio's work is
concerned. The translations of his novels and plays were conditioned by
the moral atmosphere of the times in which they were published,
particularly between 1898 and 1904. Those emasculated translations,
particularly of his novels, provided the basis for critical opinions which
dismissed d'Annunzio as a mediocrity interested largely in the seamier
and more sensual side of life. That is an accusation which it would be
inept to level against his poetry, for instance, yet only thirteen short
poems have been systematically anthologized, and that in 1893.[2]

Not that d'Annunzio's translators were bad. Arthur Symons was
well-motivated and elegant (though rather dull in his translation of
Francesca), and W. H. Woodward dealt splendidly with *La figlia di Iorio*,
while Georgina Harding (who translated probably the most important of
his novels, *Il trionfo della morte*) makes as accurate and as elegant a
translation as was possible, given the Victorian censorship and her sex.
She mistranslated thirty words or so, but her sins are, as we shall see, sins
of omission. It is useful for my purposes to consider just her work in
particular (there is too little space to dwell on other translations here)
and to do so bearing in mind factors which conditioned it, simultaneously
noting some consequences for d'Annunzio's critical fortune thereafter.

Although I shall be dwelling on the features I have so far mentioned, it is worth recalling that most Italian critics regard d'Annunzio as untranslateable anyway, because of his self-declared inimitability. One early sympathiser in Britain, Orlo Williams, noted this aspect in 1913:

> It is unfair to read d'Annunzio in translation, for the Italian language is a vital element of his art. He has created a new prose for modern Italy – a vivid, abundant, flexible medium, invariably beautiful and infinitely harmonious.[3]

The observation is not isolated; in the comments made by other British commentators there is the occasional remark by certain critics aware of that inimitable quality.

The letter to Francesco Paolo Michetti which prefaces *Il trionfo della morte*[4] gives fair warning that any translator will have a hard task; d'Annunzio had nurtured its language deliberately for five years, he was there expressing his joyous pride in a tradition which had pre-Ciceronian origins. This was to be an unrepeatable ideal of prose:

> Avevamo piú volte insieme ragionato d'un ideal libro di prosa moderno che – essendo vario di suoni e di ritmi come un poema, riunendo nel suo stile le piú diverse virtú della parola scritta – armonizzasse tutte le varietà del conoscimento e tutte le varietà del mistero; alternasse le precisioni della scienza alle seduzioni del sogno; sembrasse non imitare ma *continuare* la Natura; libero dai vincoli della favola, portasse alfine in sé creata con tutti i mezzi dell'arte letteraria la particolar vita – sensuale, sentimentale intellettuale – di un essere umano collocato nel centro della vita universa.   (p. 49)

If d'Annunzio had raised the barrier of inimitability even to his fellow Italian-speakers, what hope could there be for a translator to approach the quality of his language and style? But that was only one obstacle to his appreciation. In Britain his military and political gestures made d'Annunzio first a hero (he was given the MC in 1915) and then an object of scorn (after Fiume). But long before this, the critical climate was fixed by such puritans as Robert Buchanan. In the 1870s Buchanan set the public tone for literary ethics following the polemics between him and Dante Gabriel Rossetti. Let me briefly mention Buchanan's piece on

Rossetti's sonnet sequence, *The House of Life*, a review which further helped ruin the final years of Rossetti's existence:

> At times in reading such books as this one cannot help wishing that things had remained for ever in the asexual state described in Mr Darwin's great chapter on palingenesis. We get very weary of this protracted hankering after a person of the opposite sex.[5]

I shall return to Buchanan's views in order to illuminate other inhibitions.

Rossetti was, incidentally, one of d'Annunzio's favourite artists and poets, and since, in certain of his own poems of the *Isotteo* collection as well as in *Il piacere*, he tried to emulate and go beyond Rossetti's pre-Raphaelite ideal, those aspirations were not guaranteed to endear him to the Victorian public. I should like to convey now the atmosphere in which d'Annunzio's novels, particularly, were to be translated and reviewed during the 1890s and shortly afterwards; I shall try to show the effect which that atmosphere had on one particular work, *Il trionfo della morte*. It was an atmosphere which lasted for many years and recurred for the next fifty, along with those early critical judgements, based, as may be seen, on a false text of d'Annunzio's work. Some critics repeat almost word for word after the poet's death what had been written by Marie Louise de la Ramée (pseudonym Ouida) and others in the 1890s.

The century pullulated with puritanical organisations. In 1857 the Government published 'An Act for more effectively preventing the Sale of Obscene Books, Pictures, Prints and other Articles' (The Obscene Publications Act), probably the most effective arm of censorship, reinforced by such organisations as the National Vigilance Association (1885) or the National Social Purity Crusade (1901) or The Forward Movement for Purity (1908). To these add the Lord's Day Observance Society (1831) and a dozen missionary organisations founded during the final twenty years of the century.[6] It seems astonishing now to think that *Lady Chatterley's Lover*, which was published in Florence in 1928, had to wait until 1960 and the enterprise of Penguin Books, who were even then prosecuted for obscenity under the century-old act. Only in that year did acquittal and publication come.

That these measures had teeth we know very well from the tragic fate of Oscar Wilde. Another minor example, but relevant for us since the names of Zola and d'Annunzio were later to be linked, was the case of Henry Vizetelly, Zola's English publisher. He was prosecuted for obscenity in 1888, having published Zola's *La Terre* (*The Soil: a realist novel*). He was initially fined £100 and bound over in a further sum of £200 to keep the peace. He tried to recoup his losses by heavily expurgating the novel and reissuing it in 1889; he promptly lost his £200 and was imprisoned for three months. He died shortly afterwards, and with him the publishing house. Heinemann made no such mistake with d'Annunzio!

The measures also produced an atmosphere of what we might call auto-censorship which was to influence whole strata of society, producing guilt-feelings in the population as a whole at the thought of anything openly physical or sensual. Joyce's *Dubliners* had to wait nine years after its first submission to a publisher in 1905 before it was eventually published, largely because a typographer refused to print some of the stories, which contained seven 'bloodys', a reference to King Edward, and more to my point, a lady's legs, all of which the printer objected to. The phrase about the legs is in *Counterparts*: 'She continued to throw bold glances at him and changed the position of her legs often'.

Even d'Annunzio's critical allies see in him elements of the obscene and the sadistic which they emphasise often as much as they emphasise his merits. Edward Hutton, for instance, writes in the *Monthly Review* of 1902 a piece on *Il piacere*. 'This history of a lust is in some parts almost as ugly as that title; redeemed, indeed, by the genius of the author from the mere sordid and exciting tale of ordinary French fiction'.[7] The passage continues with a weird paradox about d'Annunzio's moral uplift:

Yet it appears to me that d'Annunzio is often quite needlessly obscene, worrying subjects usually treated with a certain care, as a maniac will twist and turn his fingers, never letting them rest for a moment the whole day long. And so, almost in spite of himself as it were, d'Annunzio often attains to a profound morality; for when he has described with the weary minuteness of the sensualist some scene of passion, one is filled with disgust, one finds the whole thing detestable, where a man of lesser passions and equal genius would have moved us to desire. (p. 148)

Perhaps among the critics before Charles Herford, W. L. Courtney was his greatest populariser and champion. Here is one of his judgements, apologising for d'Annunzio's cruelty:

> The man is still young, comparatively speaking, and for this reason, perhaps, we can understand, even if we do not altogether forgive some of his most salient characteristics. He has no pity, not much humour; he describes his scenes and analyses his characters with all that merciless severity which we associate with young and triumphant science in a dissecting room.[8]

Gerald Griffin is not so reticent in the thirties, so what can we expect the Victorians' reaction to be? I quote from Griffin:

> D'Annunzio's emphasis on the revolting, the foul, the lurid, the ghastly, the brutal and the weird, was one of the facets of that naturalism which was so rife towards the end of the nineteenth century and which was sponsored by Zola.[9]

If d'Annunzio's admirers were ambivalent in their attitudes, the eulogy which *The Times* newspaper devoted to him on 23 September 1919 contains a rather back-handed compliment, which is also indicative perhaps of a certain barbarity in our own society in the opening quarter of the century: 'Signor d'Annunzio has proved himself as good a man of action as any healthy normal Englishman, who would no more read a line of poetry than he would write one'. That kind of anti-poetic atmosphere, which many of us know, is noted in a similar context by Osbert Sitwell, in volume V of his autobiography, in an anecdote describing a lunch with an eighty-six-year-old gentleman who reminisced about his Victorian schooldays at Eton, in similar terms to *The Times'* report.

> 'I well remember, when I first went to Eton, the head boy called us together, and pointing to a little fellow with a mass of curly red hair, said, "If you ever see that boy, kick him – and if you are too far off to kick him, throw a stone" ... He was a fellow named Swinburne', he added. 'He used to write poetry for a time, I believe, but I don't know what became of him'.[10]

Sitwell comments as follows:

A poet then, of d'Annunzio's type, with his intensely Latin approach to life, will be necessarily more unpopular in Anglo-Saxon countries than even Shelley or Swinburne. Also, usually, there is less chance of kicking him. But d'Annunzio's usurpation of Fiume provided just such a rare opportunity.

The atmosphere was not conducive to sensuality or to poetry and certainly not to sensual poetry. One of d'Annunzio's greatest champions at the time was Arthur Symons (he actually translated a lot of d'Annunzio's work), but Symons himself had to endure charges of immorality and obscenity for his own compositions in Verlainean and Dannunzian moods. His *London Nights* of 1895 met with a tremendous barrage of adverse criticism and probably helped provoke the nervous illness which ruined him. A curious and nowadays amusing relict of that Victorian censorship of Symons remains in the Bodleian Library today where *London Nights* is catalogued under the symbol φ – the symbol of the Bodleian's obscene and pornographic collection – and if you want to read it in that edition you have to read it in a special corner of the library and hand the book back to a librarian when you have finished with it. It is all very innocuous, much is made of winning kisses from sensuous lips and suchlike, and the mood is very similar to Rossetti's *Nuptial Sleep* or *The Kiss*. But Symons' championing of d'Annunzio was counter-productive, since both were tarred with the same brush. Let me recall at this point Buchanan's *Fleshly School of Poetry* and his comments precisely on this kind of poem:

I have lived nearly as long in the world as they have, but never yet came across persons of the other sex who conduct themselves in the manner described. Females who bite, scratch, scream, bubble, munch, sweat, writhe, twist, wriggle, foam, and in a general way slaver over their lovers, must surely possess some extraordinary qualities to counteract their otherwise most offensive mode of conducting themselves. (p. 44)

Buchanan's obsessions included *bed* and *legs* and their associations, and, although there can be no direct influence, I feel, from his essay upon

Georgina Harding's translation of *Il trionfo della morte*, it is a fact that she usually eliminates references to these 'sensual' objects. Buchanan had noted that among the sugared sweetmeats which filled Victorian confectioners' windows, 'may be seen this year models of the female Leg, the whole definite and elegant article as far as the thigh, with a fringe of paper cut in imitation of the female drawers and embroidered in the female fashion' (p. 3). I would like to dwell on that Leg for just a while longer, because it does become relevant to most censorship questions thereafter.

> The Leg, as a disease, is subtle, secret, diabolical. It relies not merely on its own intrinsic attractions, but on its atrocious suggestions. It becomes a spectre, a portent, a mania. Turn your eyes to the English stage. Shakspere [*sic*] is demolished and lies buried under hecatombs of Leg! Open the last new poem. Its title will possibly be this or similar to this – 'Leg is enough'. Walk along the streets. The shop windows teem with Leg. Enter a music-hall – Leg again, and (O tempora! O mores!) the Can-Can. . . . It is only in fashionable rooms and in the stalls of the theatre that Leg is at a discount: but that is not because life there is more innocent and modest, but because Leg is, in the higher circles, altogether eclipsed by its two most formidable rivals – Bosom and Back.   (p. 4)

And sure enough, when Georgina Harding translated d'Annunzio's *Trionfo della morte*, the word *leg* hardly ever appears in her English version. So among the crowds at Casalbordino, the del Trigno women 'camminavano stracche, curve, con le gambe aperte' (p. 268), translated by Miss Harding as 'their feet wide apart' (p. 197). And when Ippolita's sensuality is underlined, the Victorian censorship is even more evident: 'E sotto gli occhi di lui tendendo l'una e l'altra gamba, perfette nelle loro lucide guaine, chiuse le giarrettiere su l'uno e l'altro ginocchio' (p. 310). That sentence is translated 'offered her feet, one after the other, perfect in their glistening sheath, to his gaze' (p. 137). But even in a very non-sensual piece of description such as the desperate reaction of a peasant woman whose son has been drowned, after her 'scoppii disperati del dolore' . . . 'Ella taceva; si toccava un piede, una gamba con un gesto macchinale' (p. 353). This becomes hard to censor, since there is already a *piede* in the original, so the translator draws the attention of her reader not this time to the feet but to the hand: 'She only touched a foot or a hand' (p. 269). And the peasant women again, sitting down for their rough *merenda*, 'con le gambe allargate sul terreno' (p. 269), are given the decorum of a Victorian girls' school out for a picnic, 'seated on the ground with their legs crossed under them' (p. 198). Words like *coscia, inguini, ascelle, pori* (even *i pori del legno*), *sudore* – all change in their translation into English, or are simply omitted.

And if it is thought that the preoccupation no longer exists, I note that in some parts of the United States, the *leg* of a grand piano is referred to as the *limb*, presumably to avoid *that* word. I also saw a letter in the *Guardian* on 27 March 1981, which ironically breathed a sigh of relief that we may finally accept the naked legs of pianos.

Another preoccupation of Buchanan's – as already indicated – was the word *bed*, for which he substituted *couch*. Bed, the *thalamus thalamorum* which Giorgio Aurispa, protagonist of the *Triumph of Death*, constructs for his mistress Ippolita, is a major feature of the *eremo*. Here is Buchanan again:

> Mr Rossetti in his worst poems, explains that he is speaking dramatically in the character of a husband addressing his wife. Animalism is animalism nevertheless, whether licensed or not, and indeed, one might tolerate the language of lust more readily on the lips of a lover addressing a mistress than on the lips of a husband, virtually (in these so-called *Nuptial Sonnets*) wheeling his nuptial couch into the public streets. (pp. viii–ix)

When Miss Harding has to mention bed she tries to make it clear that Giorgio lay down on 'his' bed (H. p. 65), even though it is definitely the couple's more than king-sized bed which is referred to in 'Egli andò a distendersi sul letto' (p. 121). Here is part of d'Annunzio's description of the bed:

> O se tu fossi già qui! . . . Stasera dormirò per la seconda volta nell'Eremo; dormirò solo. Se tu vedessi il letto. È un letto rustico, un monumentale altare d'Imeneo, largo quanto un'aia, profondo come il sonno del giusto. È il Talamo dei Talami. Le materasse contengono la lana d'un intero gregge e il pagliericcio contiene le foglie d'un intero campo di granoturco. Possono avere tutte queste cose caste il presentimento della tua nudità? (p. 188)

That whole passage is translated simply, 'Oh would that you were here with me' (H. p. 129). And later she translates 'Ippolita era rientrata, s'era distesa sul letto' as 'thrown herself on her bed'. There is only one bed and it is decisively shared by both of them.

There are over a thousand changes from the original to the translation. All ellipses, for instance, which may imply sensuality are avoided: 'Le mormorò nell'orecchio qualche parola. "No, no. Bisogna che siamo savi, fino a stasera, bisogna che aspettiamo. Sarà poi tanto dolce"' (p. 88), which Miss Harding translates: 'You must be good, patient and think of the charming evening that is before us' (H. p. 35). The two are on their way to an orgy of sex at Albano. Elsewhere the implications are simply omitted, as are references to olfactory images, leaving other very amusing lacunae.

There are many other examples of greater sensuality and greater grotesqueries in d'Annunzio's novel, an old hag kissing a lascivious monkey: 'Una di queste bagasce disfatte, che pareva un essere generato da un uomo nano e da una scrofa, imboccava con la sua bocca viscida una scimmia lasciva' (p. 268). In the translation this and other improprieties are simply omitted. The only contemporary critic to notice the bowdler-ising was Arthur Symons, who produced a casual but devastating review.[11] But we must pass on, leaving a summary of these attitudes to W. L. Courtney, one of d'Annunzio's assiduous critics in the first twenty years of the century: 'Our national temperament is out of sympathy with the form in which his genius finds expression' (*Maeterlinck*, p. 86). Even d'Annunzio's greatest supporters were sometimes aghast at some aspect or other of his blood-thirstiness or sadism. And his supporters or admirers included writers and critics such as Henry James, Ouida, Edward Hutton, Osbert Sitwell, all of whom admired his flair and his language, while conceding that his taste was not always suitable to the British temperament. Ouida, who achieved enormous fame in her day, wrote a very eulogistic piece as early as 1897, entitled *The Genius of D'Annunzio*, and yet her essay is studded with remarks like the follow-ing: 'What is, I think, more offensive to taste, and more injurious to art than any sensual excess in description, is mere nastiness, mere filth; and of this d'Annunzio is as guilty as Zola is, and as Zola has been, always'.[12] She is writing principally there of *Il trionfo della morte*, but she offers a general observation about d'Annunzio's novels which is pretty damning: 'In the French version the romances gain in certain points; their excessive detail is abridged, their crudities are softened, their weary analyses and too frequent obscenities are omitted' (p. 349).

Perhaps more serious than the omissions of passages reflecting sensuality or sordid reality is the deliberate excision of all references to the philosophy of Nietzsche. D'Annunzio had recently discovered the philosophy of the German thinker and it informs many of his writings during the 1880s and 1890s. The motive power behind his hero, Giorgio Aurispa, is pure Nietzsche. So entire passages of the following flavour are omitted from the Harding translation:

Dominatore forte e tirannico, franco dal giogo di ogni falsa moralità, sicuro nel sentimento della sua potenza . . . determinato ad elevarsi sopra il Bene e sopra il Male per la pura energia del suo volere, capace pur di costringere la vita a mantenergli le sue promesse.   (p. 319)

The importance of Nietzsche's influence on the novel cannot be stressed too strongly. The prefatory letter to Michetti ends with the assertion: 'Noi tendiamo l'orecchio alla voce del magnanimo Zarathustra, o Cenobiarca; e prepariamo nell'arte con sicura fede l'avvento dell'*Uebermensch*, del Superuomo' (p. 54). The rigorous excision of such material will have profound implications for the interpretation of the novel in Britain.

D'Annunzio's work is perhaps intrinsically unappreciable by a wider British audience than our academic circle, and even then prejudice against the man abounds. Contemporaries of his who wrote appreciatively in English of his writings highlight his lavish language and his Latin propensity for unveiling emotions and describing actions which the British preferred to see suppressed even in their own authors, and D. H. Lawrence and James Joyce are cases in point. Typical was the appreciative lecture delivered in 1919 by C. H. Herford, Professor of English at Manchester, who seems to have liked d'Annunzio's propensity for sex and violence:

D'Annunzio's sensuality asserts itself still, as always; but it appears here as a Rubens-like joy in intense impressions; now a coppercoloured storm sky, now a splash of blood, betrays his passion for the crude effects of flame and scarlet, most often where they signify death or ruin. He imagines voluptuously as always, but his voluptuousness here feeds not in the lust of the flesh, but in the lust of wounds and death.[13]

The sentiments are not, however, typical of the average reader of *The Times*. Take out that aspect and the plot is reduced to the triviality of Mills and Boon:

> Di sotto alla tenda piantata su la ghiaia, ancora seminudo dopo il bagno egli guardava Ippolita ch'era rimasta al sole presso le acque avvolta nell'accappatoio bianco. . . . Ella aveva disciolti i suoi capelli perché si asciugassero; e le ciocche ammassate dall'umidità le cadevano su gli omeri cosí cupe che sembravano quasi di viola. . . . Perché tu non prendi sole? chiese Ippolita d'un tratto, volgendosi verso di lui.
>
> (p. 306)[14]

Ippolita is barren after an illness; she has mild epilepsy. Neither factor is touched upon in Miss Harding's translation. In *her* version, from the excerpt above is omitted a long paragraph in which Giorgio Aurispa (or d'Annunzio) meditates on the futility of his love for this woman:

> L'inutilità del suo amore gli apparve come una trasgressione mostruosa alla suprema legge. – Ma perché dunque il suo amore, non essendo se non una lussuria inquieta, aveva quel carattere di fatalità ineluttabile? Non era l'istinto di perpetuazione il motivo unico e vero d'ogni amor sessuale? Non era questo istinto cieco ed eterno l'origine del desiderio e non doveva il desiderio avere, occulto o palese, lo scopo generativo imposto dalla Natura? Perché dunque egli era legato alla donna sterile da un vincolo cosí forte? Perché dunque la terribile 'volontà' della Specie si ostinava in lui con tanto accanimento a richiedere a strappare il tributo vitale da quella matrice devastata già dal morbo, incapace di concepire? – Mancava al suo amore la ragion prima: l'affermazione e lo sviluppo della vita di là dai limiti dell'esistenza individua. Mancava alla donna amata il piú alto mistero del sesso: 'la sofferenza di colei che partorisce'. La miseria di entrambi proveniva appunto da questa mostruosità persistente.   (p. 309)

Those sentiments could have come from a Vatican pronouncement.

Il trionfo della morte is distinguished by three main themes: the sensual love of Giorgio Aurispa for Ippolita Sanzio; the alienation which Aurispa feels at a return to his native Abruzzi and his attempts to integrate with his native environment after the sophistication of Rome; and finally the Nietzschean theme, visible in the long interior monologues which reinforce the conflict in the protagonist between his will and his periodic abandonment in instinctive sexuality. The three themes are bound together in the figure of Ippolita in various complex ways; she becomes at the end the symbol for sterility and carnal obsession, created, trained by Giorgio and finally dominating his life to such a degree that his only way of self-assertion is a suicidal plunge over the cliff which has dominated their idyllic stay in the Abruzzi. Periodically we glimpse the influence of Wagner's then fashionable *Tristan und Isolde*, blending romantic love with Nietzschean heroics. The Nietzschean theme is ignored, as I have shown, and all the passages referring to Nietzsche are expunged from the translation, seven whole pages of the Oscar Mondadori edition and sundry smaller references elsewhere. Any reflective passage, showing the mental conflict in Giorgio is shortened almost to non-existence, presumably in order to heighten the romantic interest. The complex and often brilliant study of the rancour felt by Aurispa for his father on his return to the Abruzzi, the guilty resentment he feels as he sees the same fleshly germ present in his own genes is similarly played down and all references to his father's carnality are excised. Without these details the novel becomes something out of Barbara Cartland's repertoire, and, to take the most dramatic example of the consequences of their omission (the final triumph of death) without the philosophic meditation on the impossibility of dominating one's instincts, one's flesh and one's fortune as one would wish, the final triumph of death, as I say, is nothing more than a melodramatic joint suicide. Yet it was on this truncated and bowdlerised version of the novel that critics poured their scorn – rightly so, I believe. The marvel is that in a few unfashionable reviews d'Annunzio received his due as a great stylist.

Now this truncated version of the most important work translated to date was influential since it had immediate reviews (in 1898) in a dozen important journals: *Literature, Outlook, Saturday Review, Westminster Gazette*, as well as in newspapers, the *Daily Chronicle, Daily News* and so on. It would be easily possible to digress at some length on the changes in *Il trionfo della morte* and the way this affected critical opinions.

In the case of most translations and most expurgated texts there are usually originals to hand and no great or lasting harm is done by garbled versions. Indeed in certain circumstances working on an expurgated edition and meditating on the variants sometimes produces rich results; arguably the various redactions of the *Decameron* did more for Italian and for European lexicography than any other factor. But we know that Italian was not a popularly-read language at the close of the century, and the effect of turning d'Annunzio's powerful novels into simpering Victorian love stories was to make them as transient as any threepenny romance. The result was that *Il piacere, Il trionfo della morte, Le vergini delle rocce, L'innocente* and *Il fuoco* were misunderstood and were then treated with the same passing interest as a novelette by Ouida. Marie Louise de la Ramée's sobriquet reflects her own childish pronunciation of her Christian name – Ouida (Louisa), and seems in itself comment enough upon what was required of a best-selling novelist of the time.

Notes

1. Gabriele d'Annunzio, *Tales of my Native Town*, translated by G. Mantellini, with an Introduction by Joseph Hergesheimer (London, 1920).
2. By George Greene, in his *Italian Lyrists of Today* (London, 1893); since then a handful of translations have appeared, almost capriciously, as in the *Penguin Book of Italian Verse* (London, 1958), the next 'largest' collection.
3. Orlo Williams, 'The Novels of d'Annunzio', *Edinburgh Review*, vol. 218, no. 443 (October 1913) p. 337.
4. All quotations are from the most recent edition in the Oscar Mondadori series, edited by Giansiro Ferrata (Milan, 1980). The translation by Georgina Harding (London, 1898) will here have a distinguishing H before page number references, which follow quotations in the text. In fairness to Miss Harding, I should point out that Heinemann was influenced by French censorship of *Il trionfo*, translated by Georges Herelle (Paris, 1896), whose deodorised version she often followed closely.
5. Robert Buchanan, *The Fleshly School of Poetry* (London, 1872) p. 44. The tirade had earlier appeared (under the pseudonym of Thomas Maitland) in the *Contemporary Review* of October 1871.
6. S. L. Hynes, *The Edwardian Turn of Mind* (Princeton, 1968) has good examples of the 'morality' of the period and its effect on censorship.
7. Edward Hutton, 'The Novels and Plays of d'Annunzio', *Monthly Review*, 26 (November 1902) p. 144.
8. W. L. Courtney, 'Gabriele d'Annunzio', in *The Development of Maurice Maeterlinck and Other Sketches of Foreign Writers* (London, 1904) pp. 86–7.

9. Gerald Griffin, *G. d'Annunzio, the Warrior Bard* (London, 1935) p. 277.
10. Osbert Sitwell, *Left Hand, Right Hand!* (London, 1950) p. 113.
11. In the *Saturday Review*, 1 (29 January 1898) pp. 145–6.
12. Marie Louise de la Ramée, 'The Genius of d'Annunzio', *Fortnightly Review* (March 1897) pp. 349–73.
13. C. H. Herford, 'G. d'Annunzio', *Bulletin of the John Rylands Library*, Manchester (December 1919 – July 1920) pp. 418–44, here p. 424.
14. Here I show how the Italian would appear if we cut out from the Mondadori text the excisions which Miss Harding made in her English version.

9

Voce e focalizzazione in *Senilità*

Anna Laura Lepschy

Mi propongo in questo articolo di esaminare ancora una volta la
questione del punto di vista in *Senilità*. Si tratta di un argomento a cui i
critici hanno spesso accennato. Brian Moloney scrive: 'Three characters,
moreover, are used as centres of consciousness through whom alternative points of view can be offered; Angiolina is rarely, if ever, used in
this way. Thus the narrator, after the initial pages, seldom needs overtly
to interpose his judgement between the reader and the characters. He
can limit himself on the whole to defining and explaining'.[1] Abbiamo
dunque il punto di vista di Emilio, di Amalia, e di Stefano, con una breve
comparsa del narratore all'inizio. Vediamo quello che altri critici hanno
da dire a questo proposito.

Giuseppe Pontiggia ritiene che 'l'azione è sempre vista attraverso gli
occhi di Emilio Brentani',[2] e che quando si ha un punto di vista esterno si
tratta di una stonatura, di un errore tecnico. Eduardo Saccone, nel
capitolo 'Un'educazione sentimentale' di *Il poeta travestito*, osserva che
la prospettiva narrativa 'è quella di un narratore che non solo concentra
la sua attenzione sulla coscienza del protagonista ... ma non lo lascia
mai (tranne che nel sesto capitolo), narra soltanto gli avvenimenti a cui
quello è presente, conosce tutti i suoi pensieri e sentimenti, indovina o
suppone quelli degli altri personaggi solo fin dove è possibile ad uno
spettatore intelligente, ma non eccezionale, indovinare o supporre non
azzardatamente'.[3] Qui il punto di vista è quello di un narratore che si
identifica con Emilio, tranne che nel capitolo sesto (l'episodio dell'ombrellaio, a cui assiste il Balli). Saccone va anche oltre: 'Chi narra *Senilità*
non può esser altro che Emilio Brentani' (p. 186). John Gatt-Rutter non
concorda con questa conclusione e preferisce invece distinguere il punto

122

di vista di Svevo da quello di Emilio: Svevo 'writes omnisciently, and that he judges Emilio from above is incontrovertibly clear from phrases like "he was lying", when the lie is an unconscious one'.[4]

Questa è anche la posizione di Marziano Guglielminetti che parla di un 'colloquio' fra l'attore e l'autore del romanzo,[5] un dialogo che egli documenta sintatticamente, attribuendo fra l'altro l'uso dell'imperfetto ad Emilio, e quello del condizionale passato all'autore, e sottolineando la partecipazione dell'autore: 'È arrivato cosí il momento in cui Svevo può intervenire a consolare il suo personaggio'.[6] Teresa de Lauretis riprende l'interpretazione di Guglielminetti, con le due voci contrastanti del personaggio e dell'autore, e la modifica rendendo la voce dell'autore interna invece che esterna, facendone cioè la voce della coscienza di Emilio, ma concedendo che alla fine del romanzo 'il narratore emerge, si distanzia dal personaggio, lo giudica, e lo abbandona fisso nell'immobilità formale del suo mondo simbolico'.[7]

Come si vede anche soltanto da queste poche citazioni, la questione è stata affrontata in modi diversi e contrastanti, ciascuno dei quali può essere sostenuto all'interno di una particolare interpretazione del romanzo. Senza dimenticare questo aspetto inevitabilmente soggettivo, mi propongo in questo articolo di riconsiderare il romanzo tenendo presente la sistemazione concettuale a mio parere piú utile ed efficace proposta a questo riguardo dalla critica contemporanea, cioè quella di Gérard Genette nel *Discours du récit*.[8]

Coll'espressione 'punto di vista' si designano tradizionalmente, e a volte si confondono, due nozioni che Genette cerca di distinguere nettamente: una, per cui egli usa il termine 'focalizzazione', si riferisce alla domanda 'chi vede?', e riguarda il *modo* in cui la storia viene presentata nel testo; l'altra si riferisce alla domanda 'chi parla?', e riguarda il rapporto fra narrazione (come atto narrante che produce il testo) e narrativa, che Genette esamina nella categoria della *voce*.

Per quanto riguarda la focalizzazione, Genette distingue tre tipi fondamentali: (a) la focalizzazione zero, del narratore onnisciente, che ci dice piú di quanto sappiano i personaggi; (b) la focalizzazione interna, per cui le cose sono presentate dal punto di vista di uno o piú personaggi (la focalizzazione interna è fissa, se si tratta di un unico personaggio, variabile se si tratta di piú personaggi, o multipla, per esempio nei romanzi epistolari, dove uno stesso avvenimento compare, successivamente, da diversi punti di vista); (c) la focalizzazione esterna, nei racconti obiettivi, in cui non ci vengono comunicati pensieri e sentimenti dei personaggi, ma solo loro comportamenti, come potrebbero essere, behavioristicamente, registrati da un osservatore esterno. Ci possono, beninteso, essere infrazioni alla focalizzazione adottata, alterazioni che Genette chiama 'paralipsi' (quando si danno meno informazioni del necessario), o 'paralepsi' (quando si danno piú informazioni di quanto sia consentito). Nel caso del narratore autobiografico, si può avere una polimodalità che mescola la focalizzazione del narratore e del personaggio.

Per quanto riguarda la *voce*, si tratta, fondamentalmente, della posizione del narratore rispetto all'enunciazione del testo narrato. Tradizionale, ma insufficiente, è la distinzione fra narrativa in prima e in terza persona; occorre vedere se la prima persona è quella di un personaggio (centrale, o marginale, nella storia), o quella di un narratore estraneo alla vicenda, che può comparire in punti canonici, come l'esordio e l'invocazione ('Arma virumque cano'), o piú liberamente in digressioni gnomiche rivolte agli ascoltatori.

Quando chiediamo 'chi parla?', possiamo riferirci anche a battute o riflessioni forse attribuibili a un personaggio; si tratta allora di una questione di *distanza*, che per Genette appartiene, con la focalizzazione, all'area del *modo*. C'è una distinzione fra narrativa di avvenimenti e narrativa di parole; per quest'ultima abbiamo tutta la complessa casistica del discorso riportato:[9] ma, da un lato, il discorso indiretto libero è per sua natura ambiguo e, facendoci sentire, attraverso le parole del narratore (e quindi della *voce* narrante) quelle del personaggio, si presenta come uno dei modi in cui si manifesta la focalizzazione interna; dall'altro lato, anche il discorso diretto e indiretto ci spingono dalla questione della *distanza* a quella della *voce* narrante. Genette ha ripetutamente osservato che la mimesi si riduce alla diegesi, in quanto anche le parole, citate in discorso diretto, poniamo, di Enea, sono in realtà parole che il poeta rivolge al suo ascoltatore. Questo ci riporta alla funzione del narratore. Dobbiamo distinguere tre livelli: quello dell'autore e del lettore empiricamente determinati (il primo che manda il libro all'editore, e il secondo che lo compra in libreria); quello dell'autore e del lettore *impliciti* (postulati dal testo, e da esso dotati di tutto un insieme di presupposti ideologici e culturali);[10] e infine quello del narratore e del narratario impliciti, postulati semioticamente dal testo, considerato come un messaggio rivolto dal primo al secondo.[11] Ogni testo narrativo postula un narratore implicito, sia nel caso che un narratore esplicito manchi (come in un racconto in terza persona), sia nel caso che compaia, in prima persona, un narratore esplicito che, per il fatto stesso di essere contenuto nel testo, non può esserne la fonte. Ogni narrativa ci perviene, inevitabilmente, racchiusa fra virgolette implicite che ne segnano i margini semiotici. Anche se c'è un narratore esplicito che dice 'io', la natura della narrativa è tale che noi lo possiamo venire a sapere solo attraverso un narratore implicito che ci trasmette il testo in cui tale 'io' compare. Questa pare essere la differenza semiotica cruciale fra i messaggi linguistici della vita quotidiana, in cui l''io' che compare nel messaggio si presenta come l'originatore ultimo del messaggio stesso,[12] e i messaggi narrativi, che richiedono un'emittente implicita che garantisca la loro narratività.

Anche nel caso di un romanzo in prima persona, come *La coscienza di Zeno*, dobbiamo postulare un narratore implicito che ci racconta la storia di Zeno e del Dr S. Di fatto, in *La coscienza* abbiamo due prime persone, il cui rapporto nella gerarchia narrativa non è ovvio. Il testo di Zeno pare essere in qualche modo subordinato a quello del Dr S. che gli serve da prefazione; ma è chiaro che entrambi appartengono a una stessa opera narrativa, entrambi compaiono entro lo stesso paio di virgolette implicite che stanno intorno al romanzo. Ciò risulta tanto piú nettamente quanto piú si cerchi di separare i due testi, ponendoli su livelli narrativi diversi, come accade nell'edizione inglese pubblicata da Knopf negli Stati Uniti e da Putnam in Gran Bretagna nel 1930,[13] in cui la Prefazione del Dr S. compare addirittura sulla pagina di sinistra *davanti* al frontispizio. L'uso di questo artifizio sottolinea che di un artifizio, appunto, si tratta, interno e non esterno al congegno narrativo. L'effetto è del resto 'guastato', se cosí si può dire, dal fatto che il frontispizio non solo reca il nome di Svevo in cima alla pagina, dove di solito sta il nome dell'autore (che sia cosí, allora, che va svolta l'abbreviazione 'Dr S.'?), ma anche l'avvertimento 'With an Essay on Svevo by Renato Poggioli', senza che si capisca perché questo critico debba intromettersi fra medico e paziente. Del resto, il Dr S. stesso, nella sua Prefazione, scrive: 'Io sono il dottore di cui in questa novella si parla talvolta con parole poco lusinghiere'. Quale 'novella'? L'autobiografia di Zeno, chiamata 'novella' perché contiene tante 'bugie'? O il testo completo, che contiene la Prefazione, e che nell'atto di presentarsi come documento autentico di una cura, si nega come tale chiamandosi 'novella'?

Senilità è narrato in terza persona. Chi parla è dunque un narratore, una voce narrante che non dice mai 'io'. I personaggi principali sono quattro: Emilio, Amalia, Stefano e Angiolina. Non c'è dubbio che il focalizzatore nel senso genettiano sia Emilio: 'chi vede' è Emilio, suo è il punto di vista, sia fisico, sia psicologico. Ma il testo si rivela piú complesso e sfuggente di quanto questa affermazione possa far pensare. Le questioni principali che emergono riguardano la presenza del punto di vista del narratore, e di quello degli altri personaggi, accanto o sovrapposti a quello di Emilio.

Già l'apertura, su cui spesso si sono soffermati i critici, illustra bene questa problematicità. È un passo costruito in maniera straordinaria:

> Subito, con le prime parole che le rivolse, volle avvisarla che non intendeva compromettersi in una relazione troppo seria. Parlò cioè a un dipresso cosí: – T'amo molto e per il tuo bene desidero ci si metta d'accordo di andare molto cauti. – La parola era tanto prudente ch'era difficile di crederla detta per amore altrui, e un po' piú franca avrebbe dovuto suonare cosí: – Mi piaci molto, ma nella mia vita non potrai essere giammai piú importante di un giocattolo. Ho altri doveri io, la mia carriera, la mia famiglia.
> La sua famiglia? Una sola sorella.... [14]

Il narratore conosce le intenzioni di Emilio ('volle avvisarla'), cita le sue parole in discorso diretto ('T'amo molto'), ma avverte che non sono esattamente quelle che disse ('Parlò cioè a un dipresso cosí'), e ci fornisce anche, di nuovo in discorso diretto ('Mi piaci molto') le parole che Emilio avrebbe dovuto dire se avesse parlato piú francamente. Ma neanche queste vanno bene: il narratore, dopo aver criticato la propria versione approssimativa di ciò che Emilio aveva detto, e averci comunicato le parole che Emilio avrebbe dovuto dire se fosse stato piú sincero, passa a criticare anche queste, mettendo in luce la loro insincerità e inesattezza ('La sua famiglia? Una sola sorella.... La carriera di Emilio Brentani.... Da un impieguccio ... una riputazioncella ... non gli rendeva nulla').

Il narratore pare conoscere i sentimenti e i pensieri di Emilio meglio di quanto non li conosca Emilio stesso, eppure non è un narratore onnisciente, e lascia un margine di incertezza, di ambiguità e di soggettività in quello che ci comunica. Il lettore resta spiazzato di fronte a una pagina come questa, e prova la stessa sensazione inquietante che suscitano molti passi della *Coscienza di Zeno*. Si ha l'impressione di avere accesso all'inconscio di Emilio,[15] a un discorso che viene dall'interno del personaggio e mette in questione ciò che egli pensa dei propri moventi, e allo stesso tempo che si tratti di un processo senza soggetto (l'inconscio appunto), che genera un 'io' piuttosto che esserne generato. D'altra parte una narrativa in prima persona non è detto che debba essere impermeabile ai processi dell'inconscio, e può farci sentire oltre all'io cosciente, tutto il sé con le sue contraddizioni e ambiguità. È interessante vedere come la prima pagina di *Senilità* sia traducibile in prima persona:

Subito, con le prime parole che le rivolsi, volli avvisarla che non intendevo compromettermi in una relazione troppo seria. Parlai cioè a un dipresso cosí: – T'amo molto e per il tuo bene desidero ci si metta d'accordo di andare molto cauti. – La parola era tanto prudente ch'era difficile di crederla detta per amore altrui e un po' piú franca avrebbe dovuto suonare cosí: – mi piaci molto, ma nella mia vita non potrai essere giammai piú importante di un giocattolo. Ho altri doveri io, la mia carriera, la mia famiglia.

La mia famiglia? Una sola sorella. . . .

Qui abbiamo, con la prima persona, la polimodalità caratteristica della narrativa autobiografica, in cui si mescolano la focalizzazione di narratore e di personaggio, di io narrante e di io narrato. Questa apertura, che di solito viene attribuita nell'originale, in terza persona, al punto di vista del narratore che giudica il personaggio, si presta singolarmente bene ad essere tradotta in prima persona, anzi pare quasi piú verosimile cosí, in quanto attribuisce la focalizzazione e la voce allo stesso individuo; naturalmente si perde, in prima persona, l'efficacia letteraria dell'originale, che deriva in parte dall'aver separato il punto di vista di Emilio dalla voce del narratore.

È del resto possibile vedere, anche restando alla narrativa in terza persona, i commenti del narratore come fossero riflessioni di Emilio, in stile indiretto libero; mentre cioè dice certe cose ad Angiolina, Emilio pensa che avrebbe dovuto dirne altre, e che neppure queste altre sarebbero state giuste, dato il carattere frustrato e fallimentare della sua vita.

L'indiretto libero compare anche altre volte, per i pensieri di Emilio:

Non c'era male. La luna non era sorta ancora (p. 39) ... Il suo pensiero volò ad *Ange!* Come sapeva ridere a lungo, lei, con risate prolungate e contagiose, e sorrise egli stesso pensando ... (p. 55) ... Tutto infatti sarebbe stato piú facile e piú semplice se il Balli si fosse procurato da solo la modella, e gliel'avesse poi consegnata quale amante. Ci avrebbe pensato. Esitava soltanto perché non voleva concedere al Balli una parte importante nel proprio destino. Importante? Oh, Angiolina rimaneva sempre una persona molto importante per lui. (p. 273)

In altri casi si può essere piú incerti se il punto di vista che ci viene manifestato sia quello di un Emilio a cui le proprie limitazioni non sono ignote, o se si tratti del narratore che giudica un Emilio inconsapevole dei suoi difetti:

Con un'ironia di se stesso in cui spesso si compiaceva (p. 43) ... Dicendo queste parole egli si sentí l'uomo immorale superiore che vede e vuole le cose come sono. La potente macchina da pensiero ch'egli si riteneva, era uscita dalla sua inerzia. Un'onda d'orgoglio gli gonfiò il petto. (p. 45)

Si tratta di ironia del narratore, a spese del personaggio, o di autoironia del personaggio, come la focalizzazione su Emilio indurrebbe a credere? Similmente per la considerazione di poche righe dopo: 'ma se egli fosse stato l'osservatore che credeva, si sarebbe accorto ...' (p. 47).

Cosí all'inizio dell'ultimo capitolo troviamo una riflessione che sembra venire, sia come voce sia come punto di vista, da un narratore gnomico: 'L'immagine della morte è bastevole ad occupare tutto un intelletto. ... Il pensiero di lei è come una qualità, una malattia dell'organismo' (p. 445). E il paragrafo successivo comincia con 'Di questo pensiero Emilio lungamente visse': il pensiero della morte, evidentemente; ma il testo ci fa pensare anche al pensiero espresso nel paragrafo precedente, dal quale il narratore non vuole probabilmente escludere Emilio. E la fine del capitolo ('Anni dopo egli s'incantò ad ammirare quel periodo della sua vita', p. 455) presenta una completa sovrapposizione fra il punto di vista del narratore e quello di Emilio.

Possiamo chiederci anche se gli altri personaggi emergano come focalizzatori. La figura per cui questo pare meno probabile è quella di

Angiolina, che anche nei cenni che potrebbero sembrare riferirsi al suo punto di vista ci si presenta sempre attraverso lo sguardo di Emilio. Si considerino i passi seguenti:

Quando credette di aver compreso disse: – Strano! – timidamente guardandolo sottecchi. – Nessuno mi ha mai parlato cosí. – Non aveva compreso e si sentiva lusingata al vederlo assumere un ufficio che a lui non spettava, di allontanare da lei il pericolo (p. 19) ... Angiolina aveva capito poco delle promesse, ma, visibilmente, non le occorrevano commenti per comprendere il resto (p. 21) ... Ma ella capiva ancora meno i sentimenti d'Emilio di quanto egli comprendesse i suoi (p. 39) ... Angiolina non comprese subito perché la fronte di Emilio si fosse tanto oscurata (p. 63) ... – Come puoi farmi una simile domanda! – esclamò ella veramente stupefatta. (p. 77)

Pare chiaro che in tutti questi casi, e in altri analoghi che si potrebbero citare, il lettore non si ritrova mai dal punto di vista di Angiolina, ma sempre soltanto da quello di Emilio. Le parole del narratore ci comunicano sempre l'impressione che Emilio si fa delle reazioni di Angiolina (e non è un caso che tali reazioni siano di solito di incomprensione).

Ma anche per gli altri personaggi ci sono pochi elementi che possano far pensare ad essi come focalizzatori. Il ritratto di Stefano (pp. 29–31) può ben essere visto attraverso gli occhi di Emilio, anche quando si hanno osservazioni impietose sui loro rapporti ('Circa dieci anni prima, s'era trovato fra' piedi Emilio Brentani', p. 31), che sembrano del resto piú adatte alla psicologia introspettiva di Emilio che a quella di Stefano. Anche gli scrupoli del Balli riguardo al suo intervento nei rapporti fra Emilio e Angiolina ('Si trattenne dal raccontare tutto ciò all'amico e fu l'ultimo riguardo che gli usò') finiscono col riverberarsi dolorosamente sull'amico ('Emilio non aveva alcun vantaggio del riguardo usatogli perché quel desiderio, che l'amico non osava esprimere, gli pareva anche piú grande', p. 323). Altrove la psicologia di Stefano appare mediata attraverso le reazioni di Emilio: 'Il Balli aveva capito Emilio tanto poco che dichiarò di non comprendere perché perdessero tanto tempo. ... Era la speranza, ed Emilio vi si abbandonò tutto', pp. 375–7); 'Stefano non gli credette ... Emilio impallidí' (p. 405).

Similmente, in varie occasioni in cui emergono le riflessioni e le sofferenze di Amalia, esse vengono presentate in rapporto a quelle del fratello, e anche dove Emilio non pare rendersi conto di quello che accade a Amalia ('Non s'accorgeva che quella che diceva era la parte piú pericolosa ... ella guardava dentro di sé sorpresa ...' (pp. 33–5); 'Allora al dolore d'Amalia s'aggiunse l'ira ch'egli cosí leggermente si lasciasse ingannare sulla causa delle sue lagrime' (p. 53), l'attivarsi del punto di vista di Amalia pare momentaneo, e comunque subordinato a quello di Emilio. Anche questi passi sarebbero compatibili con un racconto in prima persona, in cui Emilio, come poi Zeno, semplicemente spostasse la focalizzazione dall'io narrante all'io narrato, e potesse occasionalmente affiancare a quest'ultimo altri personaggi focalizzatori subordinati.

È del resto proprio la prova del cambiamento di voce, dalla terza alla prima persona, che ci consente di isolare i casi, non molto numerosi, in cui la focalizzazione pare non poter essere quella di Emilio. Mutare cioè la voce, adottando la prima persona, e attribuendola a turno ai personaggi coinvolti, consente di vedere se la focalizzazione è appropriata o incongrua per il personaggio in questione. Ci sono alcuni passi in cui il focalizzatore pare sia il Balli, come all'inizio del capitolo quinto (p. 123), e del capitolo sesto (p. 155), in cui, come è stato osservato, l'episodio dell'ombrellaio è riferito dal punto di vista del Balli,[16] e in qualche altra occasione, come a p. 227, e nel brano seguente:

> Ebbe qualche leggero dubbio soltanto a mezzodí quando venne a prendere Emilio all'ufficio. S'era già convinto che Amalia, innamorata di lui, si fosse confidata col fratello e che costui avesse creduto opportuno allontanarlo dalla sua casa; ora invece Emilio voleva che vi ritornasse perché Amalia non capiva per quale ragione egli non si facesse piú vedere. – Lo vorranno per convenienza – pensò il Balli con la sua consueta facilità di spiegare tutto.   (pp. 255–7)

Se proviamo a parafrasare attribuendo la prima persona o ad Emilio ('quando venne a prendermi'), o al Balli ('Ebbi qualche leggero dubbio'), vediamo che quest'ultimo è piú adatto ad essere il focalizzatore, almeno fino all'ultima frase, che sembra esprimere il punto di vista del narratore.

Qualche volta, ma piú raramente, possiamo anche avere Amalia come focalizzatore, come nel brano che comincia con 'Una sera ella lo guardò a lungo senza ch'egli se ne avvedesse' (p. 53), che sarebbe difficile ritenere presentato dal punto di vista di Emilio.

Pare di poter concludere, usando la terminologia di Genette, che la voce è quella di un narratore estraneo alla storia, che usa solo la terza persona e non dice mai 'io', ma la focalizzazione è interna e variabile (confermando l'osservazione di Moloney citata all'inizio), limitata a tre personaggi, Emilio in primo luogo, e secondariamente Stefano e Amalia. Qualche volta emergono anche, momentaneamente, tratti di focalizzazione zero, cioè osservazioni in cui il punto di vista sembra essere quello del narratore. Resta di solito peraltro un margine di incertezza; per citare un ultimo esempio, nel primo capitolo il punto di vista, come abbiamo detto, può essere attribuito al narratore (focalizzazione zero), o può essere considerato quello di un Emilio che riflette (con distacco psicologico, o cronologico) sulla sua vicenda. 'Egli s'era avvicinato a lei con l'idea di trovare un'avventura facile e breve, di quelle che egli aveva sentito descrivere tanto spesso e che a lui non erano toccate mai o mai degne di essere ricordate' (p. 19): mentre non ci sono difficoltà a voltare il passo in prima persona, e a leggerlo come una di quelle considerazioni che Zeno potrebbe fare su se stesso, meno agevolmente si presta a questa lettura l'osservazione che segue, poche righe piú sotto: 'ai rétori corruzione e salute sembrano inconciliabili', che ci riporta bruscamente al presente della narrazione e che esprime un punto di vista nel quale non riconosciamo immediatamente la psicologia di Emilio. Del resto, che in un'opera letteraria i congegni narrativi non funzionino con meccanica sistematicità non dovrebbe sorprendere né dispiacere.

Note

1. B. Moloney, *Italo Svevo* (Edinburgh, 1974) p. 42.
2. 'La tecnica narrativa di Italo Svevo', *Il Verri*, 5 (1960) p. 159.
3. E. Saccone, *Il poeta travestito* (Pisa, 1977) pp. 184–5. Il capitolo citato è stato originariamente pubblicato come articolo in *Modern Language Notes*, 82 (1967) 1–55 col titolo 'Senilità di Italo Svevo: dalla "impotenza del privato" alla "ansiosa speranza" '.
4. J. Gatt-Rutter, '*Senilità* and the Unsaid', in *Essays on Italo Svevo*, a cura di T. F. Staley, University of Tulsa Department of English, Monograph Series, 6 (Tulsa, Oklahoma, 1969) p. 32.
5. *Struttura e sintassi del romanzo italiano del primo Novecento*, Quaderni di *Sigma* (Mondoví, 1964) p. 136.
6. M. Guglielminetti, *Struttura e sintassi*, p. 138.
7. *La sintassi del desiderio. Struttura e forme del romanzo sveviano* (Ravenna, 1976) p. 125.

8. *Figures III* (Paris, 1972) pp. 65–282.
9. B. Mortara Garavelli, *La parola d'altri* (Palermo, 1985).
10. W. C. Booth, *The Rhetoric of Fiction*, 2nd ed. (Chicago, 1983); S. Chatman, *Story and Discourse* (Ithaca, 1980).
11. Cfr. S. Rimmon-Kenan, *Narrative Fiction: Contemporary Poetics* (London, 1983) p. 88.
12. Cfr. É. Benveniste, *Problèmes de linguistique générale* (Paris, 1966) parte quinta.
13. I. Svevo, *Confessions of Zeno*, translated by Beryl de Zoete: cito dall'edizione pubblicata a Londra da Putnam nel 1948.
14. I. Svevo, *Senilità* (Pordenone, 1986) edizione critica delle opere di Italo Svevo a cura di Bruno Maier, vol. II, p. 15.
15. Cfr. T. de Lauretis, *La sintassi del desiderio*, p. 135.
16. Cfr. A. L. Lepschy, *Narrativa e teatro fra due secoli* (Firenze, 1984) p. 166.

10

Schmitz, Svevo and Sexuality

Elizabeth Schächter

Ettore Schmitz was brought up in a middle-class environment with traditional nineteenth-century attitudes – much supported in his case by a strong sense of Jewish family life. He must early have come to terms with a pervasive and dominant matriarchy of mothers, aunts, sisters and wives. He grew up in this matriarchy, whose grip was tightened still further when he married into it. Doubtless the world of business was the world of men, though in Schmitz's case his mother-in-law ran even the family factory. Yet everyone, especially the men, was aware that the real business of the world was domestic, and that was the world of women. Family life was surrounded with the odour of sanctity. Of course it was tacitly accepted, especially by the husbands, that a happy bourgeois marriage was heavily dependent on adultery for its happiness and even for its odour of sanctity.

Wives, on the whole, welcomed their husbands' affection and tenderness but naturally deplored their beastliness (even when strictly necessary for conception). The beastliness of men was properly diverted towards women of the lower classes, who were apparently more accustomed to men's ways and who, in any case, were grateful for the benefits in gifts and money that compliance generally brought them. Moreover, no bourgeois gentleman with any serious pretentions to social standing seemed to be fully equipped without the possession of a mistress. The advantages accruing to both husband and wife from such an arrangement were clear, and the institution of marriage was therefore strengthened. Indeed it was most probable that (as in Zeno's case) a relationship with a mistress vastly increased the affection and tenderness the husband felt for his wife. Zeno's adultery undoubtedly improved the quality of his marriage. Perhaps at that period and among that class, it was often the case. The main difficulty is to distinguish Svevo's attitude as a creative writer from those traditional attitudes which, as Schmitz, he accepted from the society in which he lived (always assuming that these attitudes can be so separated).

I shall endeavour to demonstrate that Italo Svevo, the artist, shows, in his presentation of women, his sympathy for them, his understanding of them as human beings, indicating a psychologically perceptive and sensitive approach; whereas the man, Ettore Schmitz, was a product of his class and society, with all its inherently reactionary traditions. The women Svevo describes in his novels inevitably reflect the prevalent male prejudices – in particular the stereotype of women as either 'a madonna mother figure' or a 'whore' – a stereotype which Freud so succinctly and clearly delineated in two short papers entitled 'A Special Type of Choice of Object made by Men' and 'On the Universal Tendency to Debasement in the Sphere of Love'.[1]

Sexuality was the province of men. Women were not considered to be equal to men as sexual beings: they were either idealised and put on a pedestal (sacred love – madonna/mother) or denigrated and despised as sexual objects (profane love – the whore). A corollary to this view was that only women attractive to men had a right to happiness; to the ugly it was denied. One has but to think of the tragic fate of Amalia, the neglected and discarded sister of Emilio in *Senilità*, whose repressed sexual longings can seek an outlet only in nocturnal dreams, and of Balli's harsh judgement of women like her: 'Egli credeva fosse permesso di vivere soltanto per godere della fama, della bellezza o della forza o almeno della ricchezza. . . . Perché dunque viveva quella povera fanciulla? Era un errore evidente di madre natura'.[2] This chauvinistic attitude is not shared by Balli's creator. Svevo has considerable compassion for the condition of such women who are sexually and emotionally unfulfilled and alienated from society. This can be seen in his treatment of Amalia, to whom he devotes some of his most eloquent writing.

Sexual feelings in well-brought-up middle-class ladies were considered sinful, and if a woman succumbed to seduction, this was seen as 'il passo senza rimedio' (p. 243), bringing dishonour and disgrace. It was the road to perdition: key words such as 'perduta', 'conquistata', 'posseduta' recur throughout the three novels.

Like his friend James Joyce, Svevo drew heavily on his own life and experiences, making autobiography the myth of his fiction. Zeno is a fictional version of Svevo, and they share a great deal, even their thinning hair, their ability to play the violin, and their addiction to the cigarettes that they are determined to stop smoking but never do. The distinction between Svevo and Zeno is not easy to define with any great certainty and the danger, therefore, is that the writer will become inextricably confused with his creation. We are tempted, in other words, to use the novel to illuminate the life of its author, thus reversing a more traditional procedure. But there is, nevertheless, a good deal we can learn about the man and his attitudes, particularly his attitude to women, quite independently of his novels. Therefore, it would be useful to investigate the sources and parallels of his female fictional characters as they may be found in his life.

Ettore Schmitz came from a large, middle-class Jewish family in Trieste. He was one of eight children. His father, Francesco Schmitz, a business man, was a domineering, patriarchal figure, ambitious that his four sons should follow him in commerce.[3] His mother appears as a gentle, loving and affectionate woman, who was not authoritarian at all. Schmitz wrote to his brother Ottavio of 'tutta la bontà e la mitezza di mamma' (*Opera Omnia*, I, 31). His father died in 1892 when Schmitz was thirty-one. He remained living with his family until his mother's death three years later, on 4 October 1895. He noted the actual time of her death, seven minutes past four, in his letters and diary to his fiancée (perhaps the source of Zeno's obsession with dates). He had enjoyed a warm, loving and enduring relationship with his mother and with his four sisters, the eldest of whom, Paola, took over the maternal role after 1895. And clearly it is the maternal qualities in a wife that both Schmitz and his literary creation Zeno seek. 'Si affidava a me completamente quasi come un figlio . . . si appoggiava a me, benché di me maggiore, con una fiducia commovente, quasi filiale . . . ', wrote Livia Veneziani in the biography of her husband.[4] It seems that this fusion of the roles of wife and mother, which may perhaps represent a regression to the security of childhood in order to avoid the more complex emotional demands of mature sexuality, can be seen in *Una vita* (Alfonso's quasi-oedipal return to his mother in the country to escape from the responsibility of emotional attachment to Annetta) and in *La coscienza di Zeno* when Zeno says of himself: 'Quando la paura di morire m'assaliva, mi rivolgevo ad Augusta per averne conforto come quei bambini che porgono al bacio della mamma la manina ferita. Essa trovava sempre delle nuove parole per confortarmi' (p. 729). And there is also the smile on his mother's lips, which he recognises on Augusta's face (p. 602).

Schmitz and two of his brothers were sent away to school in Bavaria to improve their knowledge of German. It was a linguistic necessity for a business man to be fluent in at least two languages in cosmopolitan Trieste. There he experienced his first romantic attachment. The object of his affections, which were reciprocated, was the headmaster's niece. When he left the school to return to Trieste, she presented him with an inscribed copy of Shakespeare (L. Veneziani Svevo, *Vita*, p. 17). Her name was Anna Herz, a name which was to haunt him through the years and leave its mark on his fiction: Annetta is the name of Alfonso's beloved in *Una vita*. Anna is the old flame whose memory torments the narrator of the short story *Il vino generoso*; Anna is the youngest of the Malfenti sisters in *La coscienza di Zeno*; Anna is the young lover betrayed by Bacis in *Corto viaggio sentimentale*; Anna is the name of the wife in the play *La rigenerazione*. Schmitz's mother's name was Allegra and the same initial 'A' dominates the names Svevo gives to many of his other female characters: Angiolina and Amalia in *Senilità*; Ada, Augusta and Alberta Malfenti, sisters of the above-mentioned Anna in *La coscienza di Zeno*; Alberta and Alice the two cousins in the unfinished play *Con la penna d'oro*. We can feel justified in reading significance into the alphabetic properties of these names when we recall that Svevo appears to have been influenced by Freud's associate Wilhelm Stekel who drew attention to the symbolic connections between people's names and their personality and symptomatology. Furthermore Zeno comments on the literal antithesis between his name and those of the Malfenti sisters: 'Quell'iniziale mi colpí molto . . . io mi chiamo Zeno, ed avevo perciò il sentimento che stessi per prendere moglie lontano dal mio paese' (p. 651). Maybe in choosing the name Zeno, Svevo was deliberately implying an opposition between this character and those of the idealised women.

Between Anna Herz and his wife Livia Veneziani there seems to be only one other woman of importance in Schmitz's life. She was Giuseppina Zergol described as 'una fiorente ragazza del popolo' who was his mistress between 1892 and 1895 (L. Veneziani Svevo, *Vita*, p. 45). She became the prototype of Angiolina Zarri in *Senilità*. There may be significance in the similar surnames and in the juxtaposition of Angiolina's two names which encapsulates the antithesis between purity and depravity embodied in her character and symbolised in the lexical opposition of A and Z. It was initially for her that he wrote part of that novel in order to educate her (as Emilio tries to educate Angiolina). Freud noted that in this kind of loving, men feel the need to rescue the woman from her debased state.[5] In her biography Livia mentions with ill-concealed contempt that Giuseppina left Trieste to become a bareback rider in the circus (*Vita*, p. 45).

Svevo's *œuvre* contains many examples of the character of a mistress of working-class origins who is accessible, sensual, 'che vuol piacere', from his first published short story *Una lotta* of 1888 (Rosina is 'una donnina che vive sola e che riceve liberamente uomini in casa')[6] through to *La coscienza di Zeno* of 1923.

Svevo/Schmitz's recent biographer Enrico Ghidetti describes *Senilità* as 'l'implacabile resoconto ... di un disperato e degradante amore di Ettore ... una bruciante esperienza che lasciò segni indelebili nel cuore e nella memoria di Ettore' (*Italo Svevo*, pp. 114, 117). Silvio Benco, the Triestine critic, recalled meeting Schmitz at a performance of Bizet's *Carmen* and just before the third act, which includes Carmen's betrayal, he recounted to Benco 'una sua passione giovanile, le notti d'inverno passate nel gelo e nella bora a vigilare con gelosia l'uscio di una casuccia dov'era ... l'infida creatura che non meritava tanta pena' (Ghidetti, p. 117). Though many years later in a letter to Emerico Schiffrer (in 1928) he idealises it in retrospect as 'quella bella storia' (*Opera Omnia*, I, 880).

Svevo's fictional mistresses bear the imprint of Schmitz's 'degradazione del sentimento d'amore' and come, like Giuseppina Zergol, from poor working-class backgrounds. Indeed, the social *ambiente* of Lucia in *Una vita*, Angiolina in *Senilità* and Carla in *La coscienza di Zeno* are strikingly similar. Lucia is a sixteen-year-old seamstress who lives in a cramped, gloomy, impoverished home with her weak, ineffectual father, layabout brother and embittered, domineering mother. The two women are the only breadwinners of the family. Angiolina's father is mentally disturbed, her mother unkempt and dirty, and their sordid household bears the tawdry traces of luxury from her 'career'. Like Margherita, Balli's mistress, Angiolina supports the whole family with her earnings as a prostitute. Carla lives alone with her mother in two sparsely furnished rooms, eking out an existence by taking in embroidery and laundry, which is supplemented now and again by handouts from wealthy middle-class benefactors. The future prospects of such women were gloomy, as Zeno comments (slightly patronisingly):

> C'è quasi ogni settimana, nella nostra città, la sartina che ingoia la soluzione di fosforo preparata in segreto nella sua povera stanzetta, e da quel veleno rudimentale ... viene portata alla morte con la faccina ancora contratta dal dolore fisico e da quello morale che subí la sua animuccia innocente.   (p. 874)

These women have few means and no social status; they are dependent upon, and exploited by, men; their emotional needs are rarely considered; they are shown by Svevo to be in a vulnerable, subservient and humiliating situation. Svevo portrays the prevailing male attitudes towards these women as sexual playthings to be discarded at will, through the chauvinistic comments and behaviour of such sophisticated men of the world as the lawyer Macario in *Una vita* who remarks to Alfonso: 'Per saper prendere una donna che vuol darsi ci vuol poco. ... Bisogna sapere il quando ... e saputo questo quando, bisogna saper attaccare prontamente ... e essere ... quindi sicuramente vittorioso' (p. 243). Of the sculptor Balli in *Senilità* we read: 'Il suo sistema ... pareva dovesse essere la brutalità' (p. 466) and of the business man Guido Speier in *La coscienza di Zeno* when discussing women with Zeno: 'Egli si mise a dir male delle donne ... a parlare ... di tutte le altre cattive qualità delle donne ... aveva fatte sue le geniali teorie del giovine suicida Weininger ... la donna non sa essere né geniale né buona' (p. 713). Alfonso's colleague Miceni (in *Una vita*) derides him for not having 'possessed' Lucia, remarking cynically that 'una ragazza in quelle condizioni, posta accanto ad un giovine che vive in condizioni migliori, prima o poi gli si getta al collo' (p. 275). Balli's treatment of Angiolina is typical: 'Il Balli ... si rifece brusco – Lei si chiama Angiolina? ... Angiolona la chiamerò io, anzi Giolona – E da allora la chiamò sempre cosí con quelle vocali larghe, larghe, il disprezzo stesso fatto suono' (p. 468). To cite Paula Robinson: 'Balli is a notorious Don Juan who believes ... that to be a man is to be cruelly aggressive and contemptuous of women'.[7] He offers to demonstrate with Angiolina the secret of his success with women, which is to be an exemplar for Emilio. During the famous 'cena a quattro' in Chapter Four, Balli reduces everyone to subjection, including the waiter, and thus feels that he has given Emilio exactly the lesson he intended.

The character of Balli was modelled on Schmitz's close friend the artist Umberto Veruda, of whom it was said that he made a cult of cynicism about women, regarding them as a threat to art, and he refused to admit the word 'love' to his vocabulary. He never married.[8] The anecdote about him recalled by Schmitz is significant: 'So che la massima esaltazione egli [Veruda] la raggiunse un giorno, in cui schiaffeggiò al Politeama, in pubblico, la sua amante' (*Opera Omnia*, I, 880). These women were not to be acknowledged in public in the light of day: Angiolina is forced to walk behind Balli; Carla is insulted by being ignored by Zeno in the Giardino Pubblico; both Angiolina and Carla accept without question that their middle-class lovers will not marry them. If they are admired, it is for their submissiveness – it is this quality which is most highly prized by men.

In *Senilità* Balli's mistress Margherita 'fu obbligata ... a dare dei segni di sommissione perché il Balli voleva esporre il sistema che seguiva con le donne. Margherita si prestava magnificamente ... rideva molto, ma ubbidiva' (p. 465). Zeno describes Carla as 'la mia umile serva' (p. 788), 'mite e sottomessa' (p. 836), and it is 'il pregio della sua sottomissione di cui mi sembrava di poter essere sicuro' (p. 766).

For these often poorly-educated, economically deprived women living on the margins of society the only possibility of salvation, self-respect and social stability was through marriage. Only married women had any social status. Lucia's mother schemes and plots to marry off her daughter to Alfonso, and, when this fails, to one of her brother's friends. A suitor is eventually found – a printer's foreman Mario Gralli. Lucia and Gralli become engaged and for a short time Lucia is pathetically proud of her newly acquired status of 'promessa sposa' (p. 313). But her happiness is brief – Gralli jilts her after seducing her and she becomes pregnant. At first he offers to pay a monthly allowance (p. 395) in exchange for free access to the Lanucci household and Lucia's bed, and is persuaded to marry Lucia only for a large monetary settlement, offered by Alfonso: 'Era lui che aveva salvato Lucia' (p. 402). But what a salvation! Seduced, pregnant and abandoned, Lucia can be saved only by having a husband bought for her. Svevo's sympathy for her as she weeps disconsolately on discovering why Gralli agreed to marry her is plainly evident:

Lucia ringraziò singhiozzando. Ella s'era lusingata che Gralli fosse ritornato a lei per solo amore e il dolore di apprendere che cosí non era fu maggiore che non la riconoscenza. Pianse molto e si ritirò nella sua stanza (p. 403) . . . Ella continuava a piangere tenendosi sulla bocca il fazzoletto (p. 406)

Francesca, the housekeeper – mistress of Alfonso's employer Maller – hopes to improve her status by marrying her lover, and her only opportunity for such a union is to persuade Alfonso to marry his daughter Annetta. In a letter to Alfonso, Francesca implores him to return to Trieste: 'Soltanto la vostra presenza qui può salvarvi, salvarci' (p. 341). Carla gives up Zeno as soon as she has the chance of marriage to her new singing master ('un impegno piú sacro' (p. 812)), and she is delighted to take a walk with him and her mother in the afternoon.

Svevo portrays these mistresses as actively trying to shape their lives and to improve their social conditions in the only way open to them. He shows his admiration and sympathy for them in their efforts to achieve their aims, despite adverse circumstances. In *Una vita* Francesca's vigorous determination to wed her lover is all the more impressive when set against Alfonso's passive inaction. Ironically, only Angiolina – the prostitute, the debased sexual object par excellence – does not seek escape in matrimony, but seems perfectly adjusted to her way of life and is not desirous to change it. Angiolina is never described by Svevo as a prostitute, nor does he condemn her for the life she leads. On the contrary, he seems to delight in portraying her exuberant sensuality, while at the same time underlining what a burden her family responsibilities are. This unconventionally enlightened attitude is strikingly ahead of its time.

It may be interesting to note that the mothers of some of these women are often themselves treated dismissively by their daughters, who look down on them. For example, Carla in *La coscienza di Zeno* 'era tutt'altro che dolce con la madre che perciò aveva una paura folle di parlare troppo dei fatti della figlia coi suoi protettori' (p. 776). They do not seem to count – as if in having lost their beauty and sexuality they had lost their identity and value as a human being. Svevo himself describes them invariably as 'la vecchia'.

Mistresses were considered as sexual objects, and yet there is little description of physical love in the novels. This is primarily because the

three male protagonists of the three novels display an ambivalent attitude towards women and sexuality. Alfonso and Emilio are described by
several critics as 'angelists' 'divorcing love from sex and preferring to
contemplate women from afar'.[9] The French critic Jonard comments
that Emilio 'comme tout angéliste, dissocie le plaisir et l'amour,
Angiolina et Ange, la chair et l'âme, la vie et le rêve'.[10] When they,
Emilio and Alfonso, 'possess' the women they have so worshipped and
idealised, they despise and reject them: '[Emilio] aveva posseduto la
donna che odiava, non quella ch'egli amava' (p. 528), 'Il possesso . . . era
la verità propria e pura e bestiale' (p. 530). Alfonso, after his night of
love with Annetta, feels 'un malessere profondo . . . il suo disgusto
aumentava. Tutto gli dispiaceva, dal primo abbraccio . . . fino a quell'ultimo saluto' (p. 296). They thus exemplify the schizoid stereotype
described by Freud when he wrote 'where they love they do not desire,
and where they desire they cannot love'.[11]

Zeno, too, although more mature and experienced, displays the same
tendency to idealise in his attitude towards Ada whom he describes as
'divina fanciulla' and 'molto casta' and she remains for ever in his eyes an
unattainable ideal of purity precisely because he never had a physical
relationship with her. All three male characters are, as Saccone said of
Emilio, 'incorreggibilmente sognatore'.[12] Zeno is reticent about the
physical aspect of his relationship with his mistress Carla: there is no
deeply felt passion, no real intimacy, and only in his dreams does he
become assertive (not to say aggressive and sadistic). All three male
protagonists consider the sexual act as a brief, brutal and violent encounter. Alfonso's seduction of Annetta is described in these terms: 'La
costrinse bruscamente, frettoloso e brutale, e in apparenza almeno fu un
tradimento, un furto' (p. 292). For Emilio it is 'un atto breve, brutale, la
derisione di tutti i sogni, di tutti i desideri' (p. 501). Zeno recalls 'delle
scene di brutalità' (p. 790) in his relationship with Carla. The sexual
response of the women, on the other hand, is described as positive:
'Annetta fu per lui un'amante compiacente e appassionata' (p. 294),
while 'Angiolina era un'amante compiacente . . . e indovinava con un'intelligenza affinatissima i suoi desideri' (p. 532) and 'Carla era un'amante
indimenticabile' (p. 796). These comments seem to reflect the masculine
sexual fantasy that women want to be mastered and dominated by men.
Nowhere is this more strikingly illustrated than in the one prolonged
love-scene of the three novels, that between Angiolina and Emilio:

Una sera ella lo respingeva.... Egli ebbe meno vivo il desiderio di possederla che di essere, almeno una sola volta, piú rozzo di lei. La costrinse violentemente, lottando fino all'ultimo. Quando, senza fiato, cominciava a pentirsi di tanta brutalità, ebbe il conforto di un'occhiata d'ammirazione d'Angiolina. Per tutta quella sera ella fu ben sua, la femmina conquistata che ama il padrone.   (p. 542)

At a first reading of this passage, it might appear that Svevo is endorsing stereotypic male chauvinistic attitudes. But in view of the well recognised quality of irony which pervades his writings, things may not be what they seem on the surface in a Svevian text. Read from Emilio's point of view, rather than Svevo's, it could be interpreted as Emilio at last fulfilling his role of male aggressor. But since the problems of focalisation and interpretation are particularly complex in *Senilità*, it may equally be that this passage reflects not so much Emilio's enactment of the role of aggressor or Angiolina's of that of the submissive, adoring female, but rather a Svevian parody of contemporary male/female stereotypes intended to show their inadequacy as a model for real human behaviour, carrying as they do neither conviction nor truth.

Neither Alfonso nor Emilio can achieve a balanced integration of fantasy and reality, and their only solution is to withdraw from their attempt to deal adaptively with their sexuality. Alfonso, after abandoning Annetta, decides to retreat into solitude and lead an ascetic life of study and simple pleasures. Emilio's 'senilità' consists partly in his renunciation of sexuality and his contentment with the fantasy of an ideal woman who never existed.

Of all the mistresses in Svevo's novels, it is, paradoxically, the most degraded, Angiolina the prostitute, who is at the same time portrayed most unrealistically:

Una bionda dagli occhi azzurri grandi, alta e forte, ma snella e flessuosa, il volto illuminato dalla vita, un color giallo di ambra soffuso di rosa da una bella salute, camminava accanto a lui, la testa china da un lato come piegata dal peso del tanto oro che la fasciava (p. 432) . . . Il riposo di una sola notte bastava a darle l'aspetto sereno di vergine sana (p. 549)

Perhaps the key to this paradox may be found in Schmitz's own life, in the person of Livia Veneziani, his wife, whose beautiful features he worshipped. 'La sua bellezza era uno splendore, cosí vistosa, con quei suoi capelli biondissimi' (Ghidetti, p. 319). Livia Veneziani first met the Schmitz family in 1892. She was then eighteen years old, convent educated, inexperienced and chaste. Ettore Schmitz was thirty-one 'esperto ma riguardoso' (Ghidetti, p. 124). She was his second cousin and came from a very wealthy Roman Catholic family. Significantly it was what Ghidetti describes as Livia's 'gesto materno' at Ettore's mother's death-bed in October 1895 that first attracted him to her (p. 126). The combined mother/wife image of womanhood which we have noted above in his fiction, is manifest again in the biographical circumstances of his own marriage. Maier emphasises the significance of this gesture when he points out that

l'amore della madre e l'amore per Livia venivano perciò a essere due esperienze idealmente connesse . . . e anzi strettamente legate tra loro . . . consentendogli di unire in una medesima circostanza l'immagine della madre e quella di colei che sarebbe stata la buona e devota compagna della sua vita. . . . Livia [è] il simbolo, l'incarnazione stessa della virtú.[13]

Ettore and Livia became engaged on 20 December 1895. He wrote the *Diario per la fidanzata* to celebrate this important event. The diary reveals much about his attitude to women. Ghidetti describes the diary as 'un atto di purificazione' on Ettore's part to break with his sordid past (p. 123). The entry of 22 February 1896 reads: 'Io ho dietro di me un sozzo passato che mi ruinò la vita e l'intelligenza. . . . Tu invece hai un passato puro, trasparente, come l'acqua di certi laghi di montagna' (*Diario*, p. 104). Perhaps intending to raise an echo of Dante's *Vita nuova*, he claims that his engagement ushered in 'l'era novella, l'evo moderno' as he himself wrote in the diary (p. 105). In its pages he would

fissare sulla carta il mio sogno puro! Tanto puro! . . . Tanto puro che talvolta dubito veramente che si tratti d'amore perché l'amore l'ho conosciuto con tutt'altra fisonomia. Se sapessi con quale! Non la descrivo perché altrimenti non potrei consegnarti neppure questa carta. (*Opera Omnia*, I, 39)

From the diary and from his letters written in the early years of his marriage Ettore's almost pathological jealousy (which he recognises but cannot control) is only too evident. It stems partly from his perception of the contrast between his own unworthiness and Livia's idealised virtues: 'In fondo un individuo decadente come me non sa amare bene . . . la tua purezza e la tua bontà' (*Diario*, p. 72). And commenting on a wedding photograph: 'Lei virginalmente composta ma quantunque bionda e bianca giovanile e fresca. Lui invece da quel vecchio marcheur abbrutito da ogni singolo dei suoi pensieri ch'è un vizio di piú e un capello di meno' (*Opera Omnia*, I, 53). Notwithstanding, Ettore and Livia were married on 30 July 1896. Livia's mother was initially opposed to the marriage because her son-in-law was a mere 'impiegatuccio' and because of his age. He was thirteen years older than Livia and only nine years younger than his mother-in-law. It was also opposed by his artist friend Veruda who saw the marriage as a bourgeois sacrifice of Schmitz's literary aspirations (Ghidetti, p. 142). In other words, in common with the degraded women of his novels whom he portrays as seeking social salvation in marriage, Schmitz himself was perceived by Veruda as using marriage to elevate his social position from that of a lowly 'impiegatuccio' to that of a 'buon industriale e buon commerciante' (*Opera Omnia*, I, 195), much as Alfonso of *Una vita* might have done (also a mere 'impiegato') had he married his boss's daughter, Annetta.

Livia becomes a model of the wife who represents non-sexual femininity, as Ettore himself wrote to her:

Che io . . . possa starti accanto, e per spiegarsi la purezza inaudita della propria mente senta il bisogno, baciandoti, di dirti una parola che meravigliò te stessa: Sorella, è stupefacente . . . Amante mai; è veramente la parola che odio di piú perché mi ricorda delle fisonomie che ora odio. . . . Io non voglio essere violento, io voglio essere dolce e mite.[14]

In one of her letters she reciprocates this corresponding sisterly feeling:

Tu as sans doute toutes les qualités pour être un bon frère. . . . Je te remercie de tout ce que tu m'as donné . . . de la tendresse fraternelle que tu m'offres, de la douce et forte amitié qui nous lie. . . . Au revoir mon bien aimé mari, mon bon frère, mon doux ami. (*Vita*, pp. 60–1)

Livia is Augusta, Zeno's wife, without the squint, as the former herself acknowledged (*Vita*, pp. 145–6). Livia and Augusta are middle-class, respectable, religious, self-assured young women, possessing all the virtues of the perfect wife and offering stability, simplicity and strength to their neurotic and impractical husbands.

Schmitz's portrait of his wife in *Cronaca della famiglia* (1897)[15] and the first pages of the chapter in *La coscienza di Zeno* entitled 'La moglie e l'amante', are almost exact replicas of each other. In each case there is a faintly patronising tone about the perfectly adjusted bourgeois health of the two women, but also a hint of envy and admiration for their sense of security and happiness. Montale commented: 'Credo che Augusta sia il ritratto piú vivo di tutta la narrativa italiana dal Manzoni ad oggi'.[16] She has no counterpart in the other two novels, the nearest candidate being Annetta in *Una vita*.

La coscienza di Zeno was published in 1923, and Svevo could thus write about marriage from his own experience of over twenty years. 'Livia Veneziani nata per Schmitz' wrote Ettore in the *Diario per la fidanzata* (p. 118). Augusta, however, was not Zeno's first choice for a wife. He decides to court Ada (in whom he sought 'una seconda madre'), the most beautiful of the Malfenti sisters, oblivious to her own inclinations. She rejects him. One of the most comic scenes in the novel occurs when Zeno proposes to three of the sisters in one evening – and would no doubt have proposed to the youngest as well, but she was only eight at the time. Spurned by Ada and Alberta, he turns to Augusta in despair. She accepts him in a dignified manner: 'Voi, Zeno, avete bisogno di una donna che voglia vivere per voi e vi assista. Io voglio essere quella donna' (p. 706). In his parents-in-law's marriage Zeno sees the perfect model on which to base his own, a relationship which he describes as 'felicissima' and of which infidelity for the man is an essential part (pp. 653–4). Zeno too is unfaithful and accepts the double moral standards of bourgeois hypocrisy. As long as he is discreet, all is well. Augusta is represented as benefiting from Zeno's infidelities. Indeed his guilty conscience flares up every time he is with his mistress and rekindles his love for Augusta: 'Lí, accanto a Carla, rinacque intera la mia passione per Augusta. Ora non avrei avuto che un desiderio: correre dalla mia vera moglie ...' (p. 768); 'Andavo da Carla per riaccendere la mia passione per lei' (p. 767). Augusta is portrayed as steadfastly loyal, selflessly patient and long-suffering. Zeno's childish outbursts of remorse

are always soothed by her 'sorriso materno' which he constantly seeks
(p. 809). When Carla gives him up, he has the bizarre idea of sharing his
brother-in-law Guido's mistress, Carmen, reasoning that one mistress
between two is half as reprehensible as a whole one each. Unfortunately
for Zeno's conscience, Carmen does not comply.

Blissfully ignorant of Zeno's indiscretions, or so Zeno leads us to
believe, Augusta radiates happiness and contentment, and Zeno is
increasingly admired as a model husband, father and son-in-law. It is not
clear whether we are expected to assume that Zeno is aware of Augusta's
actual feelings (since he presents us with only his version of events) or
whether we are to attribute to him deliberate dissemblances in order to
mislead Dr S. We notice, for example, some discrepancy between
references to his wife's moments of unease and the later claim that 'tutti
mi volevano bene perché mia moglie era fiorente, facevano cosí delle
manifestazioni di antipatia per Guido, la cui moglie era malata'.

Zeno is shown to differ in one important respect from his younger
counterparts Alfonso and Emilio: he is not frightened of women. On the
contrary, he likes them and enjoys their company. He has warmth, a
sense of humour and spontaneity, qualities lacking in Alfonso and
Emilio. Zeno entertains them with his humorous anecdotes; he prefers
their tranquil, domestic world to the competitive, aggressive masculine
scene; he can romanticise and dream about them, or play the spoilt child.
They in turn cherish, indulge and mother him. He grows to love the
warm, affectionate, home-loving Augusta, and he describes their marriage as 'una relazione sorridente'. Since he has never idealised her, he
can establish some sort of viable relationship, even though it is mainly on
the level of childlike dependence on a mother figure. There is no real
communication between them as equals, as there was not in Schmitz's
own marriage. In her biography Livia writes: 'A me non parlava mai né
del suo tormento né delle sue ossessioni, come se volesse ... tenermi
lontana dal suo mondo tormentoso e segreto che io allora neppure
supponevo' (*Vita*, p. 64).

May we infer from Zeno's conduct that Schmitz's follows a similar
pattern? It should be mentioned that, contrary to the Italian custom,
neither Zeno nor Schmitz wore their wedding rings: 'Mi strangola',
commented Schmitz wryly (Ghidetti, p. 140). From his letters – and they
are many (Ettore wrote to Livia every day, sometimes twice, when they
were apart) – he displays the same qualities of tenderness, affection,

humour and childishness. But his jealousy (unlike Zeno's and more akin to Emilio's) is of an extremely vindictive and cruel kind, and this may be linked to the fact that he maintained an idealised image of her womanhood, which is necessarily more vulnerable to reality than a balanced one would have been. The group of letters written in 1898, when Livia spent one month alone in Salsomaggiore for health reasons, amply illustrates this: on the eve of her departure Ettore saw her packing her most elegant dresses and jewels; immediately his suspicions were aroused, exacerbated by his inferior social status and the lack of means which prevented him from joining her: 'Il povero marito di una moglie ricca è coperto di ridicolo' he writes (*Opera Omnia*, I, 76). He accuses her of betraying him: 'Se io apprendessi che tu fossi a Salsomaggiore a divertirti, io te ne punirei con tutti i mezzi che possono stare a mia disposizione . . . confesso che sono vendicativo' (p. 104). He thought to punish her by going with another woman: 'Sarebbe stata una bellissima vendetta, un vero sollievo da tanto dolore e da tanta bile, di sfogare i miei desideri . . . su un'altra donna . . . sapevo anche dove trovare la donna abbastanza desiderabile' (p. 119). That he did not do so was an act of 'heroism' on his part, for which Livia should congratulate him! 'Se io non ti ho tradita durante questo mese, è stato un vero e proprio eroismo di cui volli vantarmi perché precisamente, se tu sapessi le complicazioni dolorose della n. natura maschile, mi ammireresti' (p. 125). Here he appeals to the sexual double standard, which he expects her to accept without reservation. Fidelity is a moral obligation for a wife ('Tu non facesti invece che il tuo dovere'), but for a husband it requires heroic restraint: 'Del mio eroismo sono affranto, ammalato' (p. 125). These unjustified and vindictive remarks stem not only from Schmitz's impecunious state, but also from psychological and emotional insecurity, reflecting a childish fear of losing the woman he dared not dream of: 'Nei sogni piú arditi della mia gioventú, io non osai giammai di sperare d'avere una donna come sei tu . . . ' (p. 105). Ettore struggles to reconcile his two conflicting images of Livia as on the one hand an idealised angelic figure and on the other hand a sexualised human being. As Ghidetti points out: 'All'immagine ideale angelicata subentra la realtà di una donna: Livia diventa il simbolo vivente di una promessa mancata . . . [che] può degradare ulteriormente in tradimento, paradossalmente anche dopo la morte' (pp. 150–1). Indeed both Zeno and Schmitz suffer from a kind of posthumous jealousy, imagining their wives remarried to men much wealthier and better looking than they are (*Opera Omnia*, I, 117, 119). Zeno torments Augusta with these morbid thoughts during their honeymoon. She smiles through her tears and remarks: 'Dove troverei il tuo successore? Non vedi come sono brutta?'. 'Infatti', comments Zeno, 'probabilmente, mi sarebbe stato concesso qualche tempo di putrefazione tranquilla' (p. 729).

In a short piece entitled simply *Livia*, Schmitz fantasises about Livia's second husband:

> Era un bell'uomo, alto, diritto, forte, con bellissimi denti [Svevo had rotten teeth!] . . . last but not least era ricco. . . . Egli se la prese subito fra le braccia e le cacciò sulla bocca un bacio da conquistatore . . . ella rispose con un gesto di contentezza all'abbraccio subito cessato per un rumore alla porta (l'anima di Ettore che *buligava*). . . . Ella volle parlare di Ettore ma egli la interruppe: 'Il ricordo di quello lí non mi fa paura' disse con una superiorità calma che fece scricchiare dolorosamente la porta.   (*Opera Omnia*, III, 489–90)

In later years, when abroad on business journeys to England and France, Schmitz constantly refers to his fidelity, in spite of the many opportunities for acting otherwise, which he is careful to point out to Livia.[17] Whom is he trying to deceive? From my own conversations with his wife's sister Dora Oberti di Valnera in September 1977, it would appear that Svevo was something of a 'donnaiuolo'; and Stanislaus Joyce, in his 1932 preface to the English translation of *Senilità*, recalls an occasion when his brother's obvious and single-minded devotion to Nora was mocked by Schmitz who seemed to regard it with amusement.[18]

Last but not least (to use one of Svevo's favourite English phrases) we come to the figure of the mother-in-law. Schmitz's mother-in-law Olga Veneziani was a phenomenon, an *echt* matriarchal figure who ruled not only the vast household (comprising four daughters, a son, sons-in-law, grandchildren and servants) but also the factory until she was eighty-four years old. 'Piccola, secca, nervosa', is how she is described by her daughter (*Vita*, p. 43); she had such energy and drive that Schmitz remarked 'neppure in sogno essa sa stare ferma' (*Opera Omnia*, I, 210). She was domineering, authoritarian and dictatorial, a 'donna dragone', so much so that the workmen in the factory had nightmares about her.[19] Not only was Olga Schmitz's mother-in-law, she was also his first cousin and his employer from 1899. 'Olga mi diede ordine di dare le mie dimissioni dalla banca' he wrote to Livia on 24 May 1899; and he did (*Opera Omnia*, I, 169). Furthermore, he lived under the same roof with his parents-in-law throughout his married life. Consequently we can understand that Svevo had to be cautious in his portrayal of any fictional counterpart. Zeno is most polite, respectful and even flattering in his remarks about Signora Malfenti (his own mother-in-law): 'Mia suocera era ... una bella donna ... era elegante ... tutto in lei era mite e intonato' (p. 653). He is careful not to comment too extensively on her matrimonial manipulations which ensured that Zeno would marry Augusta: 'Provo un certo ritegno a parlarne con troppa libertà ... il suo intervento fu tanto breve ... un colpetto al momento giusto, non più forte di quanto occorse per farmi perdere il mio equilibrio labile' (p. 653).

Both Ettore Schmitz and Zeno Cosini recognised and responded to authoritarian women, to their qualities of initiative, enterprise and decisiveness, qualities singularly lacking in themselves. Svevo's appreciation of women's independence of spirit and vitality is clearly evident in his novels, as we have seen, particularly in his portrayals of the mistresses. We have also noted his implied critique of gender stereotypes which is further strengthened by the frequent use of the word 'virile' in his descriptions of women. In other words Svevo endows them with what were generally considered masculine qualities of moral and physical strength. For example we read:

[Annetta] non era una donna quando parlava di letteratura. Era un uomo nella lotta per la vita, moralmente un essere muscoloso (p. 219) ... Era Francesca ... Alfonso pensò ch'egli avrebbe riconosciuto anche a grande distanza quel corpo gracile dai movimenti virili nel vestito nero, molle (p. 303) ... La signora White ... alta, ritta ... delle linee femminili su un corpo virile ... (p. 378) ... Poi [Ada] si fece forza e mi stese la mano con un movimento deciso, virile ... (p. 417)

He also shows some women rejecting their traditional role and entering an essentially male domain. Thus Alberta Malfenti states unequivocally: 'Io non voglio sposarmi ... non ho che una meta: vorrei diventare una scrittrice' (p. 704). In fact she wins first prize for her one-act play, an achievement towards which Zeno is, to say the least, ambivalent. But a

more positive attitude is reflected in Ada's admiration for the emanci-
pated activities of British women which she describes having
encountered on her recent visit to England: 'Raccontò che le donne in
Inghilterra erano tutt'altra cosa che da noi. S'associavano per scopi di
beneficenza, religiosi o anche economici . . . raccontò di quelle donne
presidentesse, giornaliste, segretarie e propagandiste politiche'
(pp. 656–7). It would appear, then, that Svevo does not wholly endorse
the conventional view of women as expressed by Gustavo in his opinion
of his sister Lucia as 'una ragazza e quindi debole' (p. 376). Svevo is also
sensitive to the plight of those women who are tragic victims of a
patriarchal society, condemned to a life of loneliness or a loveless
marriage, as in the case of Amalia and Lucia. He conveys a sympathetic
awareness of the variety of social roles and predicaments with which the
women he creates have to contend.

In tracing the similarities and parallels between the life of the man and
the work of the artist we come to appreciate more clearly the understanding, compassion and admiration inherent in the portrayals of women,
who although perhaps not wholly convincing as living personalities, are
nevertheless much more than mere stereotyped clichés. It has become
clear, that the artist transcends the prejudices and limitations of the man
and the timelessness of his art transforms the dominant attitudes of his
age, thus perhaps contributing to a more liberal and realistic response to
one half of humanity.

Notes

1. S. Freud, *The Standard Edition of the Complete Psychological Works of
Sigmund Freud* (London, 1957) vol. XI, pp. 165–90.
2. I. Svevo, *Opera Omnia* (Milan, 1966–9) vol. II, p. 470. Further references to
the three novels contained in this volume are given after quotations in the
text.
3. *Diario di Elio Schmitz* (Milan, 1973) p. 195.
4. L. Veneziani Svevo, *Vita di mio marito* (Milan, 1976) p. 44 and p. 77.
5. S. Freud, *Complete Psychological Works*, XI, 168.
6. E. Ghidetti, *Italo Svevo* (Rome, 1980) p. 102.
7. P. Robinson, 'Senilità: the secret of Svevo's weeping Madonna', *Italian
Quarterly*, 14, no. 55 (1971) p. 68.
8. C. C. Russell, *The Writer from Trieste* (Ravenna, 1978) p. 114.
9. B. Moloney, *Italo Svevo* (Edinburgh, 1974) p. 36. Also N. Lebowitz, *Italo
Svevo* (New Jersey, 1978) p. 75.

10. N. Jonard, *Italo Svevo et la crise de la bourgeoisie européenne* (Paris, 1969) p. 126.
11. S. Freud, *Complete Psychological Works*, XI, 183.
12. E. Saccone, '*Senilità* di Italo Svevo: dalla impotenza del privato alla ansiosa speranza', *Modern Language Notes*, 82 (1967) p. 52.
13. I. Svevo, *Diario per la fidanzata* (Trieste, 1962) p. 15.
14. *Opera Omnia*, pp. 39–41. Also in a letter dated 17 June 1900, he writes: 'Penso con Tolstoi ... che i rapporti piú facili sieno quelli fra fratello e sorella. Confessa che almeno per un buon fratello a me non mancherebbe nessuna buona qualità' (p. 210).
15. I. Svevo, *Opera Omnia*, I, 65–8.
16. E. Montale, *Lettere a Italo Svevo* (Bari, 1966) p. 62.
17. *Opera Omnia*, I, 119, 247, 265, 268, 270, 275, 279, 305.
18. S. Joyce, preface to B. de Zoete's translation *As a Man Grows Older* (London, 1932) p. xi.
19. P. N. Furbank, *Italo Svevo: the man and the writer* (London, 1966) p. 43.

11

Tempo di storia e tempo di miti: teoria e prassi nel cinema durante il fascismo

Luisa Quartermaine

Il cinema è il mezzo che ha definito forse meglio di ogni altro il carattere dei costumi degli italiani del ventennio fascista, ma non è facile capirlo se non si tiene conto del contesto storico che gli aveva fatto da sfondo, della diversa personalità e individualità dei singoli protagonisti ed anche del taglio ideologico offerto dalla critica di allora.[1] Dalla documentazione a nostra disposizione riemergono contraddizioni di fondo che si manifestano in una serie di 'fascismi' piú o meno istituzionalizzati pragmaticamente con il regime.

L'incerta e ambigua adesione del cinema al fascismo, in bilico tra il condizionamento e l'evasione, crea il primo problema: se questo cinema sia, cioè, da definirsi 'cinema fascista' o 'cinema sotto il fascismo'. Il giudizio dei critici a questo proposito è contrastante.[2] Mentre Carlo Lizzani sostiene che quel cinema fu proprio un cinema immerso nel sistema, un cinema di tacito consenso,[3] e Mino Argentieri conferma che le correlazioni fra cinema italiano e fascismo sono state profonde e molteplici,[4] Gian Piero Brunetta insiste sulla necessità di riconoscere la funzione separata attribuita al cinema dal regime, che preferí sfruttare a scopi di propaganda i documentari e i cinegiornali.

Questo era avvenuto, infatti, tramite l'opera assidua dell'Istituto LUCE. Mezzo di elevata politicizzazione, i film LUCE furono prodotti con regolarità dal 1926 al 1943 e, dopo il Reale Decreto Legge del 5 agosto 1926, accompagnarono d'obbligo la proiezione dei lungometraggi nelle sale cinematografiche (2.500 sale circa nel 1930; quasi 3.000 nel 1942).

Il bilancio dei film LUCE è imponente in termini di metratura: dai due milioni del 1933 ai quattro milioni e mezzo del 1937. Il loro scopo ufficiale era di 'rinnovare' la coscienza nazionale secondo una ripetuta formula iconografica diretta alla formazione del consenso: il corporativismo, la cura della gioventú tramite l'Opera Nazionale Maternità e Infanzia, la salute fisica incoraggiata dal 'sabato fascista', il risanamento delle paludi malariche, l'esaltazione delle conquiste, della romanità, della terra (*Vita nostra*, 1925; *Duce*, 1926; *La battaglia del grano*, 1927 sono tra i titoli piú ricordati). Dopo il 1929 alle immagini si aggiunse il commento sonoro ed i messaggi propagandistici si accompagnarono a temi archeologici e di storia in cui si fa spesso avanti l'antico motivo del primato degli italiani.

La formula dei cinegiornali si fonda su strutture ripetitive in cui domina l'immagine di Mussolini in molteplici ruoli ed atteggiamenti, dal mito degli anni venti di un Mussolini interclassista e uomo del popolo (padre e contadino, in famiglia e alla trebbia, sportivo e nuotatore, pilota, automobilista, motociclista) all'eroe guerriero, fondatore dell'Impero. La regia privilegia sempre Mussolini, relegando gli altri gerarchi, e perfino il Re, al ruolo di comparse. A ragione Curzio Malaparte in *Critica fascista* sostenne che il capolavoro artistico di Mussolini non era stata 'l'Italia fascista, ma Mussolini stesso'.[5]

Anche il commento verbale si codifica sempre piú in rigide forme retoriche dove alla cronaca nazionale problematica viene sostituita una realtà concentrata sulla figura del piccolo-borghese spoliticizzato.

I giudizi negativi non mancarono. Luigi Freddi fu uno dei piú severi critici dell'attività del LUCE che, per la razione quotidiana di noia aveva 'fatto piú danno di una battaglia perduta'. Ed il critico Ernesto Cauda rincalzava:

> Non crediamo che questo istituto, pupilla del regime, abbia sfruttato in pieno la sua grandissima possibilità. . . . La LUCE dovrebbe essere la piú bella espressione del giornalismo cinematografico. Ma un giornale non può limitare il suo compito ad un'arida annotazione di fatti : . . un giornale non è un diario; esso deve commentare gli avvenimenti, metterli in rilievo. . . .[6]

Al di fuori dei cinegiornali e dei 'documentari', fu con l'avvento del sonoro che ebbe inizio il periodo ufficiale della cinematografia italiana entro l'orbita del Ministero della Cultura Popolare (Minculpop). L'adesione del cinema al regime si ebbe in modo palese con *Sole*, del 1929, con

cui esordí Alessandro Blasetti, a cui fece seguito poco dopo *Terra madre*
e *Vecchia guardia*. In essi Blasetti, riconosciuto come maestro cantore
del ventennio nero, si dimostra 'bonificatore, ruralista e squadrista'.[7] Il
valore di questi film viene identificato nell'intento (voluto o meno) di
risvegliare lo spirito nazionale, ricreando una continuità storica che
legittimasse l'operato del regime.

Se *Sole* fu un prodotto soprattutto 'di entusiasmo, di fede, di istinto'
come Blasetti stesso dichiarò,[8] di convinta adesione al regime erano stati
Camicia nera di Gioachino Forzano (1933), *Condottieri* di Luis Trenker
(1937) e *L'assedio dell'Alcazar* (1940) di Augusto Genina. L'elenco
potrebbe farsi lungo. Che il fascismo avesse ben capito la duplice valenza
del cinema, quella economica e quella culturale, divenne palese dopo gli
anni Trenta anche a livello di interventi pratici e iniziative legislative che
nel giro di pochi anni si susseguirono a ritmo incalzante.[9]

Gli anni Trenta e Quaranta erano stati anni cruciali per il regime; della
crisi del corporativismo e di quello che viene spesso definito il 'fascismo
di sinistra'. Ebbe allora inizio quell'intervento massiccio nell'economia e
nella politica che avrebbe portato di lí a poco tempo alla fase 'imperiale'
della guerra di Etiopia. Non a torto si osservò che anche il regime
fascista, come l'industria cinematografica, aveva avuto i suoi 'telefoni
bianchi': le imprese, i riti, le parole. Il piú efficace e meglio riuscito tra
questi fu certo la campagna d'Etiopia. Pirandello appunto commentava
sul Duce neo-conquistatore: 'L'autore di questa grande opera in atto è
anch'egli un Poeta che sa bene il fatto suo. Vero uomo di teatro ...
agisce, autore e protagonista, nel Teatro dei secoli'.[10]

Il mito dell'Impero era strettamente connesso al culto della romanità
che, vivo nella retorica fine ottocento, assunse piú decise caratteristiche
di *revival* nel campo letterario e artistico negli anni Venti e trovò la sua
piena realizzazione nell'architettura romano-imperiale di Piacentini e nel
modernismo monumentale 'littorio' dei progetti urbanistici proposti per
l'Esposizione Universale *E 42*. Questo progetto, secondo la testimo-
nianza di Bottai, fu una specie di 'visione profetica' maturata da
Mussolini durante la campagna di Etiopia. Intendeva esprimere 'la
vittoria abissina, l'affermazione della volontà italiana nel mondo, la
Fondazione dell'Impero'.[11]

L'entusiastico collegamento tra Roma e l'Africa, come unico possibile
sbocco espansionistico (che è alla base del gusto delle grandi parate e del
ritualismo di stampo staraciano) condiziona direttamente il cinema.

Un film che movesse dalla romanità, non da quella di cartapesta di molti film storici, ma da quella scabra, rurale e guerriera, che conquistò il mondo e giungesse alla nuova apparizione dell'Impero sui colli fatali di Roma, mettendo in rilievo i lati cesarei e nello stesso tempo umani e socialmente rivoluzionari della creazione mussoliniana, avrebbe indubbiamente una grande forza di suggestione.[12]

L'apparire netto di un profilo di tipo patriottico-oleografico viene confermato nei due filoni di cinema storico e di costume. La differenza tra i due filoni sta nel trattamento dell'affresco storico: con riferimenti il primo ad avvenimenti storici precisi, a guerre e date di valore nazionale; di invenzione romanzesca il secondo, senza un rapporto di necessità con la realtà storica, ma spesso con forma volutamente di evasione.

I film storici, non molto numerosi fino al 1939 (circa dieci per anno), si moltiplicarono dopo il '40 fino ad arrivare ad una produzione annuale di circa trenta film. La loro caratteristica costante, ben individuata da Alessandro Pavolini (Ministro della Cultura Popolare) è quella dell'attualità:

Infatti può esserci un film storico concepito con mentalità moderna ed essere infinitamente piú attuale di un film in abito d'oggi con mentalità ottocentesca. D'altra parte noi non siamo l'America. Noi abbiamo la storia nel sangue.[13]

Da annoverarsi nel filone storico è *Scipione l'Africano* di Carmine Gallone, uscito nel 1937. Il film (del tipo *Kolossal* sullo stampo del genere di successo in voga durante il periodo del 'muto'), fu fallimentare sia come iniziativa politica che industriale. Il parallelismo tra le imprese epiche di Scipione contro Annibale di cui trattava, e la contemporanea guerra d'Africa risultò, comunque, immediatamente ovvio. I discorsi di Scipione di stampo mussoliniano, la battaglia di Zama girata nei dintorni di Sabaudia (città di nuova creazione ad opera di Mussolini), l'intervento diretto nel film delle forze del ministero della Guerra, delle Colonie, dell'Areonautica e della Marina, tutto questo dimostrava l'assoluta correlazione tra passato e presente. Se il film divenne da un canto il simbolo ironico delle ambizioni sbagliate del fascismo e della sproporzione tra mezzi e retorica (e per tanto fu violentemente attaccato), d'altro canto il tema della identificazione della Roma dei Consoli e dei Cesari con il nuovo regime, rimase fatto duraturo. Insieme al volume *Scipione e la conquista mediterranea* che già Alberto Consiglio aveva pubblicato nel 1931, serví a testimoniare che la mitologia della storia come materiale di scambio, e la romanità come rievocazione di tradizioni e glorie italiane, agivano tanto a livello di élite culturale che di massa.

La guerra d'Etiopia aveva aperto la strada anche ai film coloniali. Tra questi, *Il grande appello* (1936) di Mario Camerini, i due film di Augusto Genina, *Squadrone Bianco* (1936), *L'assedio dell'Alcazar* (1940), i film di Goffredo Alessandrini, *Abuna Messias* (1939), e *Giarabub* (1942), ci riportano a fatti storici contemporanei. Le tematiche trattate sono quelle care al fascismo: l'efficacia e modernità delle forze armate, il motivo del sacrificio personale; la rinuncia dell'individualismo in favore di ideali patriottici; la rappresentazione dell'italiano fascista (spesso impersonato da Fosco Giacchetti), maschio, cupo e deciso, senza frivolità e debolezze. Accanto al tema eroico c'è spesso anche il lato umano, sentimentale che, come sostiene Gian Piero Brunetta, serviva da mascheramento.

A questi temi si aggiunge quello dell'emigrazione collegato all'immagine di un'America mitica di *Passaporto rosso* (1935). Il film di Guido Brignone, spesso annoverato tra quelli piú apertamente sostenitori della politica fascista, si sviluppa in realtà in direzioni diverse non facilmente attribuibili ad una chiara ideologia. La novità del film sta nell'alternarsi di epicità e disincanto con cui si indaga sulla mentalità degli emigrati. Il loro stato d'animo amareggiato ammette l'esistenza di una crisi non solo economica, ma soprattutto ideologica e di identità. Il film non è solo una semplice eco della momentanea politica anti-emigratoria di Mussolini, come a volte è stato interpretato. Ad entrare in crisi è la speranza e la fiducia di chi era deciso a difendere la propria dignità 'con la stessa speranza e fiducia dei primi emigranti' e di chi era alla ricerca del 'calore umano che l'Italia ufficiale non dava'.[14] Riflette quindi la delusione del mitico 'altrove' e degli Stati Uniti visti come punto di riferimento ideale, proiezione e simbolo di aspirazioni (l'America che per Pintor era soprattutto quella 'scoperta dentro di noi').[15] Preannuncia, in realtà, la delusione nei riguardi del mito americano dell'Anguilla di *La luna e i falò* di Cesare Pavese. Non si può escludere quindi una vena polemica nei riguardi del regime,[16] tanto piú che il film era stato girato in un momento in cui il fascismo preferiva accreditare nel doppio mito della terra vergine (caro alla cultura americana) e dell'alto sviluppo industriale, l'immagine positiva degli Stati Uniti e individuava nei modelli culturali americani i paragoni dell'efficienza e della giovinezza. Ancora nel 1938 Vittorio Mussolini in *Cinema* difendeva infatti quel che di mitico era nella realtà dei film americani 'la freschezza, l'audacia, la forza, l'esuberanza chiassosa ma sana'.[17] Il volto di un'America sconvolta dai problemi economici, in preda a gravi disordini interni, avrà inizio solo dopo la proclamazione delle leggi raziali.

Alla tendenza realista, definita 'borghese', il Ministero della Cultura Popolare mostrò preferire il bonario ottimismo. La formula del cosiddetto 'realismo rosa' blasettiana è apertamente sostenuta da Alessandro Pavolini: 'Non si deve scordare che il cinema dirige il suo messaggio al cuore del popolo ... quindi chiediamo allora un cinema in cui tutto sia roseo, in cui tutti abbiano dieci in condotta'.[18] Si tratta spesso di commedie sentimentali come *Rotaie* (1929), di Mario Camerini (film muto a cui piú tardi fu aggiunto il sonoro), o, sempre di Camerini, *Gli uomini che mascalzoni* (1932) e *Il cappello a tre punte* (1935), in cui ad una precisa ed accurata osservazione della società, si unisce una satira bonaria dell'ambiente italiano piccolo borghese. Sono in molti casi film in cui dopo una lettura affrettata e denigratoria si cominciano a riscoprire qualità prima trascurate: il senso dell'immaginario, la capacità di bilanciare nella giusta misura desideri fantasiosi e banalità quotidiana, soprattutto il gusto del detto e non detto e del parlare per metafora che apre lo spiraglio alla possibilità di non prendere troppo sul serio l'ideologia imperante.

Importante in questo senso è il ruolo assunto dai film comici tra gli anni Trenta e Quaranta. Filone non molto nutrito come numero di film, è tuttavia significativo per i suoi collegamenti con la vita culturale del periodo e per avere assorbito il tipo di giornalismo umoristico che si era venuto delineando soprattutto nelle riviste *Marc'Aurelio* (nata a Roma nel 1930), e *Bertoldo* (uscita a Milano nel 1936). Il principio estetico a cui si faceva appello piú o meno esplicitamente era il rifiuto della retorica fascista tramite un umorismo anticonvenzionale, che rasentava il surreale. La tecnica espressiva sia a livello letterario (con i testi di Áchille Campanile e Cesare Zavattini), sia filmico (con i film dello stesso Zavattini), richiedeva la creazione di un personaggio ilare, fortemente deformato, oppure di un personaggio provocatorio, che mostra disprezzo per il regime proprio perché non se ne cura, perché finge di non vederlo. Uno dei film piú tipici di questo filone è *Imputato, alzatevi* (1939), di Mario Mattoli, che vede il debutto del comico piemontese, Erminio

Macario. Al film collaborò anche Vittorio Metz, giornalista e redattore prima del *Marc'Aurelio*, e poi, insieme a Giovanni Mosca del *Bertoldo*. L'importanza di Metz (come del resto di Campanile e Zavattini) era nella elaborazione di un linguaggio di eleganze verbali, che riprendono ironicamente lo sperimentalismo letterario degli anni Venti e Trenta, ma utilizzate in direzione dell'irrazionale. Lo svagato diventa irriverenza, e nel caso di *Imputato, alzatevi*, contestazione indiretta nei confronti delle occasioni tradizionali di prestigio, di rispettabilità, di autorità. Il confronto diretto con la realtà sociale, che nel *Gastone* e *Gigi Er Bullo* di Ettore Petrolini si traduceva in una comicità acida e infastidita, produce in questo caso sotto il pretesto dell'evasione un effetto profondamente grottesco a testimoniare che quel concetto di società che il fascismo si era proposto negli anni Venti era entrato definitivamente in crisi.

Ma quali erano i principi fondamentali alla base della 'società fascista'?

In *Critica fascista*, la rivista quindicinale fondata da Bottai e Modigliani nel 1923 e organo del regime,[19] viene spiegato il significato 'rivoluzionario' delle ideologie del regime:

Prender possesso della vita nazionale, per il fascismo, non può significare soltanto impadronirsi del potere ed esercitarlo al posto dei dirigenti di prima: ma deve significare governare, guidare, condurre, educare gli italiani secondo lo spirito del fascismo. Questo può avvenire soltanto se i dirigenti, i guidatori-educatori hanno un'anima fascista, vivono spiritualmente in modo fascista . . . è un intero mondo spirituale che si è sostituito ad un altro.[20]

Ogni scienza – la politica, l'economia, l'arte – viene individuata come parte di un tutto. A questo si aggiungeva la visione dell'intellettuale inserito nella vita pratica, già delineata da Bottai in *Critica fascista* nel 1934. Per Bottai l'intellettuale doveva corrispondere all'uomo 'nuovo' e 'integrale' che alla solida preparazione tecnico-professionale sapesse accoppiare una efficace capacità politica.[21] Doveva innanzi tutto far sí che la cultura si inserisse nel mondo del lavoro e della produzione e che diventasse azione:

La cultura per la cultura è un tempo per la cultura; la cultura per l'azione e un altro tempo, il piú lungo, forse, e, sotto certi aspetti, il piú decisivo. . . . Il compito degli istituti fascisti di cultura si definisce proprio in questo trapasso all'azione.[22]

Che l'equazione fra cultura e vita fosse riconosciuta e apertamente perseguita dal regime è indiscusso, basta leggere ad esempio l'articolo intitolato 'Condizione letteraria' apparso in prima pagina su *Primato* il 15 ottobre del 1941.[23]

Da questa equazione trae origine anche il coinvolgimento del regime con il cinema, che ufficialmente però ebbe luogo solo nel 1936 con la fondazione della Direzione Generale per la Cinematografia ad opera di Luigi Freddi. La politica di Freddi (soprannominata 'linea Freddi') voleva il cinema inserito nell'orbita del Ministero della Cultura Popolare; era integralista (una produzione di stato, garantita da un noleggio di stato, favorita da sale cinematografiche di stato); prevedeva un ampio intervento statale sull'industria della cultura.

Il problema fu inizialmente affrontato dal fascismo in modo pragmatico, lasciando ampio spazio alle pressioni mutevoli della necessità esterna e instaurando, casomai, una spregiudicata politica fagocitante e di lusinga diretta a imbrigliare ogni opposizione. Solo cosí, per quanto riguarda il cinema del ventennio, può spiegarsi il suo oscillare verso i 'miti' americani e russi, e il confluire in esso di influenze opposte. Basti pensare che, nonostante la politica anticomunista in vigore,[24] nel 1932 e nel 1934 la Mostra d'Arte Cinematografica di Venezia favorí il lancio del cinema sovietico e che al Centro Sperimentale di Cinematografia, fondato sull'esperienza della scuola cinematografica di Mosca (ma come si è visto per diretto intervento dello stato) lavorasse Umberto Barbaro, comunista, proveniente dal Futurismo, traduttore e studioso dei testi di Ejzenstein e Pudovkin.

Il mito sovietico, è vero, s'inquadrava bene nella ricerca di un modello di società rigorosa ed efficiente. Nel luglio del 1937, sul numero 2 della rivista *Prospettive*, Curzio Malaparte aveva apertamente espresso la sua approvazione per il fenomeno rivoluzionario-fascista 'secondo una linea parallela a quella del fenomeno rivoluzionario russo'. Nei riguardi del cinema e dei mass-media in genere, questo significava, almeno in teoria, oltre ad un impegno fortemente educativo, una piú rigorosa censura sui contenuti dei film prodotti in Italia, e sulle importazioni dei film stranieri. Piú volte si era sottolineata la necessità di usare il cinema come strumento d'intervento e si era additato all'opera attiva del Gufk sovietico (l'equivalente di un ministero del cinema) come esempio da seguire. Nel 1934 ad esempio, un corsivo sul numero 12 della rivista *Cantiere*, lamentava:

> Perché la scuola di cinematografia non prende sostanza, come in Russia o in America, e non si mette alla pari degli altri rami dell'università . . .? Ancora non si è visto che il cinema è il solo mezzo di comunicazione delle masse. . . . Perché dunque non si potrebbero trasportare le energie finanziarie ed intellettuali che si sprecano in un giornalismo senza senso in un campo cinematografico ampio e magnifico?[25]

Il mito americano e russo sono componenti integranti del rapporto ambiguo tra industria e arte che si era già espresso in forma polemica negli anni Venti. Erano gli anni in cui, nel tentativo di rivalutare il cinema come fatto artistico, si era teorizzato sul film come atto creativo. Rispetto al cinema di consumo si auspicava un cinema di qualità estetica e di dignità morale, che implicasse di necessità l'impiego di una professionalità diversa. Massimo Bontempelli, consciente delle tensioni interne inerenti al mezzo filmico e, allo stesso tempo, delle sue potenzialità, cosí lo descriveva:

> Il cinema puro come tutte le purità è distruttivo. Il cinema sta nel suo nascere come spettacolo, nel dover rispondere ad una necessità: essere popolare. Esso vive in quanto c'è un milione d'occhi che guardano. Naturalmente il mestierante è distruttivo e assurdo quanto il puro. . . . L'arte cinematografica può diventare il fuoco centrale della espressione di un tempo e la piú efficace educazione di un popolo. Credo che il cinema italiano diventerà in questo secolo quello che fu l'arte italiana nel Rinascimento.[26]

Il dibattito, iniziato nelle riviste corporative, si era trasferito poi nelle riviste letterarie. È qui, infatti, che cominciò a svilupparsi la critica cinematografica di prestigio con gli interventi di Piero Gadda ed Emilio Cecchi in *Fiera letteraria*.[27] A questi si aggiunsero gli scritti di Giansiro Ferrata in *Solaria*, di Corrado Alvaro in *L'Italia letteraria*, ed i primi testi di Guglielmo Alberti in *Pegaso*.[28]

Il diretto coinvolgimento di Giovanni Gentile e Benedetto Croce nella battaglia a sostegno della dignità artistica dei film, coincise con un impegno culturale degli intellettuali nei riguardi del cinema.

Tra le riviste specializzate, *Rivista internazionale del cinema educatore*,[29] *Cinemondo*,[30] e *Cinematografo*[31] dedicarono uno spazio al cinema russo per sottolinearne il valore didattico o per additare la sintesi tra cultura e politica sul tipo della *Piatiletka*, la pianificazione e socializzazione russa.

La Russia funzionò da esempio non solo a livello organizzativo, ma anche di contenuto per l'interesse in direzione realista. Alfred Kerr nell'articolo intitolato 'I russi e il film: tecnica sovietica', additava ad un modo di fare il cinema già sostenuto da Leo Longanesi e che, nonostante il tono un po' 'strapaesano', può essere considerato uno dei molti anticipi del neorealismo:

È appunto la verità che fa difetto ai nostri film. Bisogna gettarsi nella strada, portare la macchina da presa nelle vie, nei cortili, nelle caserme, nelle stazioni. . . . Lo schermo russo ha un carattere collettivo. Esso è l'antitesi della cinematografia individualistica dell'occidente. . . . La massima parte dei personaggi viene scelta di volta in volta e viene tratta dagli ambienti piú vicini al soggetto che si vuole sviluppare. Ben spesso si tratta di veri e propri uomini della strada.[32]

Anche la rivista *Cantiere* si inserí nel dibattito sul realismo. In opposizione al gusto della bella immagine, Guglielmo Serafini, sul numero 23 del 1934, sostenne il ruolo del realismo nella traduzione in immagini della propaganda, chiarendo anche che la diversità di visione del fascismo rispetto al nazismo era dovuta al fatto che il nazismo

non è mai sceso nella realtà nazionale tedesca, esso si è esplicitamente disinteressato di ogni problema concreto . . . per proseguire alcuni balordi e ideologici concetti quale quello di razza secondo i quali non si può governare uno stato moderno.[33]

In un tipico oscillare tra est ed ovest, allo stesso tempo in cui si citavano alcuni filoni russi, si additava anche all'industria americana non solo come fenomeno di socializzazione, per avere affinato al massimo l'abilità spettacolare e per la presa sul pubblico, ma anche come fonte di ispirazione realista. Notevole, a questo proposito, è l'accostamento veramente acrobatico tra il gusto italiano e quello d'oltre oceano proposto da Vittorio Mussolini:

> Al nostro pubblico che affolla le sale cinematografiche e ai giovani in particolare, piacciono le cose chiare, poco faraginose, divertenti, piene di vita e di movimento. I pesantissimi *Traumulus* tedeschi non ci dicono niente, sono troppo lontani dal nostro spirito.... Il fatto essenziale della questione rimane espresso cosí: l'America è giovane mentre l'Europa è stravecchia.... Per fortuna nostra col Fascismo l'Italia fa parte a sé ed è estranea ad ogni corrente funesta.... È forse eresia affermare che spirito, mentalità e temperamento della giovinezza italiana, pur con le logiche e naturali differenze imprescindibili di un'altra razza, siano molto piú vicine a quelle della gioventú d'oltre oceano che a quella russa, tedesca, francese, spagnola?³⁴

Fu per questo (oltre che per la promessa di sostanziosi finanziamenti) che Mario Camerini, partito con Mario Soldati come soggettista verso l'Etiopia, si era dichiarato disposto ad abbandonare le favole bianche piccolo-borghesi per affrontare invece 'un problema cinematografico non ricalcato dalle pagine di un libro, ma scavato nella realtà viva e presente'. Il film prodotto sarà *Grande appello* (1936) lodato dal Maresciallo d'Italia Pietro Badoglio per l'accuratezza realistica delle scene che 'riproducono con esattezza le varie situazioni'.³⁵

Le poetiche del realismo quotidiano del 'colto sul vivo', legate anche ad una posizione morale, ad un modo di intendere il cinema come antievasivo, erano sostenute dai 'fascisti di sinistra' sensibili ai problemi sociali, ed appoggiate dal gruppo di cineasti che si radunava attorno alla rivista *Cinema*, uscita il 10 luglio del 1936. Tra di essi: De Santis, Lizzani, Puccini, Pietrangeli, Visconti.³⁶

Pietrino Bianchi, sotto lo pseudonimo di 'Volpone', ritornò ancora sull'argomento del realismo in *Bertoldo*, in occasione della settimana veneziana del cinema. L'articolo 'Cinema a Venezia' è una critica diretta a certo cinema italiano:

> Quello che guasta la nostra produzione e ne minora, si direbbe, l'effetto, è una certa timidezza, un complesso d'inferiorità dei registi davanti alla realtà, concreta e evidente, della nostra vita nazionale.... Questo fuggire davanti alla realtà del nostro cinematografo può voler

dire parecchie cose, ma, a nostro avviso, ne significa soprattutto una sola: l'immaturità spirituale di troppa gente che si occupa di queste cose.[37]

Gli opuscoli dei cineclub della Gioventú Universitaria Fascista, il cosiddetto GUF (in cui si formarono anche i futuri cineasti del neorealismo come Antonioni, Rossellini e Visconti), rivolsero la loro attenzione tanto al cinema americano che a quello russo, dimostrando un atteggiamento che potrebbe essere contraddittorio se non fosse che era ispirato dalla polemica contro il film d'evasione e questa non poteva attuarsi in base ai confini geopolitici. D'altra parte (ed è qui l'altra contraddizione del regime) lo stato etico fascista, presentandosi a favore dell'interesse nazionale, si poneva contro il materialismo sia russo che americano. Cosí, infatti, si era espresso Julius Evola nel 1929:

> Come la Russia, l'America ... è la precisa contraddizione della nostra cultura ... essa ha introdotto nella nostra epoca la religione della pratica, ha imposto l'interesse del guadagno, della produzione, della realizzazione meccanica.[38]

L'interesse fascista si articolò cosí in diversi momenti, seguendo una logica di necessità e pressioni interne. Dopo gli entusiasmi della guerra d'Etiopia, l'inizio dell'avvicinamento del governo alla Germania nazista portò ad un lento deterioramento della credibilità russa. Per il cinema, la posizione critica nei confronti del bolscevismo, fu la causa di un forte ridimensionamento del 'mito russo'.

Il 22 maggio 1939 l'Italia firma il 'patto d'acciaio' con la Germania. Nell'aprile del 1941 un corpo di spedizione di 60.000 soldati italiani è inviato a combattere contro la Russia. La propaganda anti-russa anche a livello di cinema si trasformerà in denigrazione. *Noi vivi* (1942) di Goffredo Alessandrini, a cui fa seguito poco dopo la seconda parte, *Addio Kira*, ne sono una prova.

Per quanto riguarda gli interventi statali e le iniziative legislative introdotte dal governo nei riguardi del cinema negli anni Venti, anche se essi furono molti, in realtà il regime si dimostrò piú abile nell'inglobare strutture nate indipendentemente che nel crearne delle sue.

A parte la già citata Unione Cinematografica Educativa (che nel 1925 subentrò al Sindacato Istruzione Cinematografica, fondato agli inizi degli anni Venti e quindi pre-fascista), l'iniziativa piú significativa fu la fondazione delle scuole di cinematografia. Alla prima, la Scuola Nazionale di Cinematografia del 1930, solo formale perché mai entrata in funzione, fece seguito nel '32 la Scuola di Cinema, che quattro anni dopo si trasformò nel Centro Sperimentale di Cinematografia. Ufficialmente sotto la presidenza del Ministro delle Corporazioni, Giuseppe Bottai, e sotto la direzione di Corrado Pavolini e Luciano Doria (in vario modo figure carismatiche del regime), in pratica queste Scuole furono affidate alla responsabilità effettiva di persone già note dello spettacolo e non direttamente dipendenti dal partito: Alessandro Blasetti nei primi due casi, Luigi Chiarini nel terzo. Furono chiamati a collaborare anche docenti rinomati e intellettuali di prestigio (come Anton Giulio Bragaglia), indipendentemente dalla loro appartenenza al partito; in alcuni casi, anzi (come per Umberto Barbaro), essi erano dichiaratamente anti-fascisti.

La scelta di Chiarini per il Centro Sperimentale va vista, però, in relazione al dissidio ideologico tra Blasetti e Freddi, uomo di cinema il primo, uomo politico il secondo. La fondazione stessa del Centro, voluta da Freddi, fu in parte una conseguenza di questo contrasto. Blasetti, infatti, pur essendo propenso a centralizzare le numerose piccole case private di produzione in un'industria pubblica unica, era anche favorevole al film sperimentale che Freddi, al contrario, osteggiava perché limitato ad un numero ridotto di spettatori. Freddi voleva un cinema come spettacolo che facesse appello ad un vasto pubblico; un cinema non politico (a questo ci avrebbero pensato i cinegiornali LUCE), ma che offrisse un'immagine nazionale di società fascista solida e permanente. Era quindi indirettamente sostenitore del genere dei film convenzionali d'evasione, contro il tipo impegnato realistico. A questa concezione del cinema aveva contribuito non solo la sua recente visita alla compatta industria cinematografica di Hollywood, ma anche e soprattutto la passata esperienza di Stefano Pittaluga, una figura abbastanza eccezionale di produttore emersa durante la crisi del cinema italiano negli anni Venti. Con l'apertura nel '26 dei nuovi studi sonori della Cines a Roma, Pittaluga era riuscito a riattivare le sorti del cinema italiano tramite l'organizzazione di una forte industria di cui lui stesso era produttore, distributore ed esercente. Freddi, al pari di Pittaluga, credeva nella necessità di progetti a lunga scadenza inseriti in un'industria centralizzata anziché parcellizzata nelle sfere private.

La linea Freddi non ebbe vita duratura perché osteggiata anche internamente al Ministero dalla politica del Ministro Alfieri. Questi, sotto la spinta di industriali privati, favoriva la riaffermazione delle molteplici case di produzione. Nel '38 la Legge Alfieri, che offriva 'premi' in misura direttamente proporzionale agli incassi dei film, significò un ritorno al controllo dettato dalle forze del mercato, ripristinando effettivamente lo *status quo*.

Quello che delle creazioni di Freddi, però, rimase fu il Centro Sperimentale. Esso produsse tanto film a lungo metraggio che documentari; diede vita a *Bianco e Nero*, una delle piú prestigiose riviste di critica cinematografica. In esso continuarono a convergere spinte diverse: creazione estetica, protezionismo industriale, fascismo e marxismo. Da esso partirono anche i rappresentanti futuri del neorealismo. Nell'accettazione del cinema americano per i dati realistici pertinenti ad una nuova coscienza sociale e nel rifiuto del medesimo come prodotto commerciale, esso rappresentò l'esempio ultimo di quello stesso conflitto tra arte e industria che si era delineato nel cinema negli anni Venti. Ma la continuità tra mass-media e tradizione artistico-letteraria e la legittimazione che il cinema aveva cercato come fatto culturale, ironicamente lo rese anche prodotto d'esportazione e piú commerciabile del prodotto di massa, perché meno legato al solo pubblico italiano. Fu proprio la possibilità di questo successo all'estero a renderlo bersaglio di due alleati imbattibili, il Governo e la Chiesa, che lo ingaggiarono in una aspra battaglia combattuta, e persa, nel dopoguerra.

Note

1. Per i dati statistici riguardanti il cinema del periodo fascista, cf. il capitolo sul cinema dal 1927 al 1944 in L. Quaglietti, *Storia economico politica del cinema italiano 1945–1980* (Roma, 1980). Per una analisi dettagliata dei film di questo periodo, rimando al mio articolo 'L'Arma piú Forte' in *Civiltà Italiana*, anno X, 1–3 (1987) di prossima pubblicazione. Mi propongo di valutare in altra sede la situazione del cinema durante il periodo badogliano e della Repubblica Sociale Italiana, che dal 1943 va fino al 1945 e che merita un capitolo a parte.
2. Tra i molti studi recenti, cf. G. P. Brunetta, *Storia del cinema italiano 1895–1945* (Roma, 1979–82) 2 voll.; *Cinema italiano tra le due guerre* (Milano, 1975); *Intellettuali cinema e propaganda tra le due guerre* (Bologna, 1973); L. Carabba, *Il cinema del ventennio nero* (Firenze, 1974); *Cinema italiano sotto il fascismo*, a cura di R. Redi (Venezia, 1979); C. Lizzani, *Storia*

del cinema italiano (Firenze, 1961); F. Savio, *Cinecittà anni trenta* (Roma, 1979) e *Ma l'amore no* (Milano, 1975).

3. Cf. il suo commento su *La Repubblica*, 18 ottobre 1976, riportato da Saracinelli e Notti, 'Il Cinema' in *L'Italia del Duce* (Rimini, 1983) p. 63.

4. M. Argentieri, *L'occhio del regime* (Firenze, 1979) p. 5.

5. Cf. 'Risposta ad un'inchiesta sull'arte fascista' in *Critica fascista*, 20 (1926).

6. Riportati in M. Argentieri, *L'occhio del regime*, p. 43 e p. 83.

7. Sono significativi alcuni commenti del tempo. *Sole* fu definito da Mussolini stesso 'l'alba del regime fascista' (cf. G. P. Brunetta, *Cinema italiano tra le due guerre*, p. 105). A Filippo Sacchi, giornalista di provata fede fascista, piacque di *Vecchia guardia* 'la magnifica marcia su Roma di largo respiro e travolgente' (*Corriere della sera*, 17 gennaio 1935); Mario Gromo dello stesso film approva 'lo squadrismo ardente e presago della vittoria ... pervaso di giovinezza impetuosa' (*La Stampa*, 19 gennaio 1935); Francesco Pasinetti lo vide come 'un film sulla Rivoluzione Fascista ... una delle opere piú vitali del cinema italiano' (in F. Pasinetti, *Storia del cinema dalle origini a oggi*, ristampa anastatica della edizione del 1939 (Venezia, 1980) pp. 307–8.

8. Cf. 'Blasetti parla dei suoi film', *Tempo*, 13 novembre 1941.

9. In ordine cronologico abbiamo: 1932: la edizione della Mostra Internazionale d'Arte Cinematografica a Venezia; 1933: decreto a favore del doppiaggio nazionale che proibisce la proiezione dei film doppiati all'estero; 1934: (10 settembre) creazione del Sottosegretariato per la Stampa e Propaganda, affidato a Galeazzo Ciano e trasformato in Ministero l'anno dopo; (18 settembre) fondazione della Direzione Generale per la Cinematografia; 1935: (13 aprile) fondazione del Centro Sperimentale di Cinematografia; (9 novembre) fondazione dell'ENIC (Ente Nazionale Industrie Cinematografiche); 1937: (28 aprile) inaugurati da Mussolini gli Studi di Cinecittà; 1938: (16 giugno) legge 'Alfieri' – si istituisce un sistema di sovvenzioni automatiche ai film in base agli incassi; (4 settembre) creazione del monopolio di stato per l'importazione dei film stranieri, entrerà in funzione l'anno seguente tramite l'ENIC. Tra gli anni Trenta e Quaranta l'intervento pubblico sembra articolato anche secondo chiare divisioni di responsabilità: CINES per la produzione; Istituto LUCE per il cinegiornale, cinema educativo, scientifico, didattico, lo sviluppo e la stampa; CINECITTÀ per i teatri di posa; ENIC-ECI per l'esercizio e la distribuzione; CINEGUF (ramo della Gioventú Universitaria Fascista) per le associazioni giovanili del cinema; CSC (Centro Sperimentale di Cinematografia) per la formazione dei quadri (cf. G. Laura, 'Il centro sperimentale di cinematografia', *Bianco e Nero*, 37, 5–6 (1976) p. 6). Gli eventi storici precipitano nel 1943 con lo sbarco in Sicilia (10 luglio), con la riunione del Gran Consiglio (25 luglio) e la deposizione di Mussolini a favore di Badoglio. L'Italia per quasi due anni sarà divisa in due: al sud il regime di Badoglio con il re; al nord la Repubblica Sociale Italiana con Mussolini. Del 22 febbraio 1944 è l'inaugurazione degli studi di Cinevillaggio a Venezia che accoglie quello che era rimasto dell'industria cinematografica romana.

10. Riportato in G. Gatti, *Vita di Gabriele d'Annunzio* (Firenze, 1956) p. 450.

11. Cf. P. Marconi, *Il quartiere dell'E42 fulcro del piano regolatore di Roma Imperiale* (Roma, 1940) pp. 9 ss. che riporta i testi di Bottai.
12. Dall'articolo anonimo 'Il cinema per l'Impero' apparso in *Lo schermo*, giugno 1936.
13. A. Pavolini, *Rapporto nazionale della cinematografia italiana*, 3 giugno 1941, riportato in Jean J. Gili, 'Film storico e film in costume', in *Cinema italiano sotto il fascismo*, a cura di R. Redi, p. 131.
14. C. Pavese, 'Ritorno all'uomo' in *La letteratura americana ed altri saggi* (Torino, 1962) p. 197.
15. G. Pintor, *Il sangue d'Europa* (Torino, 1975) p. 159.
16. Alla direzione del film prese parte anche un antifascista: Alfredo Guarini.
17. V. Mussolini, 'Emancipazione del cinema italiano', *Cinema*, 6 (1936) p. 13.
18. Riportato in *Il lungo viaggio del cinema italiano*. Antologia di 'Cinema' 1936–1943, a cura di O. Caldiron (Venezia, 1965) pp. 419–20.
19. Fu stampata a Roma da Berlutti e continuò la produzione fino al 15 luglio 1945. Bottai la diresse fino al 1930.
20. Cf. A. Nasti, 'Portatori della rivoluzione', in *Critica fascista*, 13 (1929) pp. 249–50.
21. Cf. G. Bottai, 'Appelli all'uomo', in *Critica fascista* (1934) p. 5. Il mito dello stato etico era già stato espresso come astratta utopia mazziniana durante il Risorgimento, ma è solo con Giovanni Gentile, membro del PNF dal 1923, che il concetto assume forma determinata applicata al fascismo. Il fascismo è per Gentile l'espressione finale dello stato etico, vive all'*interno* degli uomini e non *tra* gli uomini; è popolare e democratico, in contrapposizione a quello piú aristocratico del nazismo.
22. Cf. Bottai, 'Cultura in azione', in *Critica fascista* (1934) 15 settembre 1936. La citazione è riportata da Anna Panicali nel suo articolo 'L'intellettuale fascista', in *Cinema italiano sotto il fascismo*, già cit., pp. 29–50 a cui rimandiamo per una trattazione esauriente dell'argomento.
23. La rivista era stata fondata da Bottai nel marzo 1940.
24. Nel settembre del 1928 erano stati condannati 37 dirigenti comunisti tra cui Gramsci a 20 anni di reclusione e Terracini a 22 anni.
25. Riportato in Vito Zagario, 'Il modello sovietico', in *Cinema italiano sotto il fascismo*, già cit., p. 196.
26. M. Bontempelli, 'Lo schermo', in *Cinematografo*, anno 1, no. 11, 30 ottobre 1926.
27. Un numero speciale di *Fiera letteraria* del marzo 1927 fu interamente dedicato al cinema.
28. Sull'argomento cf. Glauco Viazzi, 'I primi anni della critica cinematografica in Italia', in *Ferrania*, dicembre 1956.
29. Esce a Roma nel 1929, rivista mensile di cultura cinematografica, curata dall'Istituto Internazionale per la Cinematografia Educativa. È pubblicata in cinque lingue: italiano, francese, inglese, tedesco e spagnolo.
30. Rivista mensile, esce a Milano nel 1926.
31. Nasce a Roma nel 1927. Curata da Alessandro Blasetti, è la rivista piú importante degli anni Venti. Si conclude nel 1931.

32. In *L'italiano*, 17–18 (1933).
33. G. Serafini, 'Questa egemonia', *Cantiere*, 23 (1943).
34. V. Mussolini, 'Emancipazione del cinema italiano', *Cinema*, 6, 25 settembre 1936.
35. Le due citazioni sono riportate in C. Carabba, *Il cinema del ventennio nero*, p. 73.
36. Cf. il famoso articolo di Luchino Visconti, 'Cinema antropomorfico', in *Cinema*, ottobre 1943, in cui viene sostenuto che 'il cinema americano è riuscito originale e vivo solo perché, a differenza del nostro, ha in un senso o nell'altro esercitato una funzione morale'.
37. Cf. 'Il cinematografo a Venezia', in *Bertoldo*, 13 novembre 1940. I film a cui Pietrino Bianchi si riferiva erano: *L'assedio dell'Alcazar* di Genina, *Una romantica avventura* di Camerini, e *Don Pasquale* di Mastrocinque, ambientati fuori d'Italia o in un periodo storico diverso dal contemporaneo.
38. In *Nuova Antologia*, Roma, 1 maggio 1929.

12

A resistance to the Resistance? The Italian Peasant in History, 1943–1948

Roger Absalom

> When Adam delved and Eve span,
> Who was then the gentleman?

Peasants have been and still are the object of universally negative stereotypes in almost every culture. The word 'peasant' itself is a term of abuse in our own, and even if *contadino* is not precisely that in Italian popular culture, it is still within sneering distance of *cafone* and *terrone*. Academic culture in Italy also has its *rimozioni* about peasants, if rather less blatant in expression, as can be seen by the reception and *fortuna* of Silone in literature and Nuto Revelli in history. And indeed in Italian historiography, peasants are 'the awkward class' almost by definition.[1] So much so that today's practitioners of historical materialism, neo-Crocean idealism or one of the assorted foreign structuralisms so attractive to the young and trendy might well be tempted to echo the sixteenth-century doggerel collected by Peter Burke:

> In mal far si sono astuti
> Sí li vecchi come i putti
> A me par ribaldi tutti
> Con lor non è da praticare
> De villani non te fidare

The way in which such theories have been used to elucidate, and sometimes to elude, the *questione contadina* is a useful measure of their capacity to illuminate the Italian experience in the period concerned. There are two particular questions which are a test of this: first, what account does the theory give of the successes and failures of the armed Resistance in mobilising peasants to support it? and, second, how far is there any necessary connection between the Resistance and the process whereby after the war the 'grande speranza', which between 1943 and 1948 appeared so dramatically to mobilise millions of supposedly 'inert' peasants, became the 'grande delusione' which in the following two decades demobilised them, historically speaking, with equal suddenness?

At the outbreak of war in 1939, with almost fifty per cent of the population getting their living from the land, though Italy was clearly an industrializing power, the politics, the social and economic behaviour, and the mentalities of the bulk of the population were still inseparable from a peasant past, and for nearly half of them, from a peasant present.

One aspect of the peasant experience in this critical period which makes a useful starting point for further reflection is the extraordinary response to the 'outbreak of peace' on 8 September 1943. Iris Origo tells of a peasant deserter breathlessly assuring her that 'È la pace, la pace incondizionata', and all over the countryside of central and northern Italy, innumerable bonfires were lit to celebrate the 'tutti a casa' with which there was an instantaneous mass complicity whose most visible expression was the kitting out with civilian dress of hundreds of thousands of Italian deserters and foreign escapers. Some of both kinds, and a few long-term anti-Fascists, headed for the hills and were promptly dubbed 'i ribelli' by sympathetic peasants who provided them with food and local information, but conspicuously did not join them. Neither at this stage nor later was there any sign of peasant willingness to engage in offensive actions, far less a mass uprising.

The instinctive response by the non-peasant anti-Fascist élites to these and other ambiguities of peasant attitudes in 1943–5, to what might be termed the 'resistance to the Resistance', is reflected memorably in the opening words of Nuto Revelli's introduction to his *Il mondo dei vinti*, the book which has provided us with the most complete transcript to date of the collective memory of the *mondo contadino* in the period concerned. In them he expresses his 'rabbia giovane' as a young Alpino officer just back from the Russian front and already determined to join the partisans: 'Non capivo perché la gente non scegliesse la strada aperta della ribellione. . . . Mi dicevo: "Se le madri degli alpini 'dispersi' sapessero, se avessero vissuto un attimo solo della nostra ritirata, con le mani ammazzerebbero i fascisti e i tedeschi, li strozzerebbero"'.[2]

This theme is not new in Italian radical politics: essentially it is a return to what may be termed the 'Pisacane syndrome', which sees the most oppressed social class, the peasantry, as the key to revolutionary opportunity. Today that may seem oddly anachronistic. But even if we accept the truth of Sylos Labini's remark that the peasants have solved the *questione contadina* by simply disappearing, it is also true, as Gramsci once pointed out, that 'interpretations of the past ... are not "history" but present-day politics *in nuce*'. So the last (but perhaps not the least) manifestations of the *questione contadina* may still have some relevance, provided we can find a way to retrieve them which is capable of overcoming some major structural obstacles to 'modelling' the behaviours of the protagonists concerned.

For the historian, in fact, what is still most problematic about the recent role of peasants as 'subjects' in Italian history is, precisely, the character of their 'subjectivity'. What are the questions they have asked of 'modernity' and what answers have they given themselves? What has been the nature of their participation in the processes of economic and social change which have affected the country so radically over the last century? Does, indeed, any retrievable evidence exist of the specifics of such participation? If we put aside the utterances of ideological ventriloquists, there is not much to go on: trial records, land surveys, parliamentary inquiries, the gleanings (too often manipulated) of ethnologists and social anthropologists.

And even such documentary sources as exist, and are accessible, may be misleading in various important ways, for what a literate élite culture records of the utterances in 'evidence' of a subordinate and largely illiterate one is defined by the interests and qualified by the sensibility of the former not the latter. In such circumstances the danger of inventing rather than retrieving the past looms large.

These are daunting considerations and when we turn to the way historians have dealt with the *questione contadina* in the Resistance context we may not be surprised to find that this dimension has remained largely unexplored. And in this, history is merely repeating itself. The radicals of the Risorgimento whose failure to make a 'bourgeois revolution' is traditionally lamented by the Italian Left, and of whose ideas

Pisacane's thinking is only an early expression, consistently got the peasant equation wrong precisely because they did not perceive the significance of crucial *longue durée* elements. And, ironically, to call the Resistance a 'secondo Risorgimento', as Italian historians have often done, may be a not-so-flattering truth about the anti-Fascist élites which led the struggle in 1943–5.

In the immediate post-war period, however, this was the prevalent view of the matter. Between 1945 and 1965, a period which was dominated, in Guido Quazza's words, by the 'scourge of political history', the major works on the Resistance were celebrations much more than analyses. Despite innovative sections on partisan songs and *noms de guerre*, even the stylistically outstanding piece of historical writing of this period, Roberto Battaglia's *Breve storia della Resistenza*, was politically motivated in a bad sense in its attempt to insinuate an increasingly hegemonic role in the Resistance for the Communist 'new party' designed by Palmiro Togliatti. Subsequent accounts from the same standpoint were cast, if perhaps less skilfully, in a similar mould.

Yet, as Quazza himself has recently pointed out, long before the first timid ripple of 'revisionism' appeared in the historiography of the Resistance in the late 1960s, film directors, poets, and novelists had already produced, out of their creative encounters with the social reality of 1943–5, imaginative works which clearly expressed and reflected essential characteristics which the historians were failing to confront: the real limits of the Resistance as a force for renewal and the reasons for the continuities between Fascist and Christian-Democrat Italy.

Some of Italy's finest modern literature can be found in these encounters: Cassola's *Ragazza di Bube* and *Viganó's Agnese va a morire* live in the memory. And within and around this flowering there were writers such as Pavese, Carlo Levi, Calvino, Moravia and, above all, Fenoglio who had, in the pursuit of other private and public truths also retrieved disturbing images of a peasant Italy distrustful of or indifferent to or ambiguously mobilised by anti-Fascists and Fascists alike.

For a long period such perceptiveness was not widely shared by the historians. It was not until 1964 and 1965 that the first articles giving more than a passing and triumphalistic mention to peasants, and examining their habitat and culture as significant factors in the course and outcomes of the Resistance, appeared in the pages of the latter's house-journal, *Il Movimento di Liberazione in Italia* (subsequently retitled *Italia contem-*

poranea). And even these concentrated on military and economic aspects. Almost another decade was to pass before serious historiographical attention began to be paid to the role of the peasantry in the Fascist and Resistance periods, and even here, in many of the monographs there still lurked uncritical assumptions about the creation of a 'new historic bloc of workers and peasants' which had about them more than a whiff of the then heavily-promoted 'compromesso storico'.

In 1976, finally, Guido Quazza published his seminal *Resistenza e storia d'Italia. Problemi ed ipotesi di ricerca*, signalling, or so it seemed, a new epoch in Resistance historiography as a whole and raising some of the crucial aspects of the *questione contadina*. But Quazza's challenge to Italian historians to find more convincing ways to relate Fascism and the Resistance movement to the previous and subsequent course of Italian history and at every level of enquiry, though immensely stimulating, did not elicit the anticipated response in the form of a new general history of the Resistance which could be compared with Battaglia's pioneering work of 1954. Instead, but perhaps not altogether unfortunately, the best work of the last decade has been devoted to the detailed studies not so much of the Resistance in particular areas as of particular areas in the period of the Resistance. Such studies have at last begun to take greater account of the relationship between *Resistenza* and *mondo contadino*. In Massimo Legnani's phrase, it has finally been realised that it is pointless to go on asking the same meaningless question about 'da che parte stavano i contadini'. And by 1985 Quazza, describing the findings of a comparative study of attitudes to family, work, authority and religion in a Piedmontese community (which, incidentally, showed that the answers given, down to the very words used, were virtually identical over the last 400 years), could exclaim: 'Ecco che di colpo la discussione, durata quarant'anni, sulla Resistenza tradita, muta significato, per non dire si svuota. Venti mesi di guerriglia in loco non possono trasformare la politica del Paese perché non possono mutare in profondità il tessuto sociale'.[3]

At this point it is hard not to conclude that the existing historiography of the Italian Resistance explains neither the initial mobilisation nor the subsequent demobilisation of the peasants in the period between the fall of Mussolini and the first land-reform decree, the *Lodo De Gasperi* of 1948. It may even be arguable that the latter marked not so much the start of a serious effort to defuse an unassuaged peasant hunger for land by a far-reaching programme of reform as the end, with the possible exception of a few parts of the South, of any serious desire by the peasants to benefit from one. After that, despite some powerful eddies and cross-currents, the tide of peasant syndical militancy ebbed rapidly and the wartime upsurge of psycho-cultural energy which had set it racing was diverted to other, mainly non-political, goals.

For we should not allow the apparent inertia of the peasantry's labyrinthine cultures throughout the course of post-unification history to mislead us into supposing peasants to be merely the passive objects of historical process. Least of any class is a peasantry a mere empty vessel into which the élite of the moment can pour its doctrines; on the contrary, peasant cultures can best be understood as protean collective *mentalités*, capable of assimilating to the accumulated and contradictory cognitive-affective maps of their 'wisdoms' almost any proposition from above or outside. They are able to appropriate 'symbolically', in a process not far removed from the procedures of magical ritualization, of sacralization, both disaster and the millennium, war and tyranny on the one hand and the 'world turned upside down' on the other. Events and circumstances in Italy in 1943–8, during *emergenza, resistenza* and *ricostruzione-restaurazione* need to be considered in this light if we are to characterise adequately where Italy's post-war reserves not merely of labour power but of energy, thrift and initiative came from, together with some of its most persistent social and political problems.

This type of speculative analysis is not supposed to be what historians do. Yet to common sense as well as to anthropologists sacrality reveals itself as the most persistent characteristic of cultures emerging from the direct productive relationship of human and natural environment. And sacrality, precisely because it can be manipulated by, for example, propitiatory ritual, is not merely an acknowledgement of the arbitrary uncontrollability of power, it is also *a way of controlling it*: within *this* 'cognitive map' it makes perfectly good sense to assimilate rather than resist the demands of the élite culture. The point, however, is that such assimilation also *transforms* its object, imposing a different, more protean rationality which can accommodate political and even economic paradoxes which the paradigms of the élite culture systematically exclude.[4]

And Quazza's comment on the wishful thinking which underlies forty years of Resistance historiography might be applied just as aptly to subsequent analyses of post-war development which assume the extinction almost overnight of these *longue durée* components of peasant culture followed by the apocalyptic surrender *en masse* of the Italian peasantry to urban life-styles and values.

This is not the place to establish the full implausibility of this common interpretation. But an examination of the characteristics and the behaviour of the 'social fabric' to which Quazza refers, at the moment when it became the more or less reluctant host to the Resistance movement, may provide some clues as to what kind of a force for change, both then and later, the peasants, or some of them, were.

With 8 September 1943 the peasants had to live with 'two occupations and three governments'. The most significant features of all of them, from the point of view of the peasant, were their defective legitimacy (to obey any of them automatically turned you into an outlaw for the others), and the relative resistibility of their bureaucratic attempts to organise and reorganise agricultural production and distribution. The peasant response was universal and unequivocal: large quantities of products failed to reach both the *ammassi* in Fascist-controlled areas, and the *granai del popolo* set up in the liberated South.

These phenomena cannot be dismissed simply as matters of material survival. The economy, as always, was also a moral economy. The fact that the Resistance movement claimed to have motivated and organised both the initial looting of grain stocks and the later non-delivery of produce in the unliberated areas did not by any means guarantee that adequate food supplies would always be diverted to meet its needs. For there was now another bidder for the peasant's canny attentions: the so-called 'black market' (which it would be better to define as the 'real market') which not only dominated economic production and distribution but also provided both legitimacy for law-breaking and opportunities for upwards mobility.

These were the material and moral conditions in many areas in which armed bands of the Resistance movement operated, seeking safety and room for manoeuvre in remote places but dependent increasingly on local rural populations for their survival. Inevitably they increasingly sought recruits and supplies from them. And inevitably when fair means of obtaining supplies did not suffice, they resorted to foul. Naturally: the Resistance was not a middle-class charity; it had to survive. In this kind of competition, material and moral, the Resistance could not rely on permanently occupying the high ground of peasant esteem.

Nor, in the circumstances obtaining in Italy in 1943–5, could it become a fully-fledged peasant Resistance, comparable with some of those in the Balkan countries. Although the populations of the Italian partisan republics of 1944 were peasants almost to a man, volunteers from among them rarely constituted as much as twenty per cent of partisan manpower and those that did join were usually from the peasantry's undisciplined, anarchic fringe.[5] Perhaps the most interesting of these republics, from the point of view of the *questione contadina*, was in a part of Italy already imbued with a tradition of peasant-led autonomy. This was the Astigiano, where the *Partito dei contadini* created by Alessandro Scotti in 1920 provided the Republic of Alto Monferrato with models of organisation and action by and for peasants which they had already recognised as legitimate. It is only here that we find predominantly peasant partisan bands with peasant leaders inclined to pursue peasant objectives by peasant tactics.

Yet even here the peasants turn out to be an 'awkward class' *par excellence* for those whose ideology casts peasants in the role of naturally subordinate allies of more 'advanced' classes. The awkwardness is vividly conveyed in his memoirs by Italo Nicoletto, a Communist militant of twenty years standing who in 1944 was the Political Commissar of the Monferrato Garibaldini partisans. When he first met one of the peasant partisan leaders, Primo Rocca, he found that 'non aveva molta stima di quelli che venivano dalla città, li considerava dei burocrati, dei signorini . . .'; and he went on to sum Rocca up as:

> assurto al ruolo di comandante da un'origine popolare e da un'esperienza ribellistica e sovversiva non riducibile alla formazione politica e di partito. . . . Si era avvicinato agli ideali comunisti sulla base di quello che aveva potuto leggere sulla stampa fascista, che descriveva i militanti del partito come uomini duri, feroci con i nemici, estremisti irriducibili, e vi si era riconosciuto.[6]

The Repubblica dell'Alto Monferrato is in any case an exception which appears to prove a more general rule: that the Italian peasants' relationship with Resistance was often perceived by them less as a deliverance than as an extension of that inexorably oppressive *destino contadino* characterised by Revelli as a fatalistic passivity, only rarely punctuated by collective revolt, in the face of injustice and dearth, and whose formulation in the Monferrato Anna Bravo reports as 'lavorare e sopportare'. And even in the Repubblica dell'Alto Monferrato, the attitude of the mass of peasants to those like Rocca who were their 'figli uguali e diversi' was ambivalent, seeing them both as the precursors and instruments of change, as 'un protagonista che incarna le speranze collettive', and at the same time as 'elementi di disturbo che urtano uno stato di cose accettate'.[7]

Thus, while over much of German-occupied Italy the Resistance movement may be fairly said to have developed some form of symbiotic relationship with the peasant population, the nature of the symbiosis and of the social and psychological processes which constituted it were often paradoxical and always ambiguous. Later claims that there were areas where genuine mass-participation in Resistance struggle, if not in actual combat, had really occurred, with 'every farmhouse a fortress and every ditch a trench', certainly need to be regarded as no more than metaphors for a widespread and profound hostility to Fascists and Germans which, within a tradition of devious minimal compliance with any form of authority, took whatever chance it could to make its point but rarely courted outright conflict.[8]

This deeply-rooted canniness is not easily eradicated from collective mentalities even by traumas such as those experienced by Italian peasants between 1943 and 1948. It connects with centuries, indeed with millennia, of survival against the odds of nature, fraud and force. There seems to be no intrinsic reason why its stratagems, and the forms of solidarity which underpin them, cannot be transferred to, or even rebuilt in, what have been aptly called 'cities of peasants'. Nor is there any unequivocal evidence that either the canniness or the kindness are quickly and totally deleted from the collective awareness by economic and social promotion. It is not from peasants that pure *homo economicus* is readily fashioned, but rather from grocers' daughters.

These intuitions seem to be borne out by the results of fieldwork on the attitudes and behaviour of many Italian peasants in the period considered. The Manichean choices implied by modern 'total war' were often eluded in a paradoxical acceptance of inconsistency and an admirable avoidance of rational inhumanity.

In Italy war and civil war did not, however, leave only grim, untempered memories of hatred and sorrow. There were also episodes which could be comfortably absorbed into the lengthy peasant repertory of instructive fable. Their distinctive flavour, and the trace they have left in popular culture, is neatly illustrated by a situation of 'unconditional peace' described by one informant who was an impressionable teenager at the time, living in a farmhouse at San Gervasio, near Marano Lagunare, on the coast of Friuli. The house consisted of three separate dwellings round a common courtyard, in each of which lived a family providing an evening meal, respectively, for parties of New Zealand escapers, of Italian partisans and of German coastal defence troops. Each family was aware of what the others were doing (though their guests were not) and the children were sworn to silence. No one was betrayed on either side and care was taken to ensure the failure of planned ambushes: 'Bisognava mantenere la pace. Noi si era amici di tutti'.[9]

In the post-war atmosphere of myth-making, the historiographical problematic represented by the forms of peasant participation and non-participation in the Resistance (and in its legend) was ignored, or at best, glossed over. We may perhaps begin to make better sense of it if we accept that the Italian peasants in general only participated on their own unstated terms and that these terms were the outcome more of *longue durée* factors than of the way political Italy had been made and remade. The feebleness of public and the fierce strength of private attachments, the longing for utopia and the easy tolerance of contradiction, the puritanical terrorist and the sybaritic workaholic are puzzling, frightening or irritating features of Italian social and cultural reality which still wash back into an ostensibly modern economy and politics. It seems reasonable to suspect that most of them are related to that very recent, but strongly repressed, collective experience of a process whereby elements of their own world-view, their own values and their own canniness enabled the peasants of Italy to mobilise themselves for survival, and better than survival, in radically changed social and economic, conditions. The reality and the myth of the Resistance grew alongside this process, and sometimes intermingled with it, but did not cause it.

So Nuto Revelli may have got it wrong when he called his book *Il mondo dei vinti*: perhaps, deviously as usual, the peasants are still in the fight.

Notes

1. Cf. T. Shanin, *The Awkward Class* (Oxford, 1972).
2. Nuto Revelli, *Il mondo dei vinti* (Turin, 1977) 2 vols, pp. xix–xx.
3. Guido Quazza, 'Conclusioni', in *Contadini e partigiani* (Alessandria, 1986) p. 386. He goes on to say that the *svolta decisiva* occurred during the economic boom of the 1960s; I would take issue with this as it may be as misleading as locating it in the Resistance: looking for *svolte decisive* is part of the trouble.
4. Cf. Franco Ferrarotti, *Il paradosso del sacro* (Bari, 1983) pp. 143–4: ' . . . il sacro è tale proprio in quanto si sottrae e travalica le leggi del mercato, sfida la logica delle istituzioni formali ed esalta la funzione sociale dell'utopia. . . . La genesi del sacro è nel bisogno di comunità'; see also Michael Barkun, *Disaster and the Millennium* (Yale, London, 1974) for an overview of modern theory on 'collective cultures' and how they adapt to irruptions of superior power, human or natural.
5. Moreover peasant partisans have tendencies to indiscriminate bloodthirstiness (as Fenoglio's 'Johnny' discovered early in his career), which in practice can make them more of a liability than an asset and certainly offends the susceptibilities of town-bred, middle-class leaders as much as it goes against the disciplined grain of the PCI worker-militant.
6. I. Nicoletto, *Anni della mia vita* (Brescia, 1981) p. 170, cited in Anna Bravo, 'I partigiani e la popolazione contadina nell'Astigiano', in *Contadini e partigiani*, p. 19.
7. Ibid., p. 24.
8. E. Montevecchi, *La battaglia politica dei comunisti imolesi nelle pagine della Comune, gennaio-novembre 1944* (Imola, 1965) p. 86, cited in Paolo Spriano, *Storia del Partito comunista italiano* (Turin, 1975) vol. 4, p. 361.
9. The informant was Sig.a Milan, now of Marano Lagunare, interviewed 5 July 1984; she added that she was sent on occasion to warn partisans of German plans to ambush them; and vice versa.

13

Experience and Myth in the Fiction of Giuseppe Dessí*

John C. Barnes

This paper will examine the extent to which Dessí in his fiction drew on lived experience and the manner in which he handled it. It will deal with 'lived experience' under two headings (though the distinction between them is at times blurred): Dessí's own inner experience (the auto-biographical ·strand); and his share in collective experience (which includes both local *cronaca* and the broader historical perspective).

One of the mainsprings of Dessí's earliest novel, *San Silvano*, published in 1939,[1] is the relationship between its first-person narrator, Pino, and his sister. Dessí (familiarly known as Beppe), on the other hand, had no sister. This important component in the novel, then, is plainly not based on his own experience in the obvious sense. But the writer always wished he had had a sister,[2] and appears, as it were, to have compensated for the lack in his first novel. So the relationship between brother and sister in *San Silvano* may after all be said to spring negatively from an autobiographical starting-point. Reality is remodelled according to an idealised vision.

The other central strand of this novel is the narrator's use of an extended visit to his native town, San Silvano, after several years away on the *continente*, to commune with his place of origin, increase his self-awareness, and come to terms with the fact that his youth and the world of his youth belong to the past. Here there is a considerable

* I welcome this opportunity of thanking Dessí's widow, Luisa, and his brother, Franco, for the generosity they have shown in helping me with my work on the novelist. Much of the information presented here would not have been acquired without their assistance. I am also grateful to Doug Thompson for his encouragement and advice during the evolution of this paper. Part of the research involved was funded by the British Academy and by the Carnegie Trust for the Universities of Scotland.

autobiographical element. San Silvano is clearly Villacidro, where Dessí was brought up. By the time the novel was published, Dessí had been living in continental Italy for eight years, and his visceral relationship with Villacidro was presumably then what it was years later when he described it in a television interview: 'Da ragazzo ... a Cagliari ... non facevo altro che sognare Villacidro, i boschi di Villacidro, i monti e l'aria sottile di Villacidro. Le mie radici ... sono qui, a Villacidro .... Da ragazzo, solo qui mi sentivo a casa mia, solo qui mi pareva che la vita avesse un senso. E anche ora tutte le volte che ci ritorno mi sembra di poter capire veramente tutto'.[3]

This basic autobiographical situation is consolidated by numerous sporadic. factors imported from the non-fictional world, both auto-biographical and external to the author's personality. Dessí's own favourite reading as a youth – Rilke, Leibniz, and Spinoza – is reapplied to the narrator, a writer, like Dessí in the late 1930s, who so far has published only on the *terze pagine* of newspapers. There is a pine-wood, unusual in Sardinia, planted by the narrator's grandfather, which manifestly parallels the pine-wood planted on the upper slopes of Villacidro in the 1890s by Dessí's maternal grandfather, Giuseppe Pinna, when he was the town's *sindaco*. There are memories of the absence of Dessí's father at the front in the Italo–Turkish War and on the Carso, together with memories of his parents' contrasting attitudes to their home town. There is the Ben family from Treviso, with their Venetian accent – clearly modelled on the Grandesso family, originally from Venetia, who moved to Villacidro from Emilia in 1923, when Dessí was fourteen.[4] There are fragments of nineteenth-century local history, involving smelting-works before 1856 and Tuscan charcoal-burners after that date. And although San Silvano itself is not described in detail, it is recognisable as Villacidro not only by the pine-wood but also, for instance, by the very distinctive communal laundry (*lavatoio pubblico*), where women could go and do their washing, adjacent to the house belonging to the narrator's family – and to one of the houses the Dessí family lived in.

So despite the presence of a major element of pure fabrication (the sister Dessí never had), the novel has a strong autobiographical impetus behind it, though Dessí here uses experience in a fragmentary, kaleido-scopic manner. *San Silvano* is the most Proustian of his novels, in the sense that it evinces an interest in the cultivation of memory and multi-dimensional awareness as means of self-knowledge. Russo aptly describes it as 'romanzo d'atmosfere e di suggestioni, piú che di persone e di fatti ... in cui il paese nativo è visto attraverso il dormiveglia dei ricordi'.[5] The memories in question fall into both the categories outlined at the outset of this paper, but because they constitute a *dormiveglia* the significance of both is subsumed within the category of autobiography. The author might be said to show a psychological need for a world recreated in his own image.

One of the many characters who make a fleeting appearance in *San Silvano* is Giacomo Scarbo, a cultured and highly intelligent friend of the protagonist's elder brother when they were teenagers, and 'il modello a cui tendevamo' (p. 96). Giacomo Scarbo also hovers in the background in Dessí's first book of short stories, *La sposa in città* (1939), and in the novel *I passeri* (1953). In another novel, *Introduzione alla vita di Giacomo Scarbo* (1948), he is the central figure, as a boy (up to the age of about ten); and his most substantial appearance as an older character occurs in the seventh and unfinished novel, *La scelta*. *La scelta* was to have been Dessí's autobiographical novel, as is clear both from the eighty pages of fragments he actually wrote of it and from his notes, which have been carefully studied by Anna Dolfi.[6] The choice alluded to in the title of this last novel is explicitly and generally the choice between the active life and the contemplative life, between heroism and quietism; implicitly and particularly it is the choice between two modes of anti-Fascism, that of the sword and that of the pen. Giacomo is very clearly an *alter ego* – Dessí called him 'questo amico mai esistito, al quale avrei voluto somigliare'.[7] In *La scelta* Giacomo is carefully given an identical background to the first-person narrator; for instance, both their mothers died when they were very young, so that they were both brought up by stepmothers; and in their teens they both became passionate admirers of the same authors. Potentially, then, the young narrator and the young Giacomo are the same person, but at the crucial point of choosing a destiny Giacomo (in the notes for *La scelta*) goes off to fight against Franco in the Spanish Civil War, subsequently (in *I passeri*) volunteers for service in the Second World War, and by 1943 is missing, presumed killed; while Dessí, although active underground as an anti-Fascist during the closing years of the regime, saw himself principally as a cultural *resistente* rather than as a hero.[8] This use of Giacomo Scarbo, it seems to me, is one of Dessí's most original contributions to the art of autobiographical fiction, and is similar to the creation of the sister in *San Silvano* in disclosing an aspect of autobiography by negative means.

Not only Dessí's novels but many of his short stories, too, present fairly accurate glimpses of moments in his own life. For instance, in the 1958 text 'Il distacco',[9] subsequently incorporated into the closing section of *Paese d'ombre*,[10] he relives the desperation he experienced during the First World War, between the ages of six and nine, whenever his father returned to the front for what, as the boy fully realised, could easily be the last time. Other stories, such as 'Una collana' (1937)[11] or 'Lebda' (1942),[12] recall his father and his military friends in the months immediately following the Great War. Others again, for instance 'Un'ospite di Marsiglia' (1938)[13] or 'L'uomo col cappello' (1949)[14] evoke the writer's incipient interest in girls. 'Suor Emanuela' (1940)[15] is set in the brief period he spent at a boarding-school in Cagliari, and shows how to a small extent the total lack of a feminine presence in the institution was compensated for by one of the nuns in the adjoining convent. 'Fuochi sul molo' (1959)[16] reflects a period after he moved to a state school in Cagliari, lodging with an elderly aunt who died while he was alone in the house with her. 'Il pozzo' (1956)[17] concerns the death, of typhus, when the author was seventeen, of Elisa Grandesso, the first girl he loved – an incident which is written about at length at the appropriate point in his diary.[18] A group of stories including 'Inverno' (1936)[19] and 'Cacciatore distratto' (1938),[20] both written very soon after the time recreated, arise from his love for an uneducated country girl called Natalina, who in the stories is renamed Luciana. 'Vacanza nel Nord' (1965)[21] recounts aspects of the academic year 1936–7, which Dessí spent teaching at a boarding- school in Paderno del Grappa. More unusually, 'Commiato dall'inverno',[22] of 1958, when Dessí was forty-nine, deals with the present, when he is beginning to feel old, and compares his relationship with his father when he was young to his relationship with his own son, who was born in 1943.

Although Dessí was by no means systematic, and although some of his short stories would never have been written had he not been goaded into writing them by newspaper editors with space to fill (particularly Enrico Falqui, who edited Page 3 of *Il tempo*),[23] it is legitimate to see his scattered writings as activating a loose master-plan, which it is not altogether ridiculous to compare to Petrarch's *Canzoniere*. The auto-biographical *Bildungsroman*, *La scelta*, had it been completed, might have done more than it does to clarify the master-plan. Although most of

Dessí's autobiographical texts are insubstantial when read in isolation, read together they bear witness to quite a considerable autobiographical intent. Roy Pascal, in his book *Design and Truth in Autobiography*,[24] distinguishes between autobiography, the study of a whole life, and what he calls 'autobiographical writings', which 'limit themselves to one particular experience or group of experiences that bare the core of the personality'. Dessí's autobiographical pieces obviously fall into the second of these categories, but his output as a whole goes some way, I think, towards constituting autobiography in the full sense. As we shall see later, however, such an approach by no means reveals a lack of creative imagination; for Dessí autobiographical matter is a springboard for creativity.

The element of experience in Dessí's second novel, *Michele Boschino* (1942), is largely confined to the area of *cronaca*, and to the second half of the book, which is based on a local figure in Villacidro. The model for the eponymous protagonist was a man called Giuseppe Rasinu, who used to eke out an existence by buying oranges in Villacidro and walking the ten miles to Gonnosfanadiga in the one direction or the six-and-a-half miles to San Gavino Monreale in the other, to sell them. In his later life Boschino lives in a town called Ultra, which is recognisable as Villacidro (it has, for instance, the *muraglione* of which we shall have more to say later). More precisely, he lives in a shed in the garden of one of the local families, though that part of the garden is the object of a long-standing legal wrangle with the family next door. This, too, is based on experience: indeed, the family next door, the Monti, corresponds to the Dessí family. Giuseppe Rasinu did live in a shed on land adjoining the Dessí home and technically belonging to them; and that land had been misappropriated, in Dessí's childhood, by the next-door neighbours, the Atzeri, headed by Avvocato Atzeri, and transformed in the novel into the family of Notaio Almerio.

In this case the importation from experience, although substantial, is little more than a starting-point: it would seem that, genetically speaking, the second half of the novel is the begetter of the first, which deals with Boschino's early life in another part of Sardinia, and presumably corresponds either to speculation on Dessí's part or to a more indirect form of experience if the author acquired it from Rasinu himself. Even within the *Parte seconda* the story of Boschino is only a starting-point:

the second half of the novel, unlike the first, is narrated in the first person by Filippo, a student and a neighbour of the Monti in Ultra; and the primary interest of the second half focuses on the consciousness of Filippo, in which a fascination with Boschino is a conspicuous factor. Dessí's art here could be described as an imaginative use of empathy. For the moment, however, all we need to observe about *Michele Boschino*, similar in this respect to Dessí's more autobiographical fiction, is that – like Boccaccio and many other narrative writers – Dessí is happy to take over an existing story as grist to the mill of his own creativity.

The use of external events from real life is also characteristic of Dessí's short stories. For instance 'La frana' (1950),[25] the longest of his short stories, gives an accurate account – with a few of the details altered – of a tale of financial decline, fraud, and bankruptcy which, when he was nineteen, befell his mother's side of the family and resulted in the suicide of one of his uncles. 'Le scarpe nere' (1948)[26] draws on another incident Dessí witnessed in Villacidro at the age of nineteen, when a girl of about his own age hanged herself.[27] 'La cometa' (1945)[28] reflects on the destinies of six sisters who were cousins of his. And according to some of today's oldest inhabitants of Villacidro,[29] the action of 'La ballerina di carta' (1956),[30] too, is partly based on· an episode of local *cronaca*. Evidently Signor A. in the story is modelled on a man called Oliari, who was fair-haired and came from Venetia (or perhaps from Venezia Giulia or Austria). He was interned in Villacidro with his wife and daughters during the First World War, and rented the ground floor of the Bishop's Palace. He was thought to be half mad, and, when visited by the *parroco*, Dottor Giuseppe Ortu (who subsequently became a notable local anti-Fascist), he threatened him with an axe. Later in·the War, Oliari and his family were drowned in the sinking of the *Tripoli*, a passenger ferry working between Olbia and Civitavecchia.

These reminiscences do not account for the part of Dessí's story directly reflected by the title – though it could be added that the paper ballerina herself may be connected with the writer's uncle Emanuele Pitzalis, who impressed Dessí when he was a boy by making paper frogs that jumped. But the most interesting aspect of experience exploited in this *novella*, it seems to me, lies in its setting. Brian Moloney, in his anthology of *Novelle del Novecento*, observes that the story seems to be set in Villacidro,[31] and this can be confidently confirmed. Like the town in the narrative, Villacidro *was* served by the Società delle Ferrovie

Complementari Sarde – indeed it was a terminus of the line that had its other terminus at Isili[32] – , which meant that when travelling by rail from Cagliari to Villacidro one had to leave the Ferrovie Reali and change trains at Sanluri. More importantly, the description of the town in the *novella*, with the exception of one four-letter detail, exactly reproduces Villacidro: 'Davanti all'ufficio postale si leva altissimo il Muraglione, che insieme con il Municipio forma quasi un'acropoli, non priva, a distanza, di una certa imponenza architettonica. L'altra bellezza del paese, sul versante opposto della Fluminera, è il Palazzo arcivescovile, costruito sulle rovine dell'antico castello'. Almost immediately after which, we read of 'il Muraglione e il Palazzo arcivescovile, che si vedono dalla pianura e formano un insieme caratteristico e riconoscibile, che spicca sul fondo delle pinete e nelle cartoline pubblicitarie di una locale fabbrica di liquori'.[33] The sole element of poetic licence here is the prefix *arci-*. The Bishop's Palace, dating from 1770 and rebuilt in 1838, stands on the foundations of the manor-house of the Marchesi Brondo.[34] The *pinete* are those which previously appeared in *San Silvano*, and figure so prominently in one of Dessí's novels, *Paese d'ombre*, as to find their way into the title of the English translation (*The Forests of Norbio*).[35] And the 'locale fabbrica di liquori', belonging to the Murgia family and founded in 1882, is still Villacidro's best-known manufacturing industry, producing a *liquore* known simply as Villacidro, or Villacidro Murgia.

'La ballerina di carta' and *Michele Boschino*, then, together with the frequently autobiographical character of Dessí's writing, suggest that his fiction is very much based on the *local* reality of the town in which he was brought up. And such a suggestion is not far wide of the mark. There are a number of his short stories (mainly based on his lived experiences) with other settings – settings which became familiar to him during particular phases in his life – such as Cagliari, Sassari, Pisa, Paderno del Grappa, Teramo, and so on. But a substantial proportion of his short stories are set in and around Villacidro, even if the town is never given its real-life name. What is more remarkable is that every single one of Dessí's six-and-a-half novels is set in the same restricted area. Dessí's home town is variously referred to by such names as San Silvano, Norbio, Ruinalta, Ordena, or simply V. These names are used so regularly that they become a kind of shorthand telling the reader economically that he is back on the north-eastern slopes of Monte Linas. It is true that the names shift around, so that the name San Silvano, for instance, in one novel is applied to Villacidro, in another to Sardara, and in another again to Gonnosfanadiga. But this only marginally lessens the constancy of these names, while there are others that broaden the range of this elegant literary game: the name Acquapiana, for instance, is regularly applied to Sanluri, where one had to change trains when travelling by rail between Villacidro and Cagliari.

Dessí's share in collective experience is used on a large scale in his two historical novels, *Il disertore* and *Paese d'ombre* – the last two whole novels he wrote. *Paese d'ombre*, first published in 1972, in many ways does for Sardinia what *I vecchi e i giovani* did for Sicily – each is *the* historical novel of its own island in the decades preceding and following the Unification of Italy, and each highlights the unsatisfactory side, for the island concerned, of union with the mainland. Neither of them, however, presents all the faces of its island. In Dessí's case the main focus is once again on Villacidro, though it is made to seem less exclusive to the average reader by the renaming of the town as, on this occasion, Norbio. In any case, the focus is not constantly as narrow as that, since there are inhabitants of Norbio who go and work in the coal mines of the Sulcis-Iglesiente on the other side of Monte Linas, and this leads to quite generous coverage of the severe industrial confrontations that took place there in the early years of socialism, of which the climax was the massacre at Buggerru – Sardinia's Peterloo – in 1904. The central thread of the novel, however, is the life of Dessí's own grandfather Giuseppe Pinna (1850–1920) – the one who became a distinguished *sindaco* of Villacidro. Dessí has no qualms about telling the story of his own family – he even appears himself as a child towards the end. Some of the details are altered; for instance, his mother's death of cancer in 1930 is described at some length but transferred back two generations to become the death of his great-grandmother. And there are certain passages that provide, in Manzonian fashion, the kind of intimate and historically insignificant detail that must needs be created by the novelist *ex nihilo*. But by and large the narration is remarkably truthful for a work of fiction, and the proportion of matter which Manzoni would have termed *verosimile* is much lower than it is in either Pirandello's historical novel or *I promessi sposi*.

Not all the names, either of historical people or of real places, remain unchanged. Villacidro becomes Norbio, the Pinna family becomes the Uras family, the Dessí family (which is in full the Dessí Fulgheri family) is called Fulgheri in the novel, and in fact given a simplified genealogy

which telescopes the joint genealogies of the real-life Dessí and the
real-life Fulgheri. But a remarkable number of the names are taken
straight from life. Thus Norbio has its Piazza Frontera (which includes
the post office of 'La ballerina di carta'), its Mercedarian monastery, its
Via delle Tre Marie, its *palazzo municipale*, which 'dominava piazza
Frontera come un'acropoli' (again), its Fluminera (again), its *palazzo
arcivescovile* (again), its *muraglione* (again), its Via Roma, its church of
Santa Barbara, its Monte Granatico, its Oratorio delle Anime, its
Chiesetta del Carmelo, and its Rione Castangias – just as Villacidro had.
Furthermore, many of the characters are taken from local history with
their real names, even the two most distinguished of the town's inhabit-
ants, Giuseppe Todde (1829–97), who was made Rettore of Cagliari
University (except that Dessí changes his forename to Antonio), and
Antioco Loru (1818–98), the brother of one of Dessí's great-
grandmothers, who became a Senator of the Realm. *Paese d'ombre*,
then, comfortably fits any definition of the historical novel.[36] What is
more, it has been widely publicised as a historical novel, not least by
Dessí in interviews that he gave.[37]

The same is not true of *Il disertore*, which was first published in 1958.
For the average intelligent reader, this text *may* qualify as a historical
novel but it may not do so automatically. One of its strands does very
interestingly portray the early evolution of Fascism (in 1921–2) at the
level of a remote municipality. It does include fleeting references to *a few*
events of the period, such as one of the battles of Doberdò del Lago (near
Gorizia), the march on Fiume, the First World War as a whole, the
transportation of the corpse of the Unknown Soldier from the Carso to
the capital, and the March on Rome, as well as a few nineteenth-
century events, such as the 1820 Legge delle Chiudende (Enclosures Act)
together with the unrest it entailed, and, in the second half of the
century, the commercial exploitation of Sardinia's mines by companies
based in the Italian mainland – especially Tuscany – coupled with the
destruction of much of Sardinia's natural forest to provide charcoal to
fuel the smelting-works. (These nineteenth-century events are naturally
covered more fully in *Paese d'ombre*.) Two historical characters of some
importance are mentioned by their own names: Gabriele d'Annunzio
and Giovan Battista Tuveri (1815–87), whom Lorenzo Del Piano describes as 'il piú originale e profondo scrittore politico che la Sardegna ha
avuto nella seconda metà dell'Ottocento'.[38]

With inside information, however, we know that a lot more of the novel's fabric is historical. The focal town in *Il disertore* is called Cuadu – but it can become perfectly obvious that Cuadu is, once again, Villacidro. Virtually all the distinctive features of Villacidro are there with almost no disguise beyond the change of name of the town itself: the raised *piazza* called Piazza Municipio, accommodating the Municipio and the elementary school; Piazza Frontera below it – down some steps – accommodating the post office (that same old post office) and the *Circolo di Lettura 'Regina Elena'* (*'Regina Margherita'* in the novel); the Muraglione bounding and supporting the raised *piazza* on one side; Via Roma opening out of the lower end of Piazza Frontera; the communal laundry erected in the 1890s at the instigation of *sindaco* Giuseppe Pinna (and, sure enough, at the instigation of *sindaco* Angelo Uras in *Paese d'ombre*); the stream (the Fluminera again, but unnamed this time); the Ponte del Vicario; the Chiesa del Carmelo; Rione Castangias on·the outskirts; the station fifteen minutes' walk from the town centre; and the Oratorio delle Anime in the hills above the town (amid Giuseppe Pinna's pine-trees). All that is missing on this occasion is the Bishop's Palace.

The two most prominent families in Cuadu are the long-established, aristocratic, stagnant, land-owning Manca di Tharros, and the industrial Comina, who have come to prominence more recently and done·very well out of the War. Both these families are, to a greater or lesser extent, modelled on real-life families in Villacidro. The real-life counterpart of the Comina family was – and is – the Murgia family, mentioned earlier in this paper (one of the Cominas' enterprises in the novel is indeed a distillery). Commendatore Alessandro Comina corresponds to Commendatore Gennaro Murgia, the shrewd business man who laid the foundations of the family's fortunes and opened the distillery in 1882. And both men have/had a son killed in the First World War – Benigno Comina in the one case and Sergeant Erminio Murgia in the other.

Where the Manca di Tharros family is concerned, the parallel is between Captain Roberto Manca di Tharros and Brigadier Francesco Dessí Fulgheri, the novelist's own father, though it is not a complete parallel, partly in as much as the Brigadier was fifty in 1920, whereas Roberto Manca seems somewhat younger. Nevertheless, the Dessí family was a landowning family with a touch of minor aristocracy about it (earlier generations had been counts, but the title had lapsed) and, like Roberto Manca, the Brigadier *was* a devout monarchist. What is more, he was the most senior demobilised soldier in Villacidro after the War, with the result that he did become the President of the *Sezione Combattenti*, as does Roberto Manca, and his *Sezione* did subsequently become a *fascio*, as does Roberto's – although, to be scrupulously accurate on a delicate issue, Brigadier Dessí's *fascio* was autonomous, and was later supplanted by another one acknowledging Mussolini as its ultimate leader. This Dessí's father had nothing to do with.[39]

Nor does this exhaust the wealth of detail in *Il disertore* that reflects lived experience. One of the main strands in the narrative concerns the funding and erection of a war memorial, and this may have been inspired by the fact that in 1927 or 1928 Dessí's father instigated the erection of a war memorial in the neighbouring *comune* of Gonnosfanadiga, where he was *podestà*. And the novel tells of an incident in October 1922 when a pretty girl is slightly injured by a stone thrown by a socialist, which event, partly as a matter of chivalry, it seems, proves to be the catalyst behind a significant escalation in the efforts of the proto-Fascists to stamp out socialist agitation. All of this, too, accurately reproduces the writer's recollections of the period.[40] On the other hand, there is much in the novel that, as far as I know, has no basis in lived reality: there was certainly no priest in charge of the parish of Villacidro who could be seen as a model for Don Pietro Coi,[41] and the drama of Mariangela Eca and her two sons, one of whom is the deserter of the title, also appears to be 'verosimile' rather than 'vero' in the Manzonian sense. To this extent *Il disertore* differs from *Paese d'ombre*, where virtually all the action is based on local *cronaca*. Even so, I would contend that *Il disertore*, too, comfortably fits anyone's definition of a historical novel.

The average reader would not know where a writer like Dessí is using his own experience with little or no disguise, and would read and respond to the work of fiction accordingly. But there is a sense in which Dessí was not addressing the average reader. In 1965 he wrote that his 'veri lettori' were still a small group of friends he had had in the 1930s, 'con i quali posso ancora conversare come a quel tempo, ai quali posso fare un resoconto del modo come scrivo un libro'.[42] It seems to me that there is a warning to be heeded here. We can, of course, make excellent sense of Dessí's fiction on the sole basis of the words on the page But in order to appreciate fully what Dessí was undertaking as a writer we need to penetrate his relationship with his own lived experience and that of the community of which he was part.

I have placed some emphasis on the element of repetition in Dessí's narrative texts, especially the recurrence of landmarks in the topography of Villacidro (and a parallel survey could have been conducted in relation to the rural areas outside the town). Repetition can be used to emblematise, as it is (or originally was) in heraldry, and as it is with images such as that of the laurel in the poetry of Petrarch. I should like to argue that Dessí uses repetition, together with selection, in a similarly emblematic manner, and that the constant landmarks are chosen not for purposes of convenience or verisimilitude but as symbols of the constancy of Dessí's focus on Sardinia, especially his own patch of Sardinia.[43] The effect of this use of emblematic landmarks is, paradoxically, to locate his fiction on an abstract, non-specific plane, or at least a pan-Sardinian plane. Although Dessí was especially well placed to realise that Sardinia is by no means a homogeneous island – quite apart from anything else, he lived in Sassari from 1941 to 1948, and subsequently edited the important publication *Scoperta della Sardegna*[44] – , there is none the less a potential ambiguity in much of his writing as to whether his interest embraces the whole of Sardinia or merely that part of it associated with his childhood. The topography of the fiction might suggest the latter, but *Paese d'ombre* and a good number of Dessí's essays and interviews quite clearly demonstrate that his concern is with the island as a whole,[45] at least from *Michele Boschino* onwards (since Michele hails from the centre of the Island).

Villacidro and its environs, then, are mythicised: Dessí creates an ideal vision of them to give them a broader significance. And he does the same – again by means of repetition – in relation to his own life and experiences. This is perhaps shown most clearly in the plan he drew up for *La scelta* in June 1973,[46] where a number of strands are recuperated from *San Silvano* ('Marco ... soffre di profonda nostalgia per Norbio. Torna a Norbio ogni volta che può e ama la vita all'aperto ... Giacomo Scarbo di qualche anno maggiore di Marco, personaggio fantastico, inquietante, *alter ego*'), from *I passeri* ('Giacomo Scarbo va nella Spagna a morire'), and from *Il disertore* ('Nascita del fascismo – riflessi a Norbio') as well as from the short stories ('Ritorno di Francesco dalla guerra .... Rapporti con gli ex-combattenti. Rapporti tra Marco e il padre .... Vita di Marco in collegio .... Marco e Luciana') and from

the essays ('Conoscenza di Emilio Lussu che fonda il partito sardo
d'azione . . . . Attentato a Lussu: scena della piazza . . . . Biblioteca
murata . . . . Marco e Cantimori').[47] These experiences become emblematic of the factors involved in a choice between two fundamental ways
of living one's life – the choice made with contrasting results by Dessí and
by Giacomo Scarbo.

A similar process of emblematisation is applied, thirdly, to historical
events. Dessí's writings present a constant, schematised view of the
destiny of Sardinia, and particularly his own corner of Sardinia, to which
he gives the name Parte d'Ispi (only a slight transfiguration of its
historical name, Parte d'Ippis). In practice, this mythical view begins in
1820 with the Legge delle Chiudende and its social consequences
(mentioned in both San Silvano and Il disertore before being fully
explored in Paese d'ombre). This is coupled with a lack of mutual
understanding between Sardinia and continental Italy, which, both long
before and after Unification, has been combined with a colonial relationship between the two, expressing itself first, in the exploitation by
non-Sardinians of the mines of the Iglesiente (recalled in the same three
novels, especially, again, the last), which gave rise to the development of
the Socialist leagues and the massacre of Buggerru (Il disertore and Paese
d'ombre), and second, in the cynical deforestation of the mountains of
Parte d'Ippis, also by non-Sardinians (San Silvano, Introduzione alla vita
di Giacomo Scarbo, Il disertore, Paese d'ombre).[48]

Like Dante in the Vita nuova, Dessí in San Silvano seems to have been
dimly aware of the focus of his future creative writing – in Dessí's case, on
the axis running between himself and Sardinia. His fiction, coloured by a
determinist view of life which dated from his early reading of such
authors as Leibniz and Spinoza,[49] revolves around a powerful urge to
know, to be critically aware, 'sapere chi siamo' (in Pavese's words) in
relation to the world he grew up in. La sposa in città, Dessí's first volume
of short stories, published only a few weeks before San Silvano, opens
with an introductory essay, entitled ' "La sposa in città" ', which can be
taken as a manifesto. The essay is about an unpublished short story of
Dessí's, 'La sposa in città' (1937)[50] but first the author writes about the
difficulty he has experienced in grasping reality, 'la realtà verso la quale
tendevo con tutte le mie forze e che mi sfuggiva . . . . Se disperatamente
riuscivo ad afferrarmi ad essa, solo brandelli ne restavano tra le mie mani
. . . : frammenti di realtà che . . . lievitavano nella mia fantasia'. When

he first revealed the 'mondo segreto' made up of these fermentations in
the form of a short story ('La sposa in città'), he continues, his cultured
friends liked it, which leads him to speculate thus:

Piacque forse, senza che essi se ne rendessero conto, per l'evidenza
di certe sensazioni gesti e parole che avevano poi ... un'altra storia,
segreta. Cosí che nel mio racconto c'era questa storia segreta, e una
fittizia, di vane parole disposte secondo uno schema comune, quasi
anonimo. E la prima storia, o preistoria che fosse, lievitava nella
fantasia dei miei amici, nel ricordo, animava di fatue suggestioni lo
schema del racconto. Ognuno di essi, come accade, aveva fantasticato
una storia diversa su quella traccia, e del mio racconto ricordava con
precisione solo qualche frammento .... Cosí la 'Sposa in città' visse
per diversi anni nel loro spirito. Ma in realtà era ... soltanto nella
loro fantasia.[51]

At this early stage in his career, then, Dessí saw his artistry as concealing
a 'storia segreta' beneath a 'storia fittizia'; and the 'storia segreta' was to
'lievitare nella fantasia' of the reader – in the same way as fragments of
experience had fermented in the author's imagination to produce the
narrative in the first place – thus giving life to the 'storia fittizia'.

During Dessí's career as a writer, the focus established in *San Silvano*
becomes increasingly insistent, though sometimes tending more towards
the one end of the axis (autobiography) and sometimes more towards the
other (the destiny of Sardinia). In his first novel the two sides of the
relationship are adumbrated in the interaction between Pino and his
sister (though here the novelist's personality is also fragmented and
distributed between Pino, Giulio, and Vincenzo); the relationship
between brother and sister provides the 'storia fittizia', while the 'storia
segreta' is the one about Dessí's rapport with Villacidro or Sardinia. The
formula established in ' "La sposa in città" '· can also be applied to
Michele Boschino, where another version of the same 'storia segreta',
again focusing on the whole of the Dessí–Sardinia axis (though more
explicitly involving Sardinia in its entirety), is concealed by the story of
the relationship between Filippo and Michele – though, as we have seen,
in this case the 'storia fittizia' is not wholly fictitious. But the other four
completed novels show a greater interest in Sardinia than in the novelist;
and accordingly, although the formula involving 'storia fittizia' and

'storia segreta' could probably be applied to *Introduzione alla vita di Giacomo Scarbo* and *I passeri* as well as to *San Silvano* and *Michele Boschino*, by this stage it is perhaps beginning to be less helpful.

If the focus of Dessí's fiction remains relatively constant throughout his career, his handling of lived experience alters radically and in a fairly linear manner. As we have seen, he begins, in *San Silvano*, with an extremely delicate and complex patterning of autobiographical motifs in the service of an overall autobiographical *recherche*, complicated by the inclusion of a major part of the story that originates virtually *ex nihilo* in the writer's imagination. With his next novel, *Michele Boschino*, external experience is drawn on quite heavily as sustenance for a centre of consciousness who is only in a 'secret' sense autobiographical. *Introduzione alla vita di Giacomo Scarbo* is the novel that draws least on the externals of lived experience: although the protagonist is Dessí's *alter ego*, and although, for instance, the serious accident that befalls him at the end of the novel did in fact befall not Dessí himself but his brother Franco, the most notable feature of his early years is that he is brought up by a stepmother, whereas Dessí was not. *I passeri* (1953) is a more successful novel in which the action again shows some resemblance, though not a striking one, to the vicissitudes of Dessí's own family. But here a new element is introduced: an authentic historical situation – that of the period between the liberation of Sardinia (8–13 September 1943) and the end of the Second World War. Not only does this provide an arena for the exercise of Giacomo Scarbo's *scelta* (at least in the mind of his father, who persists in believing him alive); it is also drawn on for the drama of Rita (one of the protagonists), in which a conspicuous part is played by soldiers, both Italian and American.

Until the emergence of this historical dimension, then, Dessí appears to have been drawing progressively less on the *externalia* of his own lived experience; but what *I passeri* introduces (marginally, at least) is the lived experience of a whole population. *Il disertore*, first published only five years after *I passeri*, brings the historical element from the wings on to the stage itself; during those five years Dessí evidently decided that his future role as a novelist would involve a commitment to matters of public importance.[52] As Tondo has acutely remarked, *Il disertore* seems more relevant to the second *dopoguerra* than to the first.[53] And it is the novel in which Dessí progresses furthest from his starting-point, transcending an exclusively Sardinian perspective: while *Il disertore*, like the others, can be seen as a Sardinian novel,[54] it is also the one that has the most to say about life in the wider world. With *Paese d'ombre* Dessí maintains his commitment to the public outlook, but returns to an exclusive concentration on Sardinia in the context of united Italy, highlighting the injustices of external domination and colonial exploitation that have beset the island since 1860 as they did before. And although the novel ends around 1918, it closes with an incident (the killing of Luciano Cambilargiu) which may be seen as projecting into the future, in that it replicates an incident in the early pages of the book (the killing of Don Francesco Fulgheri), thus suggesting that the Sardinians themselves are unreceptive to enlightened progress.[55] At the same time *Paese d'ombre* boldly dispenses with the element of invention *ex nihilo* at the centre of the stage (represented in *Il disertore* by the story of Mariangela, Saverio, and Don Pietro Coi).

For Dessí, reality does not lie in life's external circumstances. Whether dealing with personal or with collective experience, he always pursues reality (a 'storia segreta') behind the façade of the bare facts. As part of this pursuit, he is constantly attentive to the repercussions of events and situations in the minds and hearts of his characters. And he expects these repercussions to 'lievitare nella fantasia' of the reader. In one sense, then, it is unimportant whether the story of a Dessí narrative is taken from lived experience or invented *ex nihilo*. The fact remains, however, that Dessí draws on lived experience very heavily and in highly individual ways. In his novels, at least, he begins and ends with attempts at autobiographical fiction but gradually works towards both a fuller and a simpler treatment of experience: it need be no surprise that *La scelta* was to extend the wholesale and barely camouflaged adoption of *vita vissuta* witnessed in *Paese d'ombre* to the more intimate area of the novelist's own subjective experience (though Anna Dolfi has questioned the likelihood of its ever being completed even if the author had lived longer).[56] Shortly before the end of his life Dessí wrote, referring to *Paese d'ombre*: 'Ho sempre avuto in mente questo libro anche quando stavo scrivendo il mio primo romanzo nel 1939, *San Silvano*. Se non cominciai con *Paese d'ombre* fu perché era troppo ricco e complesso per le mie forze d'allora'.[57] This may, of course, mean that he felt he had not had enough experience to write it in 1939; but perhaps it can also be taken to mean that one of his limitations at that stage was that he felt unable fully to mythicise experience. In that case, learning how to do so was one of the most creative achievements of his career.

Notes

1. Unless otherwise stated, all references to Dessí's fiction in these notes are to the first edition in book form of the text in question, as follows. Short stories: *La sposa in città* (Modena, 1939); *Racconti vecchi e nuovi* (Rome, 1945); *La ballerina di carta* (Bologna, 1957); *Isola dell'Angelo e altri racconti* (Caltanissetta-Rome, 1957); *Lei era l'acqua* (Milan, 1966). Novels: *San Silvano* (Florence, 1939); *Michele Boschino* (Milan, 1942); *Introduzione alla vita di Giacomo Scarbo* (Venice, *s.d.* [1958]); *I passeri* (Pisa, 1955); *Il disertore* (Milan, 1961); *Paese d'ombre* (Milan, 1972); *La scelta*, edited by A. Dolfi and C. Varese (Milan, 1978 [posthumous]).
2. 'Ha sempre desiderato una sorella ma non l'ha mai avuta' (letter from Luisa Dessí to the present writer dated 3 March 1985).
3. Incorporated in the documentary *Giuseppe Dessí*, in the series *Visti da fuori*, made by M. P. Mossa and J. Onnis on behalf of the Sardinian region of Rai-Tv for presentation in 1986.
4. 'I forestieri' (*Il resto del carlino*, 5 September 1957, p. 3) is an *elzeviro* by Dessí recalling the arrival of the Grandesso family in Villacidro.
5. L. Russo, *I narratori (1850–1957)*, 3rd ed. (Milan-Messina, 1958) pp. 337–8.
6. A. Dolfi, 'Un romanzo interrotto: commento e nota al testo', in G. Dessí, *La scelta*, pp. 129–76.
7. 'Prefazione' (by the author) to G. Dessí, *I passeri* (Milan, 1965) pp. ix–xi (p. x).
8. 'Specie negli ultimi anni della sua vita, pensando a Gobetti, ai fratelli Rosselli, a Ginzburg, a Gramsci, si rammaricava di "non essere stato quello che avrebbe potuto essere". Cosí diceva. Certo è chiaro che non è stato un eroe . . . . Ma ammirava il coraggio e sapeva essere coraggioso' (letter from Luisa Dessí to the present writer dated 14 July 1982).
9. *Lei era l'acqua*, pp. 107–14.
10. *Paese d'ombre*, pp. 338–42.
11. *La sposa in città*, pp. 133–42; *Racconti vecchi e nuovi*, pp. 27–35.
12. *Racconti vecchi e nuovi*, pp. 189–200.
13. *La sposa in città*, pp. 17–44; *Racconti vecchi e nuovi*, pp. 47–71.
14. *La ballerina di carta*, pp. 104–9.
15. *Racconti vecchi e nuovi*, pp. 119–27.
16. *Lei era l'acqua*, pp. 123–46.
17. Unpublished, and kindly made available to me by Luisa Dessí. But 'Il pozzo' is due to appear in 1989 in a collection of Dessí's *inediti* to be published by Sellerio under the title *Come un tiepido vento*.
18. 'Della ragazza morta di tifo parla tanto anche nel diario' (letter from Luisa Dessí to the present writer dated 3 March 1985).
19. *La sposa in città*, pp. 143–51; *Racconti vecchi e nuovi*, pp. 19–26.
20. *La sposa in città*, pp. 153–61; *Racconti vecchi e nuovi*, pp. 73–80.
21. *Lei era l'acqua*, pp. 239–65.
22. Ibid., pp. 115–22.

22. "Falqui era un amico stimolante, un po' prepotente, affettuosamente prepotente, e quando aveva "un buco" da riempire voleva un racconto. A volte mio marito lo buttava giú in un pomeriggio e glielo dava. Se ha scritto tanti racconti lo deve anche a lui, a Falqui, che lo sgridava e lo spingeva a scuotere la sua pigrizia' (letter from Luisa Dessí to the present writer dated 3 March 1985).

24. R. Pascal, *Design and Truth in Autobiography* (London, 1960) p. 12.

25. *Isola dell'Angelo ed altri racconti*, pp. 105–98; *Lei era l'acqua*, pp. 155–237.

26. *La ballerina di carta*, pp. 83–7.

27. 'Parla della ragazza che si è impiccata anche nel diario in data 24.7.29' (letter from Luisa Dessí to the present writer dated 3 March 1985).

28. *Racconti vecchi e nuovi*, pp. 227–38; *Isola dell'Angelo ed altri racconti*, pp. 45–57; *Lei era l'acqua*, pp. 45–56.

29. My principal informant, in July 1986, was Angelo Serra, then aged 81.

30. *La ballerina di carta*, pp. 21–8; *Novelle del Novecento*, edited by B. Moloney (Manchester, 1966) pp. 41–6.

31. *Novelle del Novecento*, p. 114.

32. L. V. Bertarelli, *Guida d'Italia del Touring Club Italiano: Sardegna* (Milan, 1918) map facing page 9.

33. *La ballerina di carta*, p. 23; *Novelle del Novecento*, p. 42.

34. F. Cherchi Paba, *Villacidro* (Cagliari, 1969) pp. 13–16; C. Bolacchi and M. Sardu (eds), *Villacidro: cenni storici* (Cagliari, *s.d.* [1986]) pp. 35–8. Not that Villacidro is a cathedral town, it is in the diocese of Ales, further north. But since Ales is in an area that was relatively prone to malaria until the Americans banished the disease from the island after the Second World War, the bishops also had a palace in the much healthier setting of Villacidro, and from 1765 to 1828 Villacidro *was* virtually the seat of the Bishops of Ales.

35. G. Dessí, *The Forests of Norbio*, translated by F. Frenaye (London, 1975).

36. See, for instance, M. H. Abrams, *A Glossary of Literary Terms*, 3rd ed. (New York, 1971) p. 113: 'The historical novel takes its setting and some of its characters and events from history; the term is usually applied only if the historical milieu and events are fairly elaborately developed, and important to the central narrative'; A. F. Scott, *Current Literary Terms: a concise dictionary of their origin and use*, revised edition (London, 1979) p. 129: 'Historical novel: a narrative based upon history to represent an imaginative reconstruction of events'. Lukacs implies that his definition of the historical novel would include 'derivation of the individuality of characters from the historical peculiarity of their age' and 'an artistically faithful image of a concrete historical epoch', or 'historical truth in the artistic reflection of reality' (G. Lukacs, *The Historical Novel* (Harmondsworth, 1969) p. 15).

37. See 'Intervista a Giuseppe Dessí', edited by M. Di Cagno, *La rocca* (Assisi), 31, xiii (1 July 1972) pp. 48–9; 'Giuseppe Dessí: da Proust alle miniere', in M. Lunetta (ed.), *Sintassi dell'altrove: conversazioni e interviste letterarie* (Poggibonsi, 1978) pp. 56–61.

38. L. Del Piano, 'Giuseppe Fulgheri', in *Atti del Convegno letterario su 'La*

poetica di Giuseppe Dessí e il mito Sardegna' (Cagliari, Centro Studi di Poesia e di Storia delle Poetiche, Sezione Sarda, 1986) pp. 69–82 (p. 81).

39. The parallel between Brigadier Dessí and Roberto Manca di Tharros is made clear in a non-fictional article by the novelist about his father: 'Il frustino', in G. Dessí, *Un pezzo di luna: note, memoria e immagini della Sardegna*, edited by A. Dolfi (Sassari, 1987) pp. 119–33.

40. See 'Il frustino', pp. 126–8.

41. 'Una figura come quella del prete Coi nella vita io non l'ho mai conosciuta' (Dessí in 'Intervista a Giuseppe Dessí', edited by M. Di Cagno, *La rocca* (Assisi), 25, ix (1 May 1966) pp. 54–5 (p. 55)).

42. 'Prefazione' (by the author) to G. Dessí, *I passeri* (Milan, 1965) pp. ix–xi (p. ix).

43. It is presumably reasonable to suppose that this emblematisation also serves to create a kind of private 'shrine' which became 'sacred' because it had been associated with significant events in the novelist's childhood. All Dessí's novels except *Introduzione alla vita di Giacomo Scarbo* were written in mainland Italy; and he writes poignantly about his destiny as a Sardinian living away from Sardinia (and, not only by implication, as a Villacidrese living away from Villacidro) in his 'Introduzione' to G. Dessí (ed.), *Scoperta della Sardegna: antologia di testi di autori italiani e stranieri*, 2 vols (Milan, 1965) I, xi–xx (pp. xiii–xvi, xix–xx).

44. See note 43.

45. See J. C. Barnes, 'Cultura sarda nella narrativa di Giuseppe Dessí', in *La cultura regionale nella letteratura italiana* (forthcoming, Exeter, 1989). Even though Dessí constantly bases his fiction on the area of his childhood, there are ways in which he actively cultivates a pan-Sardinian dimension. This may be briefly illustrated by a consideration of three surnames and two place-names in *Il disertore*. The name Escano (which belongs to the *sindaco* of Cuadu) corresponds to a common surname in Villacidro, Scano, with the addition of a prosthetic *E*- characteristic of Spanish – which may be taken as recognition of the important influence exerted on Sardinia by Spain in past centuries. Isalle, another Cuadu surname in the novel, is a type of name which is common in Sassari. The name Manca di Tharros reminds at least the Sardinian reader of the name Manca di Mores, which belongs to a real-life aristocratic family, also from Sassari. At the same time the Tharros element alludes to another face of Sardinia, Tharros being an evocative archaeological site on a deserted peninsula west of Oristano – the remains of a Phoenician city half buried in sand. In the topography of the novel itself, Baddimanna (*badde* = *valle*; *manno* = *grande*) the name applied to the Coxina valley just above Villacidro, is unknown in real-life Sardinia, though there *is* an area, again near Sassari, called Baddimannu. And perhaps the most interesting name of all in this regard is the name given to Villacidro itself. The word *cuadu* in Sardinian is a past participle meaning 'hidden'; it may derive from the Latin *cubare* (= 'to lie down'). (Could the name be an allusion to the game Dessí plays with names – *hiding* the identity of his home-town under an invented name?) But the exact form of the name is

important. In Campidanese (southern Sardinian, spoken in Villacidro) the word for 'hidden' is not *cuadu* but *cuau*. *Cuadu* belongs to the Logudorese dialect, spoken in the north-east of Sardinia, including the Logudoro area. Dessí, then, is casting his net over the whole of the island.

46. The plan is reproduced in A. Dolfi, 'Un romanzo interrotto', pp. 138–9.

47. See, for example, 'Il frustino', pp. 128–9; 'Come sono diventato scrittore', in G. Dessí, *Un pezzo di luna*, pp. 187–90 (p. 190); 'Il mio incontro con l'*Orlando furioso*', in the appendix to *La scelta*, pp. 111–15; 'La Guerra insegnò a Lussu a lottare per la Sardegna', *La nuova Sardegna*, 8 April 1975, p. 3 (reprinted with omissions and the title 'Emilio Lussu, un'immagine-simbolo' in the appendix to *La scelta*, pp. 116–20; 'Il professore di liceo', in the appendix to *La scelta*, pp. 121–8). See also 'Dessí: Sardegna, "luogo remoto nel futuro" ', interview, edited by O. Cecchi, *L'Unità*, 9 July 1966, p. 8.

48. See J. C. Barnes, art. cit., note 45.

49. See A. Dolfi, 'L'ordine e la combinazione delle possibilità incostanti', in her *La parola e il tempo: saggio su Giuseppe Dessí* (Florence, 1977) pp. 9–45.

50. The short story 'La sposa in città' has never been published but is included in *Come un tiepido vento* (see note 17).

51. *La sposa in città*, pp. 12–15.

52. This is corroborated by the increasing public *impegno* shown in his essays and interviews. By and large, until the 1950s his only writing on socio-political themes had arisen from his activity as a Socialist during and immediately after the Resistance, with occasional socio-political contributions to the weekly publication *Riscossa* (Sassari, 1944–6). Otherwise, his *saggistica* had tended to concentrate on aspects of Sardinian culture, both popular and educated. Examples reproduced in *Un pezzo di luna* include 'il verismo di Grazia Deledda' (1938), 'Noialtri' (1948), 'La donna sarda' (1949), 'Paese d'ombra' (1949), 'Io e il vino' (1951), 'Sale e tempo' (1951), 'Le due facce della Sardegna' (1951), 'Proverbi e verità' (1956), 'Nostalgia di Cagliari' (1957), and 'La leggenda del Sardus Pater' (1957). 'Il frustino' (1951) may be said to represent a move towards the socio-political arena, which was later continued, for instance, in: 'Dessí: Sardegna, "luogo remoto nel futuro" ', cit.; 'A tu per tu con Dessí: in Sardegna la terra trema' [interview], edited by M. Fiori, *Sette giorni*, 342 (20 January 1974) p. 65; 'Il prezzo dell'intolleranza' (on the divorce referendum) *L'Unità*, 21 April 1974, p. 3; 'Dessí: perché mi iscrivo al Partito Comunista' (interview), edited by O. Cecchi, *Rinascita*, 31, 18 (3 May 1974) p. 32; 'Il megaporcile in Sardegna', *Paese sera*, 15 January 1976, p. 3.

53. 'Il problema è di quelli che piú hanno tormentato la coscienza europea, durante l'ultimo conflitto; al quale, piú che al precedente, sembrano riferirsi le domande che nei lunghi soliloqui il prete torna a farsi' (M. Tondo, 'Giuseppe Dessí', in *Orientamenti culturali: letteratura italiana: i contemporanei*, 3 vols (Milan, 1969) III, 559–86 (p. 582), enlarged as 'Lettura di Giuseppe Dessí', in Tondo's *Sondaggi e letture di contemporanei* (Lecce, 1974) pp. 9–69 (p. 56), and reprinted with slight further modifications as

'Giuseppe Dessí' in *Letteratura italiana: Novecento: gli scrittori e la cultura letteraria nella società italiana*, edited by G. Grana, 10 vols (Milan, 1979) VIII, 7066–100 (p. 7093)).

54. See J. C. Barnes, art. cit., note 45.
55. The observation is Claudio Varese's: 'L'ultimo capitolo ... è ... un commento che ripropone il tema stesso del racconto da un altro punto di vista, chiudendo il circolo, aperto all'inizio, dell'incontro tra la fanciullezza e il delitto. Questo balletto della beffa e dell'omertà di un carnevale di morte, questi contadini e pastori che non riconoscono l'invito razionale del loro ex-sindaco, nemico delle loro sanguinose mascherate, sono un segno e un simbolo: l'ombra grava ancora sul paese e la realtà storica e morale della Sardegna è ancora ferita' (last paragraph of his introduction to the second and subsequent editions of the novel (Milan, 1973 and 1975 (p. xiii)).
56. A. Dolfi, 'Un romanzo interrotto', pp. 137–8. See note 6.
57. Quoted by A. Dolfi in ibid., p. 168.

14

Rousseau and Calvino: an unexplored ideological perspective in *Il barone rampante*

Judith Bryce

In the mid-1950s Italo Calvino was not alone in exploring, albeit through the medium of fiction, the political and intellectual legacy of eighteenth-century Europe. In the preface to the children's edition of *Il barone rampante* published in 1965 he was to recall the contemporaneous endeavours of Italian historians in this field and particularly those individuals associated with his own Torinese *ambiente*, the publishing house of Giulio Einaudi. (The name of one established authority on the Enlightenment, Franco Venturi, springs to mind.) 'Una scherzosa invasione dell'Autore nel campo dei suoi amici studiosi' is one of the playful authorial definitions of the book proposed there.[1]

Three years later, in an interview given in October 1968 (the date is not without significance!), the subject of Calvino's much-debated *illuminismo* was raised yet again and, while unable to accept unreservedly the simple label 'neoilluminista', he nevertheless admitted to a continuing fascination with the eighteenth century, 'proprio perché lo scopro sempre piú ricco, sfaccettato, pieno di fermenti contraddittori che continuano fino ad oggi'.[2] In the study which follows, the particular 'fermenti contraddittori' on which we shall be focusing are primarily of a political nature, the aim being to propose an alternative ideological context within which to view the text under discussion.

It is generally agreed that the eighteenth century saw the emergence of concepts and values which underpin modern liberal-democratic bourgeois society: less incontrovertible perhaps is the contention that it gave birth also to more radical concepts and values which either coexisted uneasily with the above or were in open conflict with them. It is the former view of the Settecento, namely as the period which saw the

201

creation of bourgeois, technocratic values destined to triumph after the Revolution, which has given rise to the reservations of modern, left-wing ideologues, to that 'impopolarità' of *illuminismo* which Calvino ruefully noted in the 1968 interview, referring specifically to the critique of Horkheimer and Adorno whose *Dialectic of the Enlightenment* was first published in the 1940s.

Despite the risk of over-simplification, there is a sense in which it is possible to align with each of the above-mentioned sets of values the name of one of the great figures of the French Enlightenment, Voltaire and Rousseau. Of these two, it is the former who has traditionally been associated with Calvino. Corrado Rosso, in an essay entitled 'Voltaire et Rousseau dans la conscience contemporaine en Italie', rather unconvincingly connects the iconographical aptness of the solitary cat as a Rousseauian symbol with the role of the wild cat in *Il barone rampante* before going on to refer to an interview given by Calvino in *La Repubblica* in 1978 on the occasion of the bicentenary of the deaths of both Voltaire and Rousseau and to term the writer 'l'un des plus voltairiens de nos auteurs'.[3] A similar Voltairian comparison appears in an article by Norbert Jonard, 'Calvino et le siècle des lumières'. Certainly Jonard, noting the harmonious relationship established between the protagonist and the world of nature, identifies this aspect as 'le côté rousseauiste du *Barone rampante*', but the link is admittedly superficial and a couple of pages further on he asserts instead: 'Quant à son prétendu rousseauisme, il est plus apparent que réel. Même si un almanach le qualifie d'homme sauvage d'Ombreuse, Cosimo n'incarne pas le mythe du bon sauvage'.[4] By insisting rather on the Voltairian tradition Jonard is finally led to define the book as a 'divertissement pédagogique – sous tendu par l'idéologie bourgeoise du XVIIe [*sic*] siècle' (p. 110). This seems to me to be unacceptable. Instead, bearing in mind the two divergent strands of the Enlightenment legacy mentioned above, it may well prove more rewarding to view Rousseau rather than Voltaire as the ideological ancestor who looms large in *Il barone rampante*.

In 1957, the year of the first edition of the *Barone*, Galvano della Volpe, one of post-war Italy's most influential Marxist theorists, published his *Rousseau e Marx*, a volume of essays which had come to maturation during the preceding decade.[5] The significance of Voltaire is of course acknowledged, in particular his strong defence of the freedom of thought and of conscience in the Calas affair (to which both Calvino and that other much-debated *illuminista*, Leonardo Sciascia, allude more than once in their writings). For della Volpe, however, Voltaire's political and social philosophy 'è genericamente una filosofia della libertà e dell'eguaglianza borghese e specificamente una teoria dei diritti e doveri di quello *honnête homme*, o galantuomo, che è l'*homme éclairé* ò intellettuale borghese, che sostituisce, nella funzione di *élite*, lo *honnête-homme-homme-de-qualité* ossia l'aristocratico dell'*ancien régime*' (p. 116). Rousseau, by contrast, propounds a view of a truly egalitarian liberty which makes him, for della Volpe, a fundamental, although largely unrecognised precursor of Hegel and Marx. The ideological roots of Marxism are to be found in an interconnected group of key works by the Swiss *philosophe*, the *Discours sur l'origine et les fondements de l'inégalité parmi les hommes* (1755), *Émile ou de l'éducation* (1762) and the *Contrat social* (1762). Della Volpe's book was the first in a series of important re-evaluations of Rousseau which continued through the 1960s (1962 was the 250th anniversary of his birth as well as the 200th of the *Contrat social*) and on into the 1970s. Some of the prominent names associated with this scrutiny are those of Italian Marxist intellectuals and scholars such as Colletti, Cerroni, Alatri, Casini and Gerratana, the latter a friend of Calvino and translator for Einaudi of the *Contrat social* published as far back as 1945.[6]

In the course of that twice-mentioned interview of 1968 Calvino remarked upon the Quixotic character of the Baron. This is true particularly in the sense in which the Don imitates the heroes of his favourite books. Story-telling, as Jill Carlton has pointed out in a recent article, is very characteristic of Calvino.[7] Art may imitate art as when Gian dei Brughi comes to the same end (death by hanging) as the character in a novel which Cosimo is reading aloud to him. References to a range of eighteenth-century texts as well as to *Robinson Crusoe*, to *Don Quixote* and to Ariosto, form part of the intertexuality of *Il barone rampante* as Carlton argues. There is one text, however, which she does not mention and which is to be found deeply embedded in the book: that text is Rousseau's *Émile*.

There are no more overt references to Rousseau in *Il barone rampante* than to other eighteenth-century luminaries, Diderot for instance or Voltaire. The latter does indeed appear in the text as a character but, significantly perhaps, we are given a malicious portrait of a radical intellectual who has become an establishment figure, absorbed into, fêted and emasculated by smart salon society. The Rousseau references appear to be more neutral. In Chapter XIII there is an allusion to his botanical interests and John Woodhouse's edition points us in the direction of the *Confessions*.[8] In Chapter XVIII Cosimo encourages Ursula to read *La Nouvelle Héloise* (p. 128) and El Conde, leader of the aristocratic Spanish exiles, to read unspecified works. Unfortunately he found them too difficult, preferring Montesquieu – 'che era già un passo' (p. 129)! In the first flush of revolution, Cosimo delivers a lecture on Rousseau and Voltaire but his words are drowned out (an intentional irony!) by the deafening chant of the excited populace: 'Ça ira!' (p. 190). Returning to Chapter XIII, however, one of the questions put in vain by the young Cosimo to his Jansenist tutor, the Abate Fauchelafleur, is: 'Chi è il Vicario Savoiardo?'. The reference is of course to the long digression in *Émile* on natural man and belief in God, the so-called 'Profession de foi du Vicaire Savoyard'.

Let us now concentrate on *Émile*. The eponymous protagonist, the ideal, imaginary pupil, has of course an ideal *gouverneur* to accompany him through the stages of the author's innovatory educational process, while Cosimo, having only the unsatisfactory Fauchelafleur, must in a sense educate himself; nevertheless the parallels between the two books in the stages and the nature of that education (or in Cosimo's case, re-education) are striking – *Il barone rampante* is in part a retelling, admittedly in a very different key, of *Émile*.

If we briefly summarise the process in *Émile* the following sequence emerges: 1) isolation of the child from society which is corrupt, inauthentic, profoundly alienated and alienating; 2) exposure of the child to Nature encouraging a knowledge of the world through direct experience and the development of the senses rather than through a formal book-based education; 3) the encouragement of the child to fulfil real needs by himself wherever possible and above all the discouragement of superfluous needs; in short a principle of self-sufficiency ('suffer à soi'); 4) at the age of about twelve years Émile, encouraged by his tutor, has surveyed his entire natural environment and the faculty of reason begins to emerge. Formal education or even reading is still discouraged: instead there is training in manual skills; 5) between the ages of fifteen or sixteen and twenty Émile experiences the dawn of sexuality and entry into what Rousseau calls 'l'ordre moral' involving social relations and travel to complete his political education.

It is perhaps unnecessary to point out in detail the parallel development of Calvino's protagonist but one or two points should be underlined. Cosimo, like Émile, is one of a kind, a new species, the creation of an alternative mode of socialisation. Rebelling at the age of twelve, Cosimo experiences a symbolic rebirth. Thereafter in effect he follows in a slightly contracted form the same stages as Émile from 'infancy' to maturity. In the early days of his rebellion he does seem, in fact, to have regressed to infancy or even to some non-human state. As Biagio tells us 'in realtà rampava per quelle ruvide cortecce senza capir nulla, come un allocco, immagino' (p. 43). In the second stage of infancy, however, during which the child learns to eat, talk, and walk, Cosimo develops his senses atrophied by society, his mobility in the trees and his self-sufficiency (there is the Rousseauian rejection of the superfluous in the unrealized project of the 'acquedotto pensile', p. 81). In Chapter XII, after a period of outright rejection of the traditional, formal education offered by his Jansenist tutor, we see the natural, unforced awakening of the intellect: 'Cosimo era su di un noce, un pomeriggio, e leggeva. Gli era presa da poco la nostalgia di qualche libro . . .' (p. 85). The dawn of sexuality and the beginning of serious adult relations with society come close together in Chapters XVI and XVII.

In broad outline, then, there are a number of echoes in the twentieth-century text of the eighteenth-century one: I would go as far as to suggest that they are deliberate. Reading *Émile* with *Il barone rampante* in mind one is further struck by a number of similarities of detail some of which may indeed be conscious on the part of Calvino, while others may be regarded rather as sympathetic points of contact between two authors who, despite their historical distance one from the other, shared a number of social and ethical preoccupations. In this category are two statements of principle which may most conveniently be presented as parallel passages without, it must be stressed, necessarily suggesting deliberate derivation.[9]

Pour être quelque chose, pour être soi-meme et toujours un, il faut agir comme on parle; il faut être toujours décidé sur le parti que l'on doit prendre, le prendre hautement, et le suivre toujours. (p. 250)

Una persona si pone volontariamente una difficile regola e la segue fino alle ultime conseguenze, perché senza di questa non sarebbe se stesso né per se né per gli altri. (preface to *I nostri antenati*, 1960)

Dans l'ordre naturel, les hommes étant tous egaux, leur vocation commune est l'état d'homme; et quiconque est bien élevé pour celui-là ne peut mal remplir ceux qui s'y rapportent. Qu'on destine mon élève à l'épée, à l'église, au barreau, peu m'importe. Avant la vocation des parens la nature l'appelle à la vie humaine. Vivre est le métier que je lui veux apprendre. En sortant de mes mains il ne sera, j'en conviens, ni magistrat, ni soldat, ni prêtre; il sera prémierement homme: tout ce qu'un homme doit être, il saura l'être au besoin tout aussi bien que qui que ce soit; et la fortune aura beau le faire changer de place, il sera toujours à la sienne. (pp. 251–2)

– Ricordi d'essere Barone di Rondò?
– Sí, signor padre, ricordo il mio nome.
– Vorrai essere degno del nome e del titolo che porti?
– Cercherò d'esser piú degno che posso del nome d'uomo, e lo sarò cosí d'ogni suo attributo. (MUP, p. 105)

One is struck, too, by Rousseau's description of the difference between Émile, the natural man, and other human beings.

Je sais que s'obstinant à n'imaginer que ce qu'ils voyent, ils prendront le jeune homme que je figure pour un être imaginaire et fantastique, parce qu'il différe de ceux auxquels ils le comparent sans songer qu'il faut bien qu'il en différe, puisqu'élevé tout différement, affecté de sentimens tout contraires, instruit tout autrement qu'eux, il seroit beaucoup plus surprenant qu'il leur ressemblât que d'être tel que je le suppose. Ce n'est pas l'homme de l'homme, c'est l'homme de la nature. Assurément il doit être fort étranger à leurs yeux.

(p. 549)

For well-born Émile as for aristocratic Cosimo, work is regarded as an indispensable duty: 'Dans la société, où il vit nécessairement aux dépens des autres, il leur doit en travail le prix de son entretien; cela est sans exception' (p. 470). In terms of Cosimo's relations with other members of his family, too, caricatures for the most part but not devoid of pathos, a passage from *Émile* strikes a chord. In the education of children, Rousseau insists, adults should be presented as they are in reality 'non pas afin qu'ils les haïssent, mais afin qu'ils les plaignent et ne leur veuillent pas ressembler' (p. 525). In the case of the Cavalier Avvocato an unashamedly didactic chapter-ending reports that Cosimo 'riuscí a non somigliargli mai' (p. 82).[10]

One major difference between Cosimo and Émile does exist. The former is not restricted in his reading – quite the contrary! Calvino, with the benefit of hindsight, does not wish to deny his protagonist the riches of the Enlightenment, the unlimited consumption of the written word, the excitement of the pursuit of encyclopaedic knowledge. Calvino does not suffer (in the context of this particular work, at least) from Rousseau's exaggerated mistrust of books as a source of information about humankind and about the world, although he does concur with the general principle that books should not be a substitute for action or participation.[11] Three books which Émile *is* grudgingly allowed in his teens are read also by Cosimo. They are Plutarch's *Lives* (*Émile*, p. 276; *Il barone rampante*, p. 90), Fénélon's *Télémaque* (p. 578; p. 89) and Defoe's *Robinson Crusoe* (*Émile*, pp. 202–3). This latter is indeed the *only* book permitted Émile in the third stage of his development. The reference in *Il barone rampante* is an oblique one coming in a brief exchange with Viola who comments on his appearance: 'Sembri Robinson! – L'hai letto? – disse subito lui, per farsi vedere al corrente. Viola s'era già voltata . . .' (p. 151). Other indirect links with Defoe's work, however, particularly in connection with the self-sufficiency theme, are a further element shared by Rousseau and Calvino.

Let us return to the more important task of identifying the broader parallels which link the two texts under discussion. For Norbert Jonard, to requote, 'Cosimo n'incarne pas le mythe du bon sauvage'. Indeed not, but then neither does Émile. Although Cosimo's early career in the trees does mark a regression not only to infancy, as argued earlier, but to the infancy of man, to the primitive, his father's query: 'Intendete crescere come un selvaggio delle Americhe?' (p. 58), is destined eventually to receive a negative response. Calvino and Rousseau take a more positive view of the primitive than Baron Arminio and there is a strong link between Rousseau's *Discours sur l'inégalité* with its anthropological insights admired by Lévi-Strauss and the early stages of the education of

Émile, but Émile is not for all that 'un bon sauvage'. As his creator is at pains to point out:

> Il y a bien de la différence entre l'homme naturel vivant dans l'état de nature, et l'homme naturel vivant dans l'état de societé. Emile n'est pas un sauvage à releguer dans les déserts; c'est un sauvage fait pour habiter les villes. Il faut qu'il sache y trouver son nécessaire, tirer parti de leurs habitans, et vivre, sinon comme eux, du moins avec eux.
>
> (pp. 483–4)[12]

In Cosimo, as in Émile, we see the evolution of a human being from the primitive state to the civilised (the emergence of the faculty of reason is the important watershed for Rousseau) but in both individuals that evolution has taken a new path, an alternative route. What we have is a different socialisation process in which contact has not been lost with the natural man and which leads potentially towards the creation of and participation in a radically different form of human *convivenza*. It is frequently stressed that *Émile* must not be read in isolation but together with the *Contrat social* many elements of which are already apparent in the earlier work: 'l'homme de la nature et de la raison' is at the basis of a free and truly egalitarian society.[13] The subversive, revolutionary significance of both works is underscored by the orders given to burn copies of them in Paris and in Geneva in 1762.

The latter half of *Il barone rampante* concerns the protagonist's search for new ways to 'be' and at the same time to be with others. It is a time of experimentation involving the fire-fighting association, the Spanish exiles, the Masons, the French Revolution and its aftermath and a time of theorising, with political treatises such as the 'Progetto di costituzione d'uno stato ideale fondato sugli alberi' echoing in a fantastic and parodic key Rousseau's ideal *Project de constitution pour la Corse* of 1764 (Corsica, incidentally, having recently rebelled against Genoa to which Calvino's fictional Ombrosa is subject).[14] But none of these projects is successful or completely satisfying and Biagio concludes:

> Come questa passione che Cosimo sempre dimostrò per la vita associata si conciliasse con la sua perpetua fuga dal consorzio civile, non ho mai ben compreso, e ciò resta una delle non minori singolarità del suo carattere. Si direbbe che egli, piú era deciso a star rintanato tra

i suoi rami, piú sentiva il bisogno di creare nuovi rapporti col genere umano. . . . Forse se si vuole ricondurre a un unico impulso questi atteg- giamenti contraddittori, bisogna pensare che egli fosse ugualmente nemico di ogni tipo di convivenza umana vigente ai tempi suoi, e perciò tutti li fuggisse, e s'affannasse ostinatamente a sperimentarne di nuovi; ma nessuno d'essi gli pareva giusto e diverso dagli altri abbastanza; da ciò le sue continue parentesi di selvatichezza assoluta. (p. 184)

This passage is enormously suggestive in the present context. At the basis of the character of Rousseau, too, lay a similar paradox and a number of related problems – how to integrate the natural with the civilised self, how to reconcile freedom with authority, individual autonomy with the association or institution or party or society, how to reconcile the self-fulfilment of the individual with participation in the collectivity and in collective action for the common good. Bronislaw Baczko has written of the 'valeur exemplaire' of Rousseau's solitude interpreting it in terms which are relevant also to Calvino's protagonist, and indeed to Calvino himself as we shall shortly see.

Le choix de la solitude est donc une révolte morale, et par là même, sociale. Prendre du recul par rapport aux formes existantes de sociali- sation, telle est la condition indispensable aussi bien à l'affirmation de l'autonomie individuelle qu'à la conformité de l'individu avec l'idéal universel, à son élévation à 'l'humanité'. La solitude fait donc œuvre d'exemple: elle montre à 'son siècle' la possibilité d'un autre mode de vie, fondé sur un autre système des valeurs. L'idée de l'humanité et les valeurs qu'elle comporte impliquent le postulat d'une transformation de la société existante, ainsi que l'aspiration de l'individu à participer à une véritable communauté qui réaliserait ces valeurs. Ainsi, le choix de la solitude est un acte de révolte contre la réalité sociale; une révolte qui se manifeste dans une rupture entre l'individu et la société, dans la défense de son autonomie. Choisir la solitude, c'est aussi se défendre contre la réduction de sa personnalité à des rôles sociaux; c'est défendre le droit de l'individu à opposer son idéal moral et social aux rapports existants.[15]

'Une transformation de la société existante'! The emergence of Italy from the Fascist *ventennio* seemed to many to offer the possibility of a fresh start, an opportunity to experiment with a better form of human *convivenza*, and to create a new and more egalitarian society. But this early optimism was soon undermined as the politics of the cold war period, the political hegemony of the Christian Democratic Party and ominous events such as the *legge truffa* of 1953 (in effect an attack, although an abortive one, on the Italian Constitution) created a climate which gave scant encouragement to the revolutionary aspirations of the Left. Already there were signs of an impotent nostalgia for 'cette Italie meilleure qui s'était révélée pendant la résistance et les premiers temps de l'après-guerre' and, to make matters more complex, a creeping doubt about the very object of that nostalgia.[16] Within the Italian Communist Party there were literary as well as ideological problems – creative freedom versus a rigid, Zhdanovian cultural policy on one hand, and on the other a critique of the increasing bureaucratisation and ossification of the Party seen as a proponent of an authoritarian socialism à la Stalin (a failed liberator to be equated with the figure of Napoleon in *Il barone rampante*?). The story is well documented in Nello Ajello's study of the relations between Italian intellectuals and the Communist Party in this period.[17]

The years of the composition and publication of *Il barone rampante*, 1956 and 1957, only served to compound the pessimism which sounds so strongly in the opening of the final chapter: 'tutti i novatori ... sconfitti; l'assolutismo e i gesuiti rianno il campo; gli ideali della giovinezza, i lumi, le speranze ... tutto è cenere' (p. 206). The denunciation of Stalin offered a moment of hope to the innovators which was extinguished with the events in Hungary. Calvino saw the Hungarian uprising as a legitimate bid for the sort of direct democracy to which he aspired, openly expressing his dissent from the party line as laid down by Amendola on the night of 4 November. In the following year, 1957, he left the PCI in the wake of Antonio Giolitti and in a letter to Paolo Spriano of 1 August, the day of his resignation, he wrote:

> È difficile fare il comunista stando da solo. Ma io sono e resto un comunista. Se riuscirò a dimostrarti questo, t'avrò anche dimostrato che il Barone rampante non è un libro troppo lontano dalle cose che ci stanno a cuore.[18]

With this personal restatement of the solitude/solidarity paradox encountered earlier in Cosimo Piovasco and in Rousseau we return, by way of conclusion, to a final consideration of the wider relevance of the latter, in many ways the odd man out of the Enlightenment, for a reading of *Il barone rampante*. In addition to the close parallel established earlier between this text and a specific Rousseauian text, *Émile*, we should take into account the extremely complex intersection in the eighteenth-century *philosophe* of several strands of political thought which connect him to post-war Italian, and indeed European, political experience, and which have been explored in new and illuminating ways by historians and political theorists of the Left since the 1950s.

The first strand is of course the Marxist one beginning essentially with Galvano della Volpe and claiming Rousseau as an ancestor of Marx representing the democratic-egalitarian line of descent as opposed to the bourgeois-liberal line in European political thought.[19]

Secondly there is the anarchist strand, so far undifferentiated in this study. Its relevance to Calvino is clear, his 'formazione politica' well documented. Paolo Spriano has very recently reiterated its significance, viewing the writer in the fifties as engaged in a search for a synthesis of communism and anarchism.[20] Of immediate relevance as regards Rousseau in this ideological context are two studies by Carmela di Metelli Lallo, *Analisi del discorso pedagogico* and, in particular, *Componenti anarchiche nel pensiero di Jean Jacques Rousseau*.[21] While she neither claims him as an anarchist nor even as a proto-anarchist, she does convincingly identify a number of basic concepts which he shares with that doctrine: 1) it is necessary to reconstitute society *ex novo*; 2) education should be a process of deconditioning of the individual and hence a challenge to the status quo (*Émile* is important here); 3) property is the basis of inequality; 4) recognition of the importance of the individual and relating to that the concept of 'volontarismo individuale' and the necessity to be able to 'realizzare se stesso in modo autonomo operando con autodisciplina nella collaborazione coi suoi simili'. Where Rousseau diverges from anarchism it is with the concept of the social contract which conflicts with the anarchists' fundamental mistrust of the State, but even here Metelli di Lallo argues for Rousseau's anti-authoritarian concept of a dynamic, self-renewing state as against either a new totalitarianism or a static Utopia. As far as Cosimo's anarchism is concerned let it suffice to quote a passage which presents a variation on the basic paradox of his existence.

Capí questo: che le associazioni rendono l'uomo piú forte e mettono in risalto le doti migliori delle singole persone, e dànno la gioia che raramente s'ha restando per proprio conto, di vedere quanta gente c'è onesta e brava e capace e per cui vale la pena di volere cose buone. . . . Piú tardi, Cosimo dovrà capire che quando quel problema comune non c'è piú, le associazioni non sono piú buone come prima, e val meglio essere un uomo solo e non un capo.   (p. 103)

The third strand of modern political thinking which looks back to Rousseau is what came to be termed the New Left which shared with anarchism a dislike of authoritarian socialism, of bureaucratisation and the suppression of the individual. Calvino responded positively to the 'linguaggio nuovo' of 1968 – 'il momento antirepressivo, antiautoritario', 'la necessità ormai clamorosa d'una nuova forza organizzata operaia non piú burocratica e sclerotizzante' are key phrases in a short article written soon after the May events.[22] Other New Left themes, too, echo earlier concerns – volontarism, 'autogestion', the critique of alienation – while under the aegis of the New Left new groups emerged acting in areas which traditional Marxism considered irrelevant to the class struggle – notably feminism or ecology. The ecological message is one which comes through already in *Il barone rampante* of 1957 and it is yet another area in which Rousseau is now seen as a precursor. Perhaps it was with some of these themes and concepts in mind that Calvino felt able in October 1968 to assert the relevance of the Settecento 'fino ad oggi' and to remark: 'Continuo a sentire vivo lo spirito con cui undici anni fa ho scritto *Il barone rampante*'.

In conclusion, if Rousseau is indeed, as I have suggested, the particular ancestor whose hidden presence in fact dominates *Il barone rampante*, it is striking that Calvino's sympathetic response not only echoed current non-literary theoretical preoccupations with this thinker, but in fact anticipated much of the Italian and European reassessment of his continuing relevance to the second half of the twentieth century.

Notes

1. *Il barone rampante* in the series 'Letture per la scuola media' (Turin, 1965) p. 8.
2. *Una pietra sopra. Discorsi di letteratura e società* (Turin, 1980) p. 189.

3. *Mythe de l'égalité et rayonnement des lumières* (Pisa, 1980) p. 294.
4. *Forum Italicum*, 18 (1984) 93–116 (p. 106; pp. 109–10).
5. The 1957 edition was published in Rome by Editori Riuniti. I shall refer to the definitive fourth edition of 1964 by the same publisher.
6. See A. Postigliola, 'Rousseau e il marxismo italiano degli anni sessanta', *Critica marxista* (1971) 70–83 and the earlier study by C. Violi, 'Rousseau e le origini della democrazia moderna', *Critica marxista* (1966) 178–200.
7. 'The Genesis of *Il barone rampante*', *Italica*, 61 (1984) 195–206.
8. *Il barone rampante*, edited and introduced by J. R. Woodhouse (Manchester: Manchester University Press, 1970) p. 96. All textual references will be to this edition.
9. All quotations from *Émile* are from the Gallimard edition of the *Œuvres complètes* in the series Bibliothèque de la Pléiade (Paris, 1969) vol. IV.
10. Of the more trivial parallels which strike the reader (apart from the obvious similarities of agricultural pursuits and hunting exploits) are Rousseau's complaint about restrictive clothing ('L'habillement françois, gênant et mal sain pour les hommes est pernicieux surtout aux enfans', *Émile*, p. 371; *Il barone rampante*, p. 12) and his remarks on epitaphs ('Les nôtres sont couverts d'éloges; sur ceux des anciens on lisoit des faits' (*Émile*, p. 675; *Il barone rampante*, p. 209).
11. 'La lecture est le fléau de l'enfance' (*Émile*, p. 357); 'je hais les livres; ils n'apprennent qu'à parler de ce qu'on ne sait pas' (p. 454).
12. Similarly: '. . . voulant former l'homme de la nature, il ne s'agit pas pour cela d'en faire un sauvage et de le reléguer au fond des bois, mais qu'enfermé dans le tourbillon social, il suffit . . . qu'aucune autorité ne le gouverne hors celle de sa propre raison' (pp. 550–1) and 'Emile n'est pas fait pour rester toujours solitaire; membre de la societé il en doit remplir les devoirs. Fait pour vivre avec les hommes il doit les connoitre' (p. 654).
13. The connection is succintly made by Leslie Claydon: 'Preserved as in a state of nature until upon the very threshold of manhood, Émile is now treated as fitted to construct a new and better society by virtue of the fact that his preservation has kept him from the corruptions of the old. He can understand and further a sound ethical plan for living in association with his fellows', *Rousseau. On Education*, ed. Leslie F. Claydon (London, 1969) p. 112.
14. See F. Venturi, 'Francesco Dalmazzo Vasco', an essay first published in 1958 now in *Europe des Lumières. Recherches sur le 18e siècle* (Paris, The Hague, 1971) pp. 160–71.
15. *Rousseau. Solitude et communauté*, tr. C. Brendhel-Lamhout (Paris, The Hague, 1974) pp. 252–3. See, too, R. Polin, *La Politique de la solitude. Essai sur la philosophie politique de Jean-Jacques Rousseau* (Paris, 1971).
16. Interview with Calvino in *Lettres françaises*, 12 May 1966, pp. 6–9. The conversation is largely apropos of *La giornata di uno scrutatore* published in 1963 but based on the elections of 1953: 'C'est un récit que j'ai porté en moi durant dix ans'. For della Volpe on the *legge truffa* see *Rousseau e Marx*, pp. 89, 133ff., Postigliola, 'Rousseau e il marxismo', p. 77).

17. *Intellettuali e PCI, 1944–1958* (Bari, 1979) p. 395; pp. 412–13.
18. Paolo Spriano, *Le passioni di un decennio (1946–1956)* (Milan, 1986) p. 25.
19. Rousseau has been the subject of extremely divergent critical interpretations over the last two centuries. From further to the right on the political spectrum he has been seen in totally negative terms as an advocate of totalitarianism. See A. Prontera, 'I motivi totalitari ed anarchici del pensiero politico del Rousseau nelle piú recenti interpretazioni', *Bollettino di storia della filosofia dell'Università degli Studi di Lecce*, 1 (1973) 281–99.
20. *Le passioni di un decennio*, p. 15. See also the interview with Calvino, 'La generazione degli anni difficili', published in *Il paradosso*, 23–4 (Sept.-Dec. 1960) 11–18 (particularly p. 17).
21. The first was published in Padua in 1966, the second in Florence in 1970. See also Prontera's review article mentioned in note 19 above.
22. 'Per una letteratura che chieda di piú (Vittorini e il Sessantotto)' in *Una pietra sopra*, pp. 192–3.

15

Sciascia's *Todo Modo*: La Vérité en Peinture

Tom O'Neill

If the story-line of *Il contesto* seems occasionally to verge on the improbable, the fantastic pure and simple, the story-line of its sequel, *Todo modo*, far surpasses it in just such terms. It relates, through an unnamed first person narrator (who is, we quickly learn, a famous and well-established painter), a series of murders (three, to be precise) which occur during a spiritual retreat organised by an entrepreneurial, intellectual priest, Don Gaetano, for a sort of Bilderberg group of important politicians and industrialists. For its participants the retreat is clearly a holiday, but, as the narrator informs us: 'una vacanza che permetteva di riannodare fruttuose relazioni, ordire trame di potere e di ricchezza, rovesciare alleanze e restituire tradimenti'.[1] This being so, the first two murders cause little surprise, particularly the second, undoubtedly committed by the perpetrator of the first in order to avoid being blackmailed. It is the third one which produces the *coup de théâtre*, for the victim is Don Gaetano himself and the killer, of his own admission (although he is not believed), is the painter-narrator (p. 122). This double identity of the 'io narrante' is a point to which I shall return later, but for the moment we should perhaps note that in addition to painting under his own name, he also publishes detective stories under a pseudonym (p. 70). And even although Scalambri, the magistrate who is in charge of the investigation, immediately points out that the first murder is fact, not fiction (p. 70), the committing of that fact to paper by the painter-narrator and the identification of him (like the Agatha Christie narrator referred to in the text)[2] as one of the murderers hints that perhaps the distinction between fact and fiction is not as clear-cut as it may seem. It should not surprise us, therefore, that the text opens with a clear reference to Pirandello (p. 3)[3]

215

and that in addition to other specifically Pirandellian references (to *Sei personaggi*, for example)[4] it proceeds *pirandellianamente* to break down the divide between life and literature (p. 3) and to multiply by refraction the lives of the characters, especially Don Gaetano.

If *Todo modo* seems at first sight more fantastic and improbable than *Il contesto*, if fiction seems to reign unbridled at the expense of fact to the extent that we as readers, marvelling at the author's extreme of *fantasia*, mutter, like one of the retreatants, 'cose dell'altro mondo' (p. 38), we should perhaps, if only to convince ourselves that on occasions truth is indeed stranger than fiction (and, moreover, belongs to this world), turn to *Nero su nero*, a diary kept by Sciascia for some ten years, between 1969 and 1979, when it was published.[5] A reading of pages 53–6 of this later text reveals that the basic story-line of *Todo modo* has its source in reality where it would seem to be a coalescence of two distinct but nevertheless real occurrences: the presence of the author as a member of the jury for the award of a literary prize in a hotel in which a retreat was also coincidentally taking place and his presence, on another occasion, at a Catholic conference on the subject of hope.[6] The details of comparison need not unduly detain us here. The wife, who accompanies her husband by car to the retreat and who excites the imagination of the painter-narrator (p. 22), is already present at length in the diary (p. 54). The atmosphere at the outset, 'di una compagnoneria facile e sguaiata: gridi di sorpresa, abbracci, manate, scherzosi insulti' (p. 23), repeats almost to the letter what is in the diary: '... si incontravano con espressioni di sorpresa e di gioia, scherzosi insulti, abbracci e manate. E magari si erano lasciati la sera avanti, giú in città: ma il ritrovarsi all'appuntamento di ogni anno, tutti insieme, svegliava in loro una compagnoneria facile e sguaiata: ...' (pp. 53–4). Direct comments, authorial and otherwise, in the novel are already present in the diary. The painter-narrator's remark that he felt 'come un cane in chiesa' (p. 37) repeats the words of a Catholic from Brianza at the conference on hope: ' "Sono un democristiano, credevo che un cattolico potesse e dovesse andare alla Democrazia Cristiana. Ma qui mi sento come un cane in chiesa" ' (p. 57). The reproach of Don Gaetano to two reluctant meditators: ' "Avvocato, onorevole! Mi meraviglio di voi: ancora qui a parlare delle vostre e nostre miserie! Andate in camera a meditare sulle parole di sua eminenza!" ' (p. 38) find their origin in the ' "Avvocato, mi meraviglio di lei! Vada a meditare in camera" ' (p. 54). The description of the recitation of the rosary at dusk, too:

E in quel momento anche chi, come me e come il cuoco, li vedeva nell'abietta mistificazione e nel grottesco, scopriva che c'era qualcosa di vero, vera paura, vera pena, in quel loro andare nel buio dicendo preghiere: qualcosa che veramente attingeva all'esercizio spirituale: quasi che fossero e si sentissero disperati, nella confusione di una bolgia, sul punto della metamorfosi. E veniva facile pensare alla dantesca bolgia dei ladri. (p. 46)

has its clear textual counterpart in the diary:

E in quel momento, anche chi (come me) li vedeva nell'abietta mistificazione e nel grottesco, scopriva che c'era qualcosa di vero, qualcosa che veramente attingeva all'esercizio spirituale, in quel loro andare su e giú al buio, in quel biascicare preghiere, in quel confondersi e aggrovigliarsi: quella nota di isteria, di paura; quasi che per un attimo si sentissero, disperati, nella confusione di una bolgia, sul punto della metamorfosi. Appunto come nella dantesca bolgia dei ladri. E che l'attimo potesse diventare eternità. (p. 55)

But if pages 53–6 of *Nero su nero* provide us with the starting-point in reality of *Todo modo*, other pages are more illuminating still. The painter-narrator's question, for example, to his fellow diners, 'cosa pensassero della restaurazione del diavolo operata da Paolo VI' (p. 33), has already been answered by Sciascia himself in *Nero su nero*: 'La sola cosa per cui ho avuto un moto di simpatia per Paolo VI è stata la resurrezione da lui operata del diavolo' (p. 221). And should the reader think I am hinting at a simplistic identification of painter-narrator and author *tout court*, forgetful of that Pirandello-like split personality typical of many of Sciascia's characters, let him look at what Don Gaetano (and not the painter-narrator) has to say apropos of the *Commentari* of Enea Silvio Piccolomini, Pius II (pp. 35–6), and what Sciascia has to say in a similar, no less Stendhalian, vein in *Nero su nero* (pp. 140–1).[7] Given the nature of the novel, though, perhaps the presiding genius is not so much Stendhal or Pirandello as Borges.

The most illuminating reference would seem to be the short story

concerning two rival theologians who, having spent their lives espousing
diametrically opposite views, turn out in paradise to be one and the same
person.[8] Sciascia refers to it specifically in an *elzeviro* entitled 'Il cerchio
del fanatismo: l'inquisitore', which was published in *La Stampa* on 13
April 1975, less than six months after the publication of *Todo modo*. His
reference in it to the enmity of fanatics being specular ('L'inimicizia dei
fanatici è propriamente speculare') undoubtedly illuminates in retrospect much of the mirror imagery of *Todo modo*, but Borges's presence is
also more general, linked not to this or that specific text but to the
construction (and, today, we might add, deconstruction) of the text as
such. Already thirty years before *Todo modo*, the author had spoken of
Borges in these terms:

> Pensate ai racconti di mistero di Edgar Poe, a certi racconti fantastici
> di Max Beerbohm, a quelli surreali di Savinio; e al loico arabesco di
> Ortega, e ancora a Savinio per quel gusto della citazione, vera o
> apocrifa, ma in ogni caso, nella funzionalità del gioco, apocrifa –
> pensate a una fusione di questi elementi nella personalità di un uomo
> del nostro tempo ossessionato dalla storia: e avrete, con buona appros-
> simazione, l'immagine dello scrittore argentino Jorge Luis Borges.[9]

Closer in time and space, the clearest clue to a Borgesian reading of *Todo
modo* is given by Sciascia himself, yet again in *Nero su nero*:

> Leggo la *Vita di Antonio* di Atanasio. Hanno ragione F. & L.: un
> inganno, una mistificazione, un libro interamente creato – testo,
> traduzione, introduzione e note – da Borges o da un borgesiano.
> Faccio però la constatazione che di libri simili, da qualche tempo, ne
> sto leggendo molti: Clemente d'Alessandria, Lattanzio, Agostino,
> Anselmo, Ambrogio. Accade qualcosa a me o sta accadendo a tutti
> qualcosa per cui questi libri ritornano, per cui nella nostra inquietu-
> dine – borgesianamente – li reinventiamo?   (p. 163)

Do we not have here in sufficient number those *auctores* of the patristic
tradition who will turn up in the novel? And, more importantly, are we
not provided with the key whereby they should be read? It would not be
unreasonable, I think, to link this passage of what Sciascia was reading at
a given point in time and how he was reading with a different but similar

set of names in *Todo modo*. Michelozzi, the first murder victim, is having a lively discussion with Don Gaetano over lunch, at the end of which the painter-narrator affirms: 'Ero piuttosto interessato a Origene, a Ireneo e allo Pseudo Dionigi, ma in senso del tutto eterodosso. Alla Borges, tanto per intenderci' (pp. 50–1). The names are, of course, different, but the method of reading is the same: hetero – or, if we prefer – unorthodox. Within the novel itself, the reference in the text to Dionysius the pseudo-Areopagite is anticipated in the lengthy quotation from his *Mystical Theology* which serves as a preface, but what unlocks it, so to speak, is the reference in that same preface to the 'bella teologa ginevrina' referred to by Casanova in his *Storia della mia vita*: 'Lasciò cadere l'ultimo velo del pudore, citando San Clemente d'Alessandria'. Sciascia himself provides us with the details of the reference ('tomo VIII, capitolo IV, episodio della bella teologa ginevrina') in *Nero su nero* (p. 94), but it is in another, later volume of essays, *Cruciverba*, that we find the real key when, apropos of a question of incest in the *Icosameron*, he talks of Casanova's excessive preoccupation and precaution

a giustificare e sommergere la rappresentazione dell'incesto sotto una valanga di dottrina teologica e morale di indiscutibile (ossia di discuti-bilissima, come sempre quando si abbandona alle digressioni di teologia e di morale) autorità.   (p. 60)

The juxtaposition or, perhaps, more accurately, the downgrading of the purely spiritual and speculative to the impurely carnal and pragmatic at the very outset of the novel should be seen as a cautionary note to the reader not to read what follows literally, not to believe unilaterally what is said or quoted in support of a given argument for there are always at least two sides to it. Let the reader be what Borges requires every man of culture to be and what the very subject-matter of *Todo modo* too demands, a theologian, but let him be, as Sciascia would want him, a 'teologo ateo'.[10]

In an interview given to Giovanni Giuga for *La fiera letteraria* in July 1974, Sciascia referred to *Todo modo*, then half-written, as a tale 'sui cattolici, sulla politica dei cattolici; l'altra faccia del *contesto*, insomma'. There are, I believe, compelling arguments for considering the two novels as a sort of literary diptych (indeed, possibly a triptych, with *Candido* constituting the third work), but here let me simply suggest one possible link. The text that lies at the heart of *Il contesto* is Voltaire's *Traité sur la tolérance* of 1763. It is not mentioned in *Todo modo* where references to Voltaire are few and far between: a fleeting remark (apropos of English painters) 'che per dipingere bene bisogna avere i piedi caldi' (p. 18) and, more significantly, a comparison between Voltaire and Pascal, perhaps more precisely, a mystical osmosis in which the differences between them (which are, after all, what matters) are ironed out:

> È stato detto che il razionalismo di Voltaire ha uno sfondo teologico incommensurabile all'uomo quanto quello di Pascal. Io direi anche che il candore di Candide vale esattamente quanto lo spavento di Pascal, se non è addirittura la stessa cosa.   (p. 105)

I shall have occasion to return to this particular episode later on, but it might not be totally irrelevant here to note *en passant* a certain similarity between Riches as he speaks to Rogas in the central pages of *Il contesto* and Don Gaetano as he speaks to the painter-narrator here. 'Si spostò in avanti sulla poltrona', runs the text of *Il contesto*, 's'inclinò verso Rogas con un sorriso accattivante, gli occhi lucidi di febbrile ansietà'.[11] 'Riaprí gli occhi', runs the text of *Todo modo*, 's'inclinò verso di me sulla scrivania. – È stato detto che il razionalismo di Voltaire . . .'. 'Come accade nei manicomi', thinks Rogas in the sentence immediately following, 'dove sempre incontri quello che ti blocca a confidarti la sua utopia, la sua civitas dei, il suo falansterio'. But the fanatical single-mindedness of Riches, intent over a lifetime to prove Voltaire wrong in theory and consequently to deny tolerance in practice is no less a distinctive feature of Don Gaetano. 'Lei è un fanatico', exclaims the painter-narrator at one point. 'Crede che potrei non esserlo, con questa veste?', replies his antagonist (p. 48). Voltaire's *Traité* may not be named as such in *Todo modo*, but there can be no doubt that it is still, as always, the target.[12]

   If this is so, perhaps we should pay less attention to the implied antithesis Voltaire–Pascal in the novel and concentrate instead on how Don Gaetano argues. If we do so, we might conclude (in a fashion which would no doubt please the painter-narrator with his trinity fixation) that he employs three methods: like Stendhal, he mixes fact with fiction, what is true with what is not; like Borges, he uses texts 'in senso del tutto eterodosso' (p. 51); but above all, unlike Voltaire, he argues fanatically, single-mindedly, reductively, ironing out those nuances and subtleties that constitute differences, not black on white, but 'nero su nero'.

Although even early on in the novel there are pages that stop the reader in his relentless drive for more information and make him think again, and hard, on what is being said and discussed – pages 46–9, for example, with Don Gaetano's paradoxical affirmation, highlighted through reference to Géricault's *The Raft of the 'Medusa'*, that the shipwreck or last judgement has already taken place and the survivors (not all of whom, it is clear, will be saved: already, theologically, a thorny problem) are swimming in an attempt to reach the raft – it is really only with the second half of page 76, with its allusion to Dostoyevsky (whose presence, it might be said, can be felt not very far beneath the surface throughout the novel), that the denseness of the text begins to increase and reaches perhaps its densest point some twenty or so pages later in yet another discussion between the painter-narrator and Don Gaetano in terms of Luke, chapter 12, verse 49, but especially Voltaire and Pascal. The painter-narrator, on returning to his room immediately after this discussion, finds by his bed a black-bound copy of the *Pensées* with its marker placed in such a position that upon opening the text at the appropriate point, his eye alights on the *pensée* at the top of the right-hand page, number 460, which he reads, and then continues on until number 477. 'Poiché la sua vera natura è andata perduta', runs the text of Pascal, 'tutto diventa la sua natura, come, essendo perduto il vero bene, tutto diventa il suo vero bene' (p. 107): 'La vraie nature étant perdue, tout devient sa nature; come, la véritable bien étant perdu, tout devient son véritable bien'.

Calvino, in a letter to Sciascia conveying his immediate impression of the novel which he had just read, tells how he failed to track down *pensées* 460–477 in the Livre de Poche edition he had at home and how equally unsuccessful he was upon going to the nearest bookshop to double-check in another edition, the Garnier one. Was he missing, he wondered, a theological link to enable him logically to solve the mystery?[13] Possibly, but I suspect not. The actual number attributed by Sciascia to what is a genuine *pensée* does not correspond, as far as I have been able to ascertain, to any of the four commonly used arrangements of the original material. It may intentionally allude to an entirely different *pensée*, one which was, as Calvino discovered, an 'elogio delle lunettes' and which could, he went on, 'entrare benissimo nelle tue divagazioni sugli occhiali'.[14] This is entirely possible and imaginatively neat, but no less possible is that Stendhalian mixture of fact and fiction, of true and false which, as I have suggested, is one of the ways Don Gaetano argues.

But leaving aside Stendhal, and indeed Borges, it is perhaps that third, decidedly un- if not anti-Voltairean, way of reading that is most appropriate here. The decontextualisation of the *pensée* in question confers upon it an absolute quality which its very language with its twice-repeated 'tutto' helps to underline; and that repetition in its turn sends us back, even if only musically, to the rule of Ignatius which gives the novel its title: 'todo modo, todo modo, todo modo ... para buscar y hallar la voluntad divina ...'. *One Way or Another* runs the title in a recent English translation, but I doubt whether that really catches its note of fanaticism. And yet it is precisely that we are talking about. I have already referred to all-important differences between Voltaire and Pascal being ironed out (see page 105 of the text). Here, a page and a half later, Pascal's true or sovereign good is indistinguishable from its opposite, total, indiscriminate evil; and to close the circle wherein tolerance has given way to fanaticism, the *pensée* also sends us back to the allusion to Dostoyevsky in which, it is claimed, the existence of God allows us, so to speak, *carte blanche*:

– Veda: credere che Cristo abbia voluto fermare il male è l'errore piú vecchio e piú diffuso del mondo cristiano. 'Dio non esiste, dunque nulla ci è permesso.' Queste grandi parole, nessuno ha mai veramente tentato di rovesciarle: piccola, ovvia, banale operazione. 'Dio esiste, dunque tutto ci è permesso.' Nessuno, dico, tranne Cristo. E nella sua vera essenza, questo è il cristianesimo: che tutto ci è permesso. Il delitto, il dolore, la morte: crede sarebbero possibili, se Dio non ci fosse?
– Dunque il trionfo del male ...
– Non il male, non il trionfo del male: bisognerebbe decollare da queste parole, dalle parole.... Eppure non abbiamo che parole....
(pp. 76–7)

The fanaticism with which the text is concerned manifests itself in a number of ways and I have already alluded to some of these. There is, for example, the fanaticism of thought whereby traditional logical procedures are reversed in favour of paradox (p. 48). There is also, as we have seen, the fanaticism of reading in which orthodoxy is subverted by heterodoxy with the result that intrinsically incompatible texts become, as it were, interchangeable: Voltaire with Pascal, and, more strikingly, the Areopagite with Casanova. Inexorably, though, our attention is made to focus beyond these specific illustrations on the writer's basic tool, language, and on the act of writing itself. It is surely not by chance that those crucial thirty pages of the novel, pages 76–106, start and end with considerations regarding precisely these. Thus, in the first instance, when the painter-narrator objects to Don Gaetano that his definition of Christianity ('. . . tutto ci è permesso. Il delitto, il dolore, la morte . . .') effectively means the triumph of evil, the priest replies:

> bisognerebbe decollare da queste parole, dalle parole. . . . Eppure non abbiamo che parole. . . . Bisognerebbe entrare nell'inesprimibile senza sentire la necessità di esprimerlo. . . . Ma lei, capisco, non sa che farsene dell'inesprimibile; e dunque scendiamo. . . . Scendiamo, ecco, alle antiche accuse, alle antiche difese. A Tertulliano, per esempio. . . .
>
> (pp. 76–7)

The passage is immediately striking because it contrasts words, which are all we have and which, perhaps because of that, define our basic humanity ('opera naturale è ch'uom favella', as Dante puts it), with what cannot be expressed; and it does so in such a way as to imply (particularly in its choice of verbs: 'decollare' as opposed to 'scendere') a crystalline clarity in the latter and a muddy opaqueness in the former. Unconsciously or otherwise, it may perhaps be a reminiscence of John (chapter 3, verse 19: '. . . but people love the darkness rather than the light . . .'); but its more immediate source, as the second sentence clearly points out ('Bisognerebbe entrare nell'inesprimibile senza sentire la necessità di esprimerlo . . .') is the citation of the Areopagite which serves as a preface to the novel. At first sight both passages would seem to serve the same purpose, but only at first sight, for whereas Dionysius's clear intention is to define as closely as he can the ultimately ineffable godhead,[15] Don Gaetano's no less clear intention is merely to obfuscate. That this is generally so is underlined by his retort to the painter-narrator a moment later: 'Ecco che lei torna alle parole che decidono, alle parole che dividono: migliore, peggiore; giusto, ingiusto; bianco, nero' (pp. 77–8). And that in practice Don Gaetano pays little heed to the nuances of what a text says can be seen in his use of Luke: 'Ricorda il Vangelo di Luca? L'ha mai letto? . . . "Io sono venuto a portare fuoco sulla terra; e che voglio, se già divampa? Ora devo essere battezzato di un battesimo, e come sono angustiato fin tanto che ciò non si compia" ' (p. 103). The precise reference is to chapter 12, verse 49, but, as Philippe Renard points out, the words of Luke, 'Ignem veni mittere in terram, et quod volo nisi ut accendatur' (I came to set the earth on fire, and how I wish it were already kindled) are altered by Don Gaetano, or, perhaps, in the context, more appropriately, rewritten by him so that they might more easily be appropriated to the context and significance he wishes to give them.[16]

   In the light of what I have said in the last paragraph, this corruption of the 'puro segno' of the gospel text into 'contorto cirillico' need not surprise us.[17] And just as it has been prepared for by a whole series of earlier references in the text (Dionysius, Casanova, Sereni, Borges, and so on), in its turn it prepares us, first of all, for the conversion of Voltairean rationalism into its Pascalian equivalent with the consequent elimination of all differences (to which I have already referred); and secondly, subsequent on this practical illustration, the enunciation that:

E forse si possono oggi riscrivere tutti i libri che sono stati scritti; e altro anzi non si fa, riaprendoli con chiavi false, grimaldelli e, mi consenta un doppiosenso banale ma pertinente, piedi di porco. Tutti. Tranne *Candide*.   (pp. 105–6)

At this point, I believe, the painter-narrator decides to kill Don Gaetano and does so like Rogas before him, as Sciascia himself has said, 'per affermare un ordine morale'.[18] In terms of this particular story and the genre to which it belongs, this is undoubtedly sufficient motivation, but is it the only one or, for that matter, the most important one? For *Todo modo* is not *Il contesto* and the painter-narrator is not Rogas. Is he perhaps, then, given that the story is told in the first person, the author himself? In general terms, of course, all fictional characters reflect in some degree and in some fashion their creator; and with much care and circumspection it would be possible, I believe, if we knew nothing of the man Sciascia, to construct a picture of him from his works which in terms of what counts, his intellectual make-up, would be essentially faithful.

But through a whole series of interviews, and one in particular, the book-length *La Sicilia come metafora*,[19] we do in fact know a great deal about him, so that JoAnn Cannon can affirm, drawing on precisely such material, that the shooting of Don Gaetano exorcises the temptation of mysticism to which the rational writer had been attracted.[20] But the exorcism is not that simple or perhaps it is the authorial persona which is in reality much more complex. Perhaps every book that has ever been written can nowadays be re-written. Except *Candide*. On this last point Don Gaetano was to be proved wrong three years later by the publication in 1977 of *Candido ovvero Un sogno fatto in Sicilia*.

The re-writing of the one text which could not be re-written did not, of course, signal a recrudescence of mysticism, but it did highlight another problem and one to which the painter-narrator of *Todo modo* had already alluded. Painting, genuine painting, he had affirmed paradoxically, 'si volge a tutto quel che non sarebbe da dipingere' (p. 18); and, later, in a more personal key, 'tutto, dentro di me e intorno a me, era ormai da anni finzione' (p. 26). The key term is 'finzione' which, I suspect, not by chance was already present in that prose re-writing of Leopardi's 'L'infinito' in the novel's opening page ('. . . lungamente mi appartavo in un luogo, che mi fingevo remoto e inaccessibile . . . '). Be that as it may, clearly in the context of *Todo modo* its implications are negative – fiction as opposed to fact, literature as opposed to life. And it would seem that if the painter-narrator is in part the author, in the wake of *Todo modo* he abandons fiction, fictional literature in favour of life. The novel appeared in November 1974. The following year Sciascia was elected as an independent Communist councillor in Palermo and continued as such until early 1977 when, as a result of friction with the PCI (in part imaginatively transcribed in *Candido*), he resigned. Two years later he was to be elected as a Radical to both the Italian and European parliaments, opting for Rome rather than Strasbourg, and he continued as a deputy until the elections in June 1983.

'Je vous dois la vérité en peinture', says Cézanne in a letter of 23 October 1905 to Émile Mâle, 'et je vous la dirai'. Sciascia's text too, starting with its dust-jacket on which is reproduced Rutilio Manetti's *Temptation of Saint Augustine*, would also seem concerned with a representation of truth through painting. The novel is literally studded with references to painters and paintings and these, like their literary counterparts, would seem to increase in denseness as the novel approaches its climax. After the reading of Pascal in the bedroom, literature almost literally gives way to painting as the painter-narrator distractedly etches out a nude for Scalambri while his mind, working independently, homes in on a possible (albeit not specified) solution to the first murder (pp. 107–8). Lunchtime the following day, the last (public) exchange between the painter-narrator and Don Gaetano, has its starting-point in the painter-narrator's gift for Scalambri and proceeds to a discussion on religious art between Don Gaetano and the painter-narrator, more specifically, on the representation of the figure, the face of Christ, be it that of Antonello da Messina in the museum at Piacenza[21] or, in modern times, the *Miserere* of Rouault or Redon's *Tentation*. Much might be said of this discussion (pp. 112–13) but I would simply like to hazard one suggestion. The painter-narrator at the beginning refuses to be tempted by Don Gaetano into painting a Christ figure for the chapel, but at the close of the discussion he says he does not feel able but wishes to ('Non sento ma voglio'). And he does in fact, with no great difficulty. Might it be that, having killed Don Gaetano, he reacquires that sense of the sacred that enables him, the manifestation of evil having been eliminated, to contemplate and depict the good, 'a piedi caldi', so to speak?[22]

Painting with warm feet, reading texts authoritatively, that is to say, as their author actually intended they be read rather than whimsically, as may be the reader's (or critic's) wont, would seem to be the crux of the problem. And if at first sight the ending of *Todo modo* with its lack of closure, its open-endedness, would seem in Barthesian terms to favour the *scriptible* over the *lisible*, a comparison with, say, the Chinese boxes of Calvino's *Le città invisibili* (1972) or *Se una notte d'inverno un viaggiatore* would highlight the need for caution.

If it were at all necessary, for already, early on in the novel in what is clearly very close to a personal confession (pp. 25–6), the painter-narrator recognises the gulf that separates literature from life and, consequently, also from truth. Let the reader henceforth elaborate his own fiction: ' "fatevelo da voi, un grande pittore ve lo ha già firmato" '. Let him become, in short, the novelist, for the novelist who is Sciascia will write no more. The writer who is Sciascia will continue to write. The high degree of readability of the text will be unchanged, the stylistic admixture of lyricism and allusiveness will be what it always was, but after *Todo modo* the subject matter becomes invariably non-fiction.

Notes

1. Leonardo Sciascia, *Todo modo* (Turin: Einaudi, 1974) p. 27.
2. Ibid., p. 120. For this reference to *And Then There Were None* (originally *Ten Little Niggers*), see Stefano Tani, *The Doomed Detective. The Contribution of the Detective Novel to Postmodern American and Italian Fiction* (Carbondale and Edwardsville, 1984) p. 126, n. 18. In more general terms, Claude Ambroise, *Invito alla lettura di Sciascia*, 2nd ed. (Milan, 1978), asserts that '*Todo modo* è un modo di gareggiare con il *Roger Ackroyd* di Agatha Christie ...' (p. 205).
3. The quotation, from Giacomo Debenedetti, was first cited by Sciascia in *Pirandello e il pirandellismo* (Caltanissetta-Rome: Sciascia, 1953) p. 55. It turns up again in essence in *Cruciverba* (Turin: Einaudi, 1983), in a paragraph which, with its references to Savinio and Stendhal, would seem to me basic for understanding the nature of literary identity and consequently literary autobiography in a writer like Sciascia (p. 213).
4. *Todo modo*, pp. 25–6. See also Ambroise, *Invito*, p. 154 and p. 207.
5. Leonardo Sciascia, *Nero su nero* (Turin: Einaudi, 1979).
6. Although the relevant pages of *Nero su nero* are pages of a diary, nevertheless they are pages already at one remove from the geographical location and psychological frame of mind which gave rise to them. For a geographically more specific description of the location as well as a more decidedly and literally ('esasperato, fuori delle grazie di dio') angry Sciascia, see Bruno Arcurio, 'Il laboratorio di Leonardo Sciascia', *Italyan Filolojisi*, anno IX, n. 10 (1977) pp. 103–15, but especially pp. 106–7.
7. It should be noted *en passant* that Don Gaetano's definition of the author of *Storia di due amanti* as an 'eroe stendhaliano avant la lettre' (p. 36) is exactly the phrase used a decade later in the blurb of the *Storia* brought out by Sellerio in 1985. The blurb, although unsigned, is likely to have been written by Sciascia who had cooperated closely with Sellerio from 1970 until fairly recently. See Bianca Stancanelli, 'Leonardo non abita piú qui', *Panorama*, anno XXV, n. 1080–1 (4 gennaio 1987) p. 110.
8. See 'The Theologians' (from *Fictions*) in Jorge Luis Borges, *Labyrinths* (Harmondsworth, 1985) pp. 150–8.
9. Cited by Sciascia himself in 'Un affascinante teologo ateo', *Corriere della sera*, 30 settembre 1979.
10. See the final paragraph of 'Un affascinante teologo ateo', *cit*.
11. Leonardo Sciascia, *Il contesto* (Turin: Einaudi, 1971) p. 89.
12. See *Nero su nero*, p. 21: '... è da notare come Voltaire resti ancora e sempre il nemico ...'.
13. See Italo Calvino, 'Lettere a L. Sciascia', *Forum Italicum*, 15, 1 (Spring 1981) pp. 62–72, but especially pp. 70–2. The letter in question is dated Paris, 5 October 1974.
14. *Pensée* 266 in the Brunschvicg edition or 942 in the Lafuma text.
15. See Michael Haren, *Medieval Thought. The Western Intellectual Tradition from Antiquity to the 13th Century* (London, 1985) pp. 75–6.

16. See Philippe Renard, 'Les lunettes de Sciascia', *Italianistica*, 6, 2 (1977) 392–3.
17. *Todo modo*, p. 29. The poet in question is Vittorio Sereni and the text cited is 'La ragazza d'Atene' from *Diario d'Algeria*.
18. See 'Sciascia risponde ai suoi inquisitori', *Il tempo illustrato*, 27 febbraio 1972, cited in Ricciarda Ricorda, 'Sciascia ovvero la retorica della citazione', *Studi Novecenteschi*, 6, 16 (marzo 1977) p. 78, n. 35.
19. Leonardo Sciascia, *La Sicilia come metafora. Intervista di Marcelle Padovani* (Milan: Mondadori, 1979).
20. See JoAnn Cannon, '*Todo modo* and the Enlightened Hero of Leonardo Sciascia', *Symposium*, 35 (1981–2) p. 285; and *La Sicilia come metafora*, pp. 63–7.
21. *Todo modo*, p. 112: 'Per me, una delle piú inquietanti immagini di Cristo, è quella di Antonello, che si trova oggi, mi pare, al museo di Piacenza: quella maschera di ottusa sofferenza ... Terribile ...'. The words are Don Gaetano's, but in terms of the partially autobiographical nature of the character, see what the writer Sciascia says apropos of Antonello in 'L'ordine delle somiglianze', in *Cruciverba*, p. 27: 'E si potrebbero fare osservazioni consimili anche sugli Ecce Homo sui Crocifissi sul Salvator Mundi: volti di ottuso dolore, maschere di carnale sofferenza ...'. The essay had originally appeared as a 'Presentazione' to *L'opera completa di Antonello da Messina* (Milan, 1967).
22. The sense of the sacred and the contemplation of the good are, of course, in purely lay terms, as the lengthy quotation from Gide's *Caves du Vatican* indicates. On the Gidean ending of the novel, see JoAnn Cannon's finely nuanced conclusions '*Todo modo* and the Enlightened Hero', pp. 290–1). On the significance of the painter-narrator's head of Christ, see, instead, the no less finely reasoned page of Ambroise (*Invito*, p. 162).

POSTSCRIPTUM. In the letter referred to in note 13, Calvino regretted he did not have to hand 'l'edizione Einaudi con le tavole delle corrispondenze stabilita dal nostro compianto Paolo Serini'. Since completing this paper, I have been able to consult the Einaudi edition of the *Pensieri*. In it 460 corresponds to what Sciascia transcribes and, moreover, it is to be found on the right-hand page, albeit the second on the page rather than, as is stated in *Todo modo*, the first. 477, at which point the painter-narrator stops reading, corresponds to the end of the section entitled 'La soluzione biblica del problema dell'uomo', in itself the first part of Section VII, LA RELIGIONE CRISTIANA.

16

Some Thoughts on Internal and External Monologue in the Writings of Natalia Ginzburg

Alan Bullock

In 1963 Natalia Ginzburg was interviewed for the magazine *L'Europeo* by the well-known journalist Oriana Fallaci, whose report appeared in print on 14 July of that year under the title 'Parole in famiglia'. In it Ginzburg describes how she emerged from a period of creative impotence or writer's block by discovering the novels of Ivy Compton-Burnett during the three years she spent in London, from 1959 to 1961. Her return to creative writing with renewed vigour and a desire to make full use of a new ability to produce dialogue of her own – an ability which according to some critics she indulged to excess in 1961 in *Le voci della sera* – inevitably draws attention to her narrative technique in her earlier work, where alongside what we may describe as a conventional use of dialogue between characters involved in the action we also find an extensive use of internal monologue and individual pronouncements which are in themselves sufficient to give us the measure of what would in real life be an exchange between two people.

Both these techniques are clearly discernible in Ginzburg's first published work, the short story *Un'assenza*, written in 1933, in which the protagonist Maurizio reflects on the insignificance of his life and the emptiness of his marriage during his wife's temporary absence on a trip out of town. It begins with a conventional third-person narration, but already in the second paragraph we have the beginnings of an internal monologue, printed in inverted commas: '"Anna è a San Remo"', and this is followed a few lines later by a transcript of Maurizio's conversation with his small child, in which, however, we are only told what he, Maurizio, says: 'Chi era che faceva i capricci un momento fa? ... Ora vatti a vestire, caro Villi'.[1] This may appear at first sight a relatively obvious device relating to the difference in status between the two characters, but is soon revealed as something rather more subtle at the end of this same paragraph when in alluding to an exchange between Maurizio and his wife Ginzburg likewise merely reproduces the latter's comments, and, furthermore, restricts them to a single phrase which perfectly encapsulates Anna's disparaging attitude to her husband and his domestic needs: 'Questa non è un'osteria' (p. 370), a patronising approach which is akin to Maurizio's comment to his son: '. . . i bambini cattivi non mi piacciono' (p. 369).

As the story progresses conventional narrative is rapidly overtaken by internal monologue. The conversation between Maurizio and Anna on the subject of his employment occupies a whole paragraph and includes straightforward dialogue, but it is a mixture of imagination and memory, not a real conversation at all. Maurizio's childhood reminiscences, which his wife likewise finds so unappealing, are also dealt with in flashback, and after two short paragraphs of straightforward description we reach the finale, Maurizio's *crise de conscience* and momentary thoughts of suicide, a long paragraph occupying over a page of text in the 1964 edition (pp. 372–4) in which there is a single exchange between husband and wife, once again presented in a context combining narration, memory – the word 'ricordava' occurs three times in quick succession – and reflection, conveyed as before through internal monologue and emphasised by the use of inverted commas. A short narrative paragraph rounds off the story in appropriately ironic vein.

In *Casa al mare*, written four years later, the narrative shifts from third to first person, a device which precludes any use of internal monologue among the other characters but at the same time allows greater scope for reflection and self-analysis, an opportunity which the author makes full use of in order to communicate the narrator's changing state of mind. On receiving his friend Walter's request to visit him and provide some counselling in relation to a problem which is troubling him the writer's first reaction is 'un turbamento vago, come un po' di paura e d'angustia' at the thought of becoming involved in someone else's affairs (*Cinque romanzi brevi*, p. 375). But after his arrival in the small seaside resort this soon gives way to feelings of contentment and fulfilment: 'Mi sentivo molto a mio agio e la mia salute ne godeva' (p. 378): to the extent that he finds the thought of returning to his normal life intolerable, and this despite the fact that no counselling of any kind has taken place:

Il pensiero di dovermene andare mi rattristava.... Il ricordo del lavoro, della città, di mia madre, mi riusciva spiacevole e lo evitavo. Mi sembrava d'esser là da un tempo indeterminato, lunghissimo. Gli altri non accennavano mai alla mia partenza e neppure parevano rammentare che mi avevano chiamato per un consiglio. Non davo alcun consiglio e nessuno me ne chiedeva.   (p. 378)

This relaxed passivity changes gradually in turn to increasingly strong feelings of attraction for his friend's wife, which dominate him completely and that he reacts to with pathetic attempts at self-delusion: 'Avrei dovuto partire subito. Ma non ne fui capace. Sul principio mi dissi che non c'era nulla di vero. Finsi con me stesso di credere d'aver dato importanza a cose che non ne avevano alcuna' (p. 379). Alongside this wealth of detail there are also frequent instances of what we may call 'one-sided communications' in which Walter and Vilma speak about the breakdown of their marriage without any visible feed-back from the narrator, while on the one occasion on which we see him speak directly to the wife she replies by silently embracing him. The essential artificiality of this procedure in no way detracts from the credibility of the story, which rather acquires a greater intensity from the conciseness of the whole, while any doubts as to its effectiveness are cleverly dispelled by the scene where the narrator confronts Walter after his seduction by Vilma the previous evening and in which his silence is now justified in naturalistic terms by his feelings of 'pena e disgusto' (p. 380) and the fact that 'il dolore e la vergogna m'impedivano di parlare' (p. 381). Thus in a mere seven pages we are made fully aware of the different personalities of the characters and the oppressive atmosphere in which they live out their lives.

When she produced her next story, *Mio marito*, a grim demonstration of the destructive force of sexual passion, Ginzburg had accompanied her husband Leone to the Abruzzi, where he had been exiled in 1940 by the Fascist authorities, a traumatic upheaval which inevitably affected her writing. We know from her introduction to *Cinque romanzi brevi* that in contrast to her two previous short stories, based on imagination and dealing with situations entirely divorced from her own experience, the background to *Mio marito* was based directly on her village environment, and that the doctor whose destructive passion is at the centre of things was the exact physical replica of her own village doctor at that

time. This shift towards the incorporation of direct experience is not total
– indeed the author tells us that for the role of the female narrator she
imagined 'una donna quanto piú possibile diversa e lontana da me' (p. 10)
– but it none the less resulted in a very different package in which
alongside passages of narration we find not only crucial exchanges
between husband and wife in which both parties speak to each other on
the printed page but also descriptions of a protracted childbirth and a
suicide which are far more dramatic than anything Ginzburg had
previously attempted. If the structure of this tale is thus basically more
conventional than in those which precede it the story also contains the
first example of a technique which Ginzburg was to make extensive use of
twenty years later, that is the extended speech by a single character in
which a whole personality is delineated, here represented by the
sequence in which the husband first tells his wife about his obsessive
passion for the peasant girl Mariuccia. In addition, as in *Casa al mare*, the
first person narration allows the author, now able to empathise more
fully with her female protagonist, ample scope to chart the changing
feelings of her character, from the monotonous resignation of her
unmarried state at the beginning of the story, through her initial
happiness at her new role as country doctor's wife, her disillusion at the
news of her husband's sexual enthralment, and her final awareness that
all her efforts to cope with the situation have been in vain.

   Five years later with the war over and a new life before her Ginzburg
abandoned the peasant environment which had been her home, and, at
least to some extent, her inspiration during her husband's exile, and
turned once more to an analysis of her original background in *È stato
cosí*, the protagonist of which is a well-educated but essentially naïve
young woman from the middle classes. The novel begins as she shoots
her husband Alberto, who is about to leave home for a trip with his
mistress, and then recounts in a long flashback everything that has led to
this fatal gesture from the time of their first meeting. The technique here
is essentially that of *Mio marito*, in which long passages of narration
alternate with exchanges of dialogue in moments of particular significance, but the process of analysis is far more detailed than in the
earlier work, partly because of the difference in length but also, clearly,
because this time the woman at the centre of the action is not only better
educated but also more emotionally involved, however misguidedly,
with her partner, and correspondingly more anxious to understand him.

The result is a greater intensity of analysis and an unrelenting desire on the part of the protagonist to interrogate both herself and her husband, something which increases their respective feelings of alienation and draws from Alberto the unfeeling comment that 'dovevo guarire di quel vizio che avevo di guardare sempre fisso dentro di me' (*Cinque romanzi brevi*, p. 105), while elsewhere we read that 'pensavo che nella mia vita non avevo mai fatto altro che guardare fisso fisso nel pozzo buio che avevo dentro di me' (p. 147). On the last page of the novel we discover that what we have been reading is the protagonist's confession, written out in the pages of her shopping-book before she commits suicide, in other words an extended monologue in which she explains everything that has happened, an account in which every detail is important. Earlier on in one of the breaks in the flashback in which the narrative briefly returns to the present she has contemplated making this confession to the police and emphasised her need to speak without interruption: 'Bisognava che io chiedessi che mi lasciassero raccontare ogni cosa, proprio dal primo giorno, magari anche certi particolari che parevano banali ma invece avevano avuto una grande importanza. Era una faccenda un po' lunga ma dovevano lasciarmi parlare' (p. 114).

Typical of this kind of apparently banal but in reality deeply revealing incident is the scene set in the confused and contradictory period preceding her marriage to Alberto in which the narrator calls on some friends in order to obtain news of him during his absence but is too shy to mention the object of her visit. As a result she is subjected to a lecture on the most efficient method for cleaning domestic windows delivered by the lady of the house, who then gives her something to drink and sends her away:

> Sono andata dai Gaudenzi un giorno per vedere se ce lo trovavo o se dicevano qualcosa di lui. Non c'era il dottore, c'era soltanto la moglie che stava lavando i vetri. Son rimasta a guardare come strofinava i vetri e m'ha spiegato che prima si deve fare con dei giornali e cenere sciolta nell'acqua e poi fregare pian piano con uno straccio di lana e allora vengono lucidi che è uno splendore. E poi è scesa giú dalla scala e m'ha fatta la cioccolata ma non mi diceva niente di lui e cosí me ne sono andata via. (p. 92)

Surrounded on all sides by insensitivity and incomprehension, unable to communicate with the one person who attempts to help her, the outrageously promiscuous Francesca, the narrator sinks ever deeper into depression and despair, to the point where she can only break the mould by an act of violence whose repercussions are no less fatal for herself. No longer a verbal account delivered to a policeman 'dalla faccia olivastra dietro al tavolo' (p. 155) her final confession is thus addressed to whom it may concern, a kind of personal bequest to society.

With *Le voci della sera* in 1961, an analysis of the stultifying effect of village life on youthful sensibilities and possibly Ginzburg's most famous novel, we find not only the renewed ability to create dialogue, to which I have already referred, but also the rebirth of 'one-sided communication', here used to maximum effect in the opening and closing sections of the book, where Elsa's mother Matilde babbles away incessantly, releasing a flood of trivia which initially produces only minimal reaction in her daughter, and that only after a direct appeal –'Ma possibile che non si possa avere da te, qualche volta, il miracolo d'una parola?' (*Cinque romanzi brevi*, p. 274) – and ends with complete and utter silence, more eloquent than any protest or complaint. The same device is used, albeit less pointedly, throughout the novel, interspersed with passages in which the author provides both sides of the conversation and sections involving straightforward narration. Both these alternatives hark back to Ginzburg's earlier work but appear here in a more refined form than hitherto; the conversations, in many cases apparently simplistic or even trivial, are reminiscent of those found in *La strada che va in città* from 1941, but range here over a much wider area, as one would expect from an environment which is essentially middle-, rather than working-, class, and in the process expose even more tellingly the limitations of the people concerned, while large sections of the narration consist of an extended flashback which recalls the structure of *È stato cosí* but is here likewise applied over a wider area to a collection of characters each of whom has a distinct personality which we see develop from first youth to maturity.

If, as has been suggested elsewhere, *Le voci della sera* is the work in which Ginzburg's talents are most evenly distributed, the most striking of these in terms of structure is undoubtedly the refinement of the monologue. This has now developed from a kind of primitive stream of consciousness device in *Un'assenza* and a retrospective analysis in *È stato cosí*, both of which focus on a person who is alone with his or her thoughts in a distressing moment of truth, to a context in which a character indulges his or her personal interests while pretending to carry on a conversation with a fellow human being. The difference is considerable in terms of what one might call audience participation, in that while one undoubtedly responds to Maurizio in *Un'assenza* and the unnamed protagonist of *È stato cosí* they clearly represent extreme examples of human misfortune which are by definition uncommon, while Matilde in *Le voci della sera* is immediately recognisable as that all too common phenomenon: the crushing bore from whom escape is impossible and whose interminable soliloquies flourish spontaneously in the presence of a captive audience.

It is this concentration on self-expression that is the most striking aspect of Ginzburg's use of monologue, now externalised and relating no longer to an extreme situation in which dramatic intensity justifies extended speech, as in the passage from *Mio marito* to which I have already referred, but, instead, to a context of everyday normality in which characters who suffer from verbal diarrhoea have achieved the goal referred to ironically by the Producer in Pirandello's *Sei personaggi in cerca d'autore*: 'Ah, comodo, se ogni personaggio potesse in un bel monologo ... venire a scodellare davanti al pubblico tutto quel che gli bolle in pentola!'.[2]

Having perfected this technique Ginzburg used it to the full in a context where it might at first sight have seemed singularly inappropriate: the theatre, where it is of course essential that audiences should not be bored, something she has skilfully avoided by ensuring that her speakers are all interesting characters with fascinating personalities. Thus in her first play, *Ti ho sposato per allegria*, the protagonist Giuliana is presented as an indestructible creature who keeps bouncing back like the proverbial rubber ball however distressing or destructive her treatment at the hands of other people, possessed as she is of a boundless optimism that, unknown to her, is her most attractive characteristic and has unwittingly procured her a constant husband. In *L'inserzione*, dating from the same year, 1965, we see the reverse of the coin in Teresa, a woman who instead of bouncing back has ricocheted from crisis to crisis throughout her life, not only never learning from her misfortunes but also being progressively diminished by them to the point where she eventually loses control completely and commits murder. Both women are incorrigible talkers, both obsessed with the need to pour out their life's experiences to a receptive ear, and both given an ideal opportunity to do so; in Giuliana's case the passive recipient is the maid, Vittoria, conscious of her inferior social position and permanently open-mouthed at her mistress's range of disasters, all recounted with a bubbling enthusiasm which is a constant source of comic effect; in Teresa's it is the naïve young student Elena, too tender-hearted for her own good and whose status as a prospective tenant ensures that she must humour her future landlady if she is to be accepted for the room. In *Fragola e panna*, from 1966, the relationship is reversed in that the compulsive talker is the inferior vessel: a young girl, Barbara, who has left her husband and child and who recounts with moving simplicity the story of her affair with a middle-aged man to her lover's wife, Flaminia, in the naïve belief that it will leave the latter emotionally indifferent. Her behaviour immediately creates a crisis in Flaminia, whose jealous outbursts reveal not just the instinctive feelings of resentment appropriate to dishonoured wives but also, more importantly, a realisation of the essential futility of her whole existence and a full awareness of the contempt that she feels for her husband, a. selfish nonentity who ruthlessly exploits the advantages deriving from his sex and his status to indulge his emotions in total disregard for his obligations. Flaminia's long and lucid analysis of her feelings are the natural counterpoint to Barbara's ingenuous account of her adolescent infatuation, and it is no surprise that she follows this speech with obsessive repetitions of Barbara's key phrase 'Dove vado? Non so dove andare'.[3] Meanwhile Tosca the servant is also describing at some length her feelings of alienation on living in the country in a series of anguished statements that fall consistently on deaf ears and which while contributing superficially to comic effect also represent yet another existential crisis which is no less real for being set on a lower social level.

One year later, in 1967, we find a further refinement which does away entirely with the physical presence of the listener while maintaining the necessary link which enables the monologue to take shape and develop. This concerns that most characteristic of modern items the telephone, which appears in a minor capacity in *L'inserzione* before coming into its own in *La segretaria*, where we find two mammoth speeches from Sofia, in Acts I and III respectively, that give us a complete picture of that character's personality and her impossible emotional situation. In terms of structure the absence of the person at the other end of the phone enables Ginzburg to recreate the 'one-sided communications' apparent in her earlier work in a naturalistic manner which is clearly more appropriate in a theatrical context, while at the same time ensuring a greater concentration on the character who is in the spotlight, whose flow is uninterrupted by any comment from her partner in the exercise. The same technique is used in *La porta sbagliata* of 1968, where Stefano's phone-calls to his mother and his mother-in-law, each of whom receives a radically different account of the domestic scene, splendidly convey the chaos and confusion of a household where everyone is either neurotic or frustrated and the practicalities of day-to-day existence go by the board. Alongside the phone-calls we also find in this play, as in *La segretaria*, scenes in which someone gives an account of himself or herself in the presence of another character, but this parallel technique, maintained from her earliest work in the theatre, is abandoned altogether in Ginzburg's last play to date, *La parrucca*, written in 1971, a one-acter with a single character who spends almost all her time on the phone to her mother, whose assistance she needs to pay the hotel bill and to whom she recounts at some length the extravagant details of her emotional life inside and outside the matrimonial home. She eventually rings off and informs her husband that she is pregnant by her lover, only to discover that he has long left the bathroom next door and has not heard a single word of her confession; as a result the play turns out to have been a monologue in every sense of the word.

   Caro Michele, written in 1973, represents the next stage in Natalia Ginzburg's development of the monologue. As the title implies the book consists mainly, though not entirely, of letters to and from Michele, a young man obliged to leave the country at short notice for obscure political reasons which are never clarified, and whose absence, by creating a situation in which contact is only possible through letters, fosters in his mother Adriana an awareness of the importance of true communication, previously only seen at its most basic level of maternal guidance and scolding. Undistracted by his presence and the attendant need to discharge her maternal role Adriana's first letter to her son wavers between trivial comments about dirty washing and more significant reflections on her state of mind, and when, shortly after this, her husband, Michele's father, dies, the old pattern is definitely broken and the letters become increasingly a form of correspondence between two equals in which Adriana examines her life and her relationships past and present with those around her. Here we have what is perhaps a perfect synthesis: an externalisation of individual feelings and reflections expressed in isolation, and thus as a monologue, which is at the same time addressed to a specific person whose personality and circumstances condition, at least in part, the contents of the message. The same is true of the letters sent to Michele by Mara, a girl who is his mirror image but whose problems, in essence no less crucial, are treated from a comic standpoint. Meanwhile Michele himself is gradually revealed through *his* letters – only two of which are addressed to his mother – as a typical example of failure and incompetence, blundering through life full of good hopes and intentions but totally incapable of learning from experience.

Ginzburg's discovery of the epistolary novel, a genre which may at first seem somewhat old-fashioned in a social context where, as she herself has said, people tend to communicate exclusively by telephone,[4] has, if anything, deepened her powers of analysis and opened up a new vein of investigation. Its development has not been a sudden thing: her two short stories *Borghesia* and *Famiglia*, published four years after *Caro Michele*, function on an entirely different plane in which the author appears to have forsaken monologue of any kind in favour of an extended narrative flow which combines the descriptions of events and the reactions of the characters concerned, together with a limited use of dialogue, in a complex whole which is outside the scope of this paper. However it is clear with the benefit of hindsight that in the ten years following the publication of *Caro Michele* Ginzburg had become at the same time increasingly aware of the power of the letter as a means of in-depth examination, witness her most recent work *La città e la casa*, which appeared in 1984. Preceded one year earlier by a long account of Alessandro Manzoni's family history, in which extensive quotations from published correspondence alternate with linking passages of narration and comment, a work in which people and events are determined by historical fact and thus restrict the author to a predetermined range of plot and characterisation, we now have a novel which is totally fictional and consists entirely of letters exchanged between a wide range of well-defined individuals whom the author has been able to create with total freedom and whose communications she has structured in such a way as to reveal their inner essence in a masterly exposition of thoughts and feelings that represents the final stage in Ginzburg's use of the monologue. The protagonist of this most recent novel is Giuseppe, a journalist in the throes of the male menopause, who decides to tear up his roots in Rome and move to Princeton, where he has a brother who can help him make a fresh start. Conscious of the fact that he is about to enter a new phase of his life cycle in which his actions will determine the remainder of his existence he is anxious to make a complete break with his old routine in exchange for an idyllic retirement in which he can be a gentleman of leisure and devote himself to scholarship, something which he has clearly been unable to do while working for a newspaper in a large capital city. His feelings are expressed with clarity and precision in the first of his letters to Lucrezia, a woman with whom he has had a long and chequered relationship and to whom he has no inhibitions about confessing his innermost feelings:

> Non ho soldi. Mi sono stancato di scrivere articoli sui giornali. I giornali mi fanno schifo. . . . Ho voglia di abitare a Princeton, città piccolissima. . . . Ho voglia di vivere in una piccolissima città dell'America. . . . Là ci sono molte biblioteche. Finalmente mi farò una cultura. Avrò pace per lavorare e studiare, e non chiedo altro. Voglio prepararmi cosí alla mia vecchiaia. Non ho mai combinato niente e presto avrò cinquant'anni. . . . Da un po' di tempo, quello che decido di fare, voglio deciderlo e farlo per sempre.[5]

At the same time Giuseppe is aware that his radical change of life-style is not without danger in someone òf his generation and that he is taking a serious risk in abandoning well-trodden paths, however unexciting, for a context which is completely unknown, a fact which he glosses over in his long letter to Lucrezia but feels moved to mention in the much shorter note he sends his brother at the very beginning of the novel: 'Vengo in America come uno che ha deciso di buttarsi nell'acqua, e spera di uscirne fuori o morto, o nuovo e diverso' (pp. 3–4). Like so many Ginzburg characters Giuseppe is caught in a moment of truth, at the crossroads of his life, and the special intensity implicit in such a situation explains not only his desire to analyse his every feeling at length but also his need to recall the failure of his marriage and discuss in detail the negative nature of his relationship with his son, whose hippy life-style and uninhibited homosexuality recall the protagonist's rootless existence in *Caro Michele* and the ambiguous relationship between that young man and the character Osvaldo. Like Michele before him Alberico is murdered in circumstances which are never made quite clear, and which abruptly terminate the gradual development of warmth and affection between the son and his parent, one of the many key themes in the novel. Just as Adriana was paradoxically only able to communicate with her son by letter after his departure from Rome had prevented verbal exchanges face to face so Ginzburg shows Giuseppe and Alberico taking this process a stage further by a mutual revelation of thoughts and feelings in relation to the experiences they undergo, many of which are deeply traumatic and act as a kind of catalyst in giving new life to a rapport which had previously been virtually non-existent in everything but name. This degree of intimacy, clearly unthinkable under normal circumstances, is the direct result of having to express oneself by letter, i.e. in a kind of monologue dictated by the need to externalise the essence of one's feelings or beliefs untrammelled by the distractions of small talk and physical proximity in a medium which allows – indeed obliges – the subject to sharpen his mind in a high degree of concentration. Indeed the mere fact of being obliged to write a letter to someone who cannot be reached in any other way frequently seems to induce a contemplative state of mind in which individuals analyse their deepest sentiments, communicate intimate truths about themselves, and lose all inhibition in what they feel able and willing to set down on paper. Thus Lucrezia replies to Giuseppe's letter with an evocation of their old affair in which past events are recalled not for reasons of nostalgia but to focus on their significance, often unnoticed at the time in the intensity of the moment, or to isolate specific flashes of awareness which proved fundamental in the course of the relationship. She now realises, for instance, that her desire to leave her husband and move in with Giuseppe would have been a terrible mistake, even if he had agreed to her wish to formalise things between them, 'perché già eravamo stanchi, tu di me e io di te. Ma non lo sapevo, non l'avevo capito' (p. 21), and her most powerful feeling at the time, a self-righteous contempt for her lover, now turns out, ironically, to have been the source of her salvation. Lucrezia's submissive relationship with her mother is likewise recounted in this same letter with an intensity and a wealth of detail that gives us the full measure of her personality and her obsessive need to attach herself limpet-like to those she believes able to protect her from adult responsibility, something which brings her much pain and soul-searching before the book is ended.

Ginzburg's sense of humour also ensures that the information provided and the conclusions drawn from all this are not exclusively distressing, or, at least, not always communicated in an atmosphere of gloom and doom. Thus Albina, another of the characters, writes to Giuseppe on hearing of his intention to leave Rome, and after having confessed that 'quando ti ho conosciuto mi ero innamorata di te' (p. 29), goes on to inform him with equal candour that 'nemmeno tu sei tanto bello ... perché sei magro, verde e secco' (p. 30). Albina is a sensitive soul who has difficulty in reconciling her emotions, easily awakened, with the practical expression of her feelings, a serious impediment to achieving a balanced life-style, which, however, she renders by the essentially comic statement: 'Io ho l'innamoramento facile, ma il letto difficile' (p. 30). If the particular intimacy of these confessions is in some measure due to Giuseppe's imminent departure, something which encourages both women to be especially honest in their revelations, they are themselves astonished at the extent of their communication; thus Lucrezia half apologises for having written a 'lunghissima lettera' (p. 26) which she realises is more than a simple evocation of times past: 'Non è che ti ho raccontato un gran che di nuovo. Molte cose di me le sai. Te le ho già raccontate mille volte. Ma era per dirti com'ero io e cosa mi è successo a me, a venticinque anni' (p. 26) while Albina, whose motive for writing in the first place is purely and simply the fact that Giuseppe has not answered a phone-call in which she wanted to invite herself to dinner, ends by stating, with some surprise: 'Volevo scriverti solo due parole, e invece ti ho scritto una vera e lunga lettera' (p. 31). These communications are in effect not simply 'highly literate phone calls', as Ian Thomson has described them,[6] or, more disparagingly, in the words of another critic, expressions from a 'colorful coterie of letter-writing friends',[7] but rather a skilful exploitation of a traditional format which acquires a new relevance in the fragmented context of contemporary urban life, affording access to a dimension in which individuals find they can analyse and clarify their behaviour, their experience, and their very nature, not only to their correspondents but also, in the process, to themselves. If the overall result of this is indeed what Thomson has described as 'finely-spun despair' this is consistent with Ginzburg's essentially pessimistic vision of life, which she is now able to convey with supreme intensity through a medium which relies entirely on her use of a type of monologue which is both internal in its creation and external in its function, and whose workings will undoubtedly repay further study in due course.

Notes

1. *Un'assenza*, in *Cinque romanzi brevi* (Turin: Einaudi, 1964) p. 369.
2. L. Pirandello, *Sei personaggi in cerca d'autore*, in *Maschere nude* (Verona: Mondadori, 1955) vol. I, p. 95.
3. *Fragola e panna*, in *Ti ho sposato per allegria e altre commedie* (Turin: Einaudi, 1968) pp. 152, 155, 156, 157.
4. 'Oggi c'è il telefono. . . . Al telefono si parla senza pensare, senza rivolgersi all'altro in tono assorto e intimo' (G. Nascimbeni, 'Ginzburg: "Il mio Manzoni giú dal piedistallo"', *Corriere della sera*, 5 febbraio 1983, p. 3).
5. *La città e la casa* (Turin: Einaudi, 1984) p. 7.
6. I. Thomson, 'Finely-spun despair' in *The Sunday Times*, 19 October 1986, p. 54.
7. R. Signorelli-Papas, review of *La città e la casa* in *World Literature Today*, 60 1 (1986) p. 89.